T0247837

GODS OF THUNDER

GODS OF THUNDER

HOW CLIMATE CHANGE, TRAVEL, AND SPIRITUALITY RESHAPED PRECOLONIAL AMERICA

TIMOTHY R. PAUKETAT

Oxford University Press is a department of the University of Oxford. It furthers the University's objective of excellence in research, scholarship, and education by publishing worldwide. Oxford is a registered trademark of Oxford University Press in the UK and certain other countries.

Published in the United States of America by Oxford University Press
198 Madison Avenue, New York, NY 10016, United States of America.

CIP data is on file at the Library of Congress
ISBN 978–0–19–764510–9

DOI: 10.1093/oso/9780197645109.001.0001

1 3 5 7 9 8 6 4 2

Printed by Sheridan Books, Inc., United States of America

To Ross Hassig: anthropologist, mentor, curmudgeon.
He will never read this book.

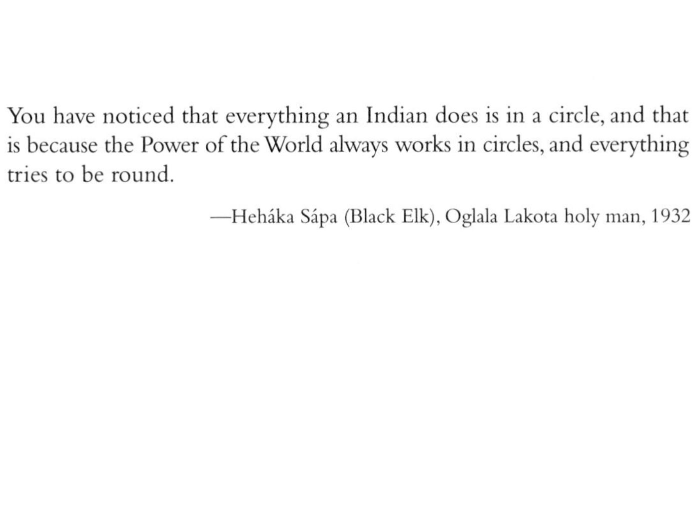

You have noticed that everything an Indian does is in a circle, and that is because the Power of the World always works in circles, and everything tries to be round.

—Heháka Sápa (Black Elk), Oglala Lakota holy man, 1932

Contents

Acknowledgments

This book is both a result of my National Endowment for the Humanities fellowship (NEH FA-58536-15 FLLW) in 2015–2016, and a request by Stefan Vranka, executive editor, Oxford University Press, that I write a cross-border history of precontact North America. It is also the second in a two-part history of medieval-era Greater Mesoamerica—a historically amorphous chunk of the continent from the Yucatan Peninsula up through Mexico into the American Southwest and, then, over into the Deep South and up the Mississippi Valley. The first volume was *Cahokia: Ancient America's Great City on the Mississippi* (Penguin, 2009). For this second volume, I am grateful both to Stefan and to Jason Boffetti, program officer for NEH, who helped me juggle both the fellowship and a collaborative research grant.

With regard to the NEH research grant, I am also indebted to my co-principal investigators, Drs. Susan Alt, Laura Kozuch and Thomas Emerson. They managed the grant when I wandered off to ancient landscapes and modern universities in Belize, Bolivia, Brazil, Chile, China, England, Guatemala, Mexico, Missouri, Illinois, Arizona, and New Mexico to develop the content for this book. Susan joined me in some of these, and our hosts and friends on those trips include Anna Guengerich, Ross Hassig, Frances Hayashida, John Janusek, Zhichun Jing, Lisa Lucero, Preston Miracle, Eduardo Neves, John Robb, Andrew Roddick, Wolfgang Schüler, Anna Sofaer, Andrés Troncoso, and Rob Weiner. I also thank the Institute of Archaeology at the Chinese Academy of Social Sciences, the Shanghai Archaeology Forum, the Museum of Archaeology and Ethnology at the University of São Paolo, the University of Chile, the Solstice Project, and the

McDonald Institute for Archaeological Research at Cambridge University. For their permissions to reproduce images for this book, I am grateful to the Amerind Foundation, the Emerald Acropolis Project, the Illinois Department of Transportation, the Illinois State Archaeological Survey, the Xibun Archaeological Research Project, and Susan Alt, Pete Bostrom, David Boyle, Tamira Brennan, David Dove, Thomas Emerson, Eric Kaldahl, Brad Koldehoff, Maria Martinez, and Tricia McAnany. The text has benefited from the critical eyes and encouragement of Stefan Vranka, Peter Jimenez, F. Terry Norris, and anonymous reviewers of an earlier version.

Long before the fellowship and travels that gave birth to this book, the ideas herein were gestating as part of a series of scholarly seminars on Indigenous cosmologies in the Americas at the Santa Fe Institute (SFI). These roundtable-style seminars took place in Santa Fe, New Mexico, between 2005 and 2011 and were the brainchild of George Gumerman, with the help of Stephen Lekson, Ben Nelson, Linda Cordell, and myself. Supported by SFI founder and Nobel laureate Murray Gell-Mann and funded by Jerry Murdock and SFI, George made the meetings happen. The insightful Indigenous archaeologist and gentleman scholar Robert L. Hall was at a couple of these meetings, and his studies are referenced often in this book.[1]

In the 2010s and early 2020s, Steve Lekson, Gerardo Gutierrez, and I again explored ancient Mesoamerican-Southwestern-Mississippian connections via three Crow Canyon Archaeological Center tours and a School for Advanced Research seminar that took place in both the American Southwest and Midwest. The tours were organized by Sarah Payne and David Boyle. They and a series of tour participants—especially Susan Markley—contributed ideas to the discussions that make their way into this book. Phil Tuwaletstiwa took part in one of the Crow Canyon tours and one SFI seminar, and I benefited from his and Judy Tuwaletstiwa's thoughtful insights and hospitality on several occasions. The SAR seminar was organized by Brenda Todd and Danielle Benden. I thank all of the organizers and participants of each of these events for helping to shape the ideas that end up here.

Of course, the human history upon which this book is based must, in the final analysis, be credited to the hundreds of generations of Indigenous North Americans who lived and died on this, their continent, so that we could ruminate on the deeper meanings of their time on earth. They built the great centers through which the reader will pass, although most will necessarily remain anonymous, as they perhaps were even in their own time.

In the same vein, let us acknowledge the precious materials and phenomena of (and around which Native people built) the centers. Such materials and phenomena were and are alive, so to speak, and helped to give the places herein their vibrancies and legacies. Accordingly, this book must also be credited to the earth, the waters, and the sky above, which deserve our attention and need our help to mitigate the many serious threats posed to them by the worst forces of the modern world.

In my own journey, I have been profoundly affected by several of the places in this book for what they do to the visitor. Go and immerse your being in the dark trickling waters of Actun Tunichil Muknal. Stand amid the breathtaking monuments of Aztec, Cahokia, Carson, Chaco, Chichen Itza, and Teotihuacan. Witness the timeless sweep of Chimney Rock's horizon. Walk through the intimately stratified history of Cuicuilco, Tenochtitlan, and Tlatelolco. Hear the jungle sounds of Tikal, and feel the earth's breath at Wupatki. Even in ruins, these places have the power to inspire.

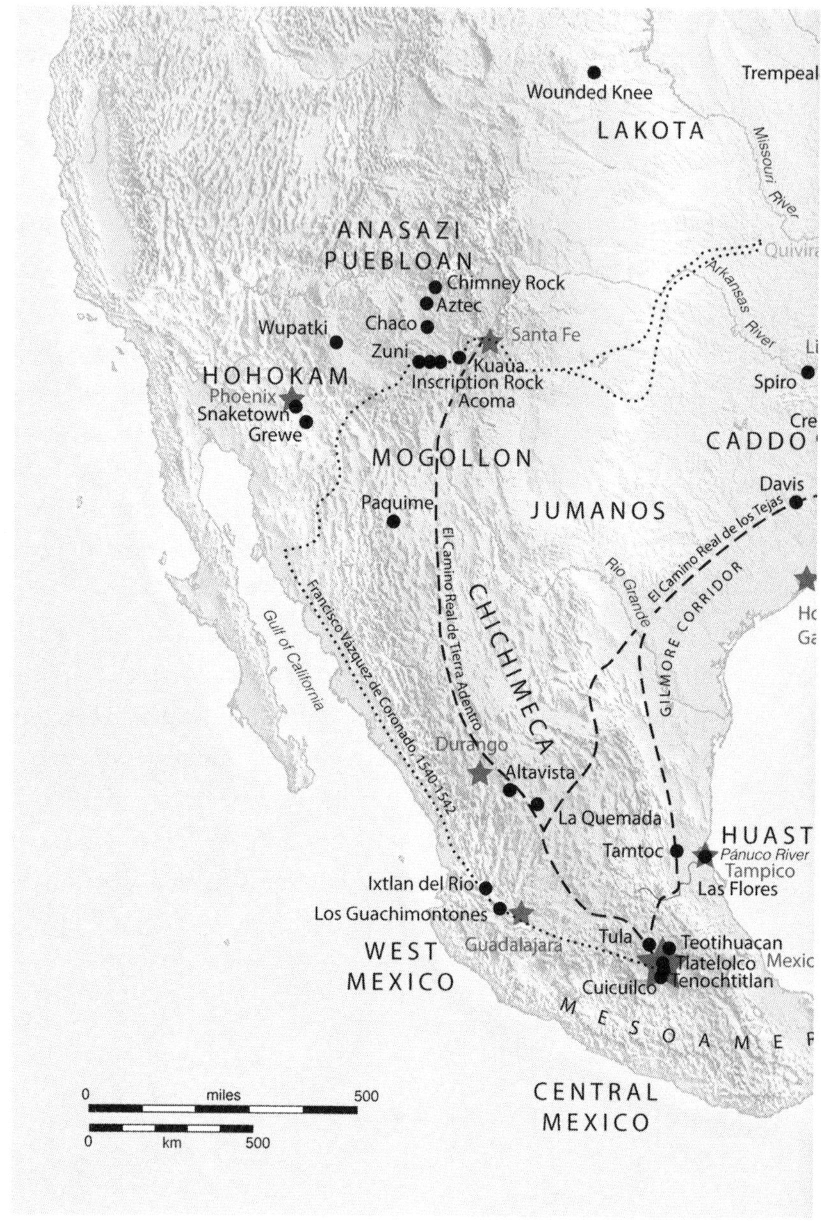

Map showing routes and locations mentioned in text (dots = archaeological sites, stars = modern cities).

eau
OHIO
HOPEWELL
Newark
Chillecothe
St. Louis
Emerald
Ohio River
Cahokia
Thebes Gap
ttle Rock
Mississippi River
Cherry Valley
Toltec
nshaw
MISSISSIPPIA
Poverty Point
Apalachee
ouston/
alveston
Gulf of Mexico
ECA
Merida
Chichen Itza
Uxmal
o City
MAYA
Belize City
Tikal
Actun Tunichil Muknal
R I C A
Copan

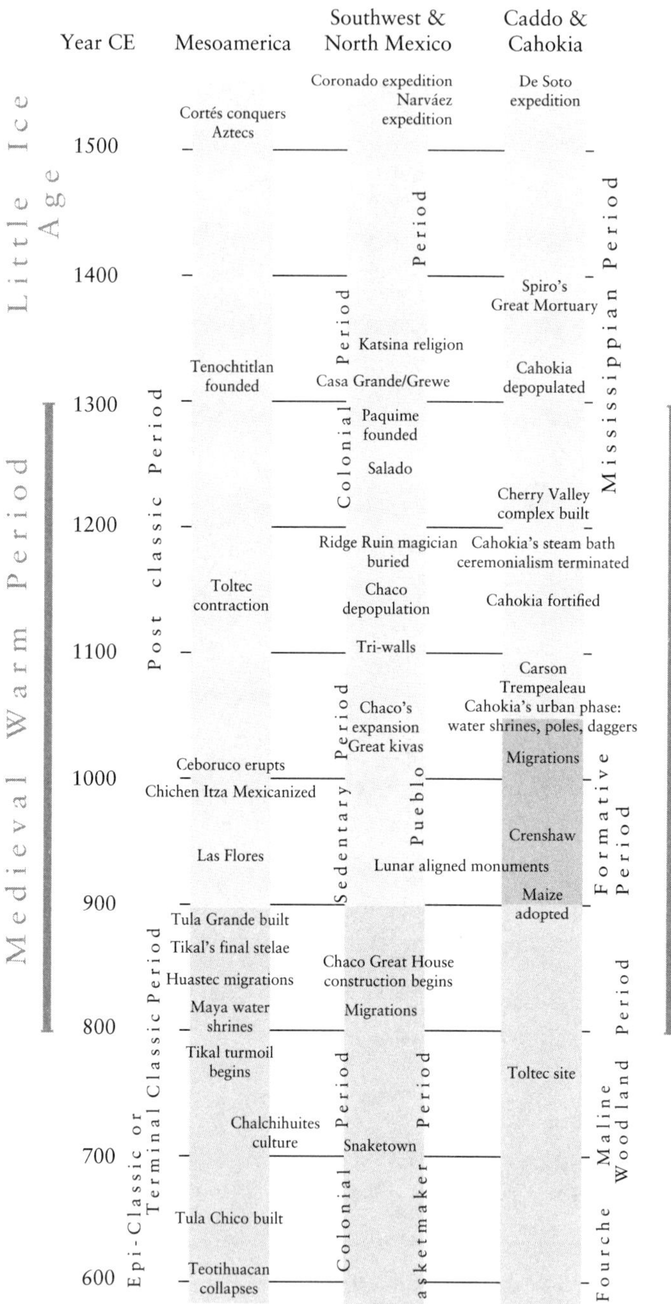

Timeline of precolonial America

Introduction

In Search of Medieval America

The medieval period of seven to twelve centuries ago is better known in Europe and the Old World. But it was a global phenomenon. It happened in the New World, too. To climatologists, this epoch is known as the Medieval Climate Anomaly or the Medieval Warm Period (800–1300 CE).[1] To archaeologists, it was a time of great change, a period when cultural patterns were put into place that lasted into the modern era. This book is a travel guide to that most consequential period of history in North America.

By travel guide, I mean that the book leads you down the same paths walked by Indigenous people a millennium ago and, more recently, the trails trod by Spanish conquistadors just a few centuries ago. By consequential period, I mean one in which climate change helped to alter the course of human history. And by history, I don't mean the written word. History is never simply recounted through writing. It is a physical narrative written into the earth, moved along by flowing waters and blowing winds, and recorded by anonymous authors through the ruins of shrines, monuments, ceremonial centers, and cities.

North American history includes the lands now partitioned as the United States, Canada, Mexico, Guatemala, Belize, El Salvador, and Honduras. But ignore today's borders, especially the modern US-Mexico border. They mattered little to most people before March 2,

1836, when Texas declared its independence from Mexico. The history herein heeds modern political boundaries no more than it does a strict separation of nature and culture.

The chapters that follow will freely cross modern borders and cover a lot of ground. In so doing, this book will provide an explanation of *how* history unfolded in one particular two- to three-century chunk of time in places that few of us think about today. Knowing how this history happened is possible because archaeology allows a sweeping survey of some remarkable Native civilizations that, we now know, developed alongside each other during the period 800–1300 CE.

At the end of each chapter, you'll be encouraged to think about these parallels in detail by visiting key cultural sites featured in the chapter. As you do, you will also see the evidence for a series of new religions, religious movements, or cults starting in the 800s and extending through the 1000s. These were all part of one big history, one big movement—both literally and figuratively—that saw great journeys, pilgrimages, and migrations.

This big history is, in actuality, even bigger than portrayed in this book, since the Medieval Climate Anomaly was global, with the most dramatic impacts known from the Northern Hemisphere in Europe, Asia, North Africa, and North America. Most readers will already be familiar with the word "medieval" because it denotes a well-known European historical period dating to the second half of the so-called Middle Ages, the period after the collapse of Rome and before the Renaissance. But keep in mind that European medieval cultural history was enabled by global climatic conditions in no way restricted to Europe. And the medieval climatic era itself was a result of centuries of reduced volcanic activity on earth that, in turn, allowed more solar radiation to reach the surface, heating the air and oceans and, from there, producing historically anomalous atmospheric and oceanic circulation patterns.

In northern Europe, the combination led to warming trends that enabled farmers to expand or intensify their production.[2] What followed was the age of Vikings, who were able to increase their agricultural output, grow their populations, and then conduct a series of long-distance raids across seas formerly blocked by ice during northern European winters. The first recorded Viking raid was 793 CE. By the mid-800s, Vikings were marauding and colonizing much of northern Europe as far west as Iceland. By the 900s, they had traveled far to the west across the North Atlantic to Greenland and, by the early 1000s, Newfoundland, a feat only possible thanks to warmer sea temperatures. To the east, they reached Kiev in present-day Ukraine, raided along the coasts of the Iberian Peninsula, and sailed into the Mediterranean and Black Seas, one Viking man stopping in Istanbul to etch some runic script onto the floor of the Hagia Sofia.

By 1066, Christianized Viking or Norse descendants in northern France invaded England, just one of several large-scale population shifts that defined European social history during the eleventh and twelfth centuries, all thanks to the Medieval Climate Anomaly. These included Teutonic migrations into the Baltic regions of eastern Europe, an Anglo-Norman migration into Ireland, and German movements into Transylvania. Predictably, climate and migration also laid the foundations for the growth of the late medieval European state, which up to the year 1100 had been weak and feudal. By the beginning of the twelfth century, and at the height of the medieval warming, those formerly feeble governments were able to more reliably gather up the surplus foods and tribute of farmers, converting these resources into manpower and infrastructure to expand control of hinterland zones. Even the European Crusades into Palestine, a great extension of medieval European political-military might, could be understood as indirectly caused by the Medieval Climate Anomaly.[3]

The Crusades also continued the pattern of great journeys by nobles and their followers similar to the travels of the earlier Vikings. The first Crusade began in 1096 CE and led to the siege of Jerusalem in 1099. Besides this and later religiously motivated military movements, there were many other medieval journeys by princes, scholars, merchants, and would-be elites into distant lands. People traveled in order to learn about the wider world, the ulterior motives almost always being to legitimate their prestige, authority, or control back home.[4] Such people were often celebrated in sagas and stories or commemorated in monuments. The travels of Charlemagne—the so-called father of Europe, as canonized by the pope—helped him expand his realm and found the Carolingian Empire in the late 700s, even while the Vikings were confronting Charlemagne's soldiers in northern Europe.

European rulers routinely journeyed to Rome or Jerusalem to have their authority affirmed by the pope. Likewise, Islamic sultans and caliphs traveled to Mecca to pay homage to the powers on which their own authority rested. So did medieval Islamic merchants, whose travels to the Indian Ocean helped to spread Islam all the way to Sumatra and the Philippines by the 800s. At the same time, merchants carried Islam along the Silk Road into China, the same road taken by Marco Polo beginning in the 1270s.

The medieval climatic conditions affected other parts of the Old World in ways quite unlike Europe. In Central Asia, the lands became colder and drier, effects that extended into China up until the mid-tenth century. Likewise, the Nile basin and much of the Sahara of North Africa dried up, with the Nile itself reaching its lowest levels in the late tenth and early eleventh centuries. Meanwhile, the monsoon winds and rains increased in South Asia, supporting the growth of a series of states in medieval India, Thailand, Myanmar, Cambodia, and Vietnam.

The rulers and elites of the South Asian states frequently adopted the Hindu religion, which helped to provide a supernatural basis for their ever-expanding claims to rights, properties, and territories in the eyes of their commoner populations and fellow aristocrats in neighboring provinces. In coastal India, the Chola kingdom expanded into an empire in 848 CE, allowing its statemen and merchants to continue spreading Hinduism into Southeast Asia. There, one Hindu ruler of the Angkor state, named Jayavarman II, had ascended to the status of universal god-king over his domain in Cambodia in 802 CE. He and his successors expanded their domain into an interregional power, the Khmer Empire, the likes of which Southeast Asia had not previously seen. Its capital city of Angkor, with its well-known Hindu temples such as Angkor Wat and its great reservoirs of water such as Tonle Sap, was by 1150 CE home to more than 700,000 people. Its population rivaled Rome's during that imperial city's own heyday.[5]

The correspondence of dates and events and the prevalence of journeys by rulers, merchants, and proselytizers and the spread of Islam and Hinduism during the medieval era in the Old World makes a compelling case that climate change enabled historical development. The same was true in the New World, where equally profound social changes were occurring. These changes were sometimes realized during pronounced El Niño periods, episodes every three to five years when equatorial waters of the Pacific warmed above average, affecting the weather up and down North and South America's western coastlines and interior zones. For instance, in South America, the mountainous interiors east of the coasts became drier, possibly contributing to the failure and abandonment of two Middle Horizon cities, Wari and Tiwanaku. Both had been founded in the first half of the first millennium CE, with the cities peaking around the years 500 and 800, respectively. And both were abandoned by 1100.[6]

In western North America, the drier medieval climate and more pronounced El Niños made human habitation nearly impossible in southern California's Mojave Desert. To the north, conditions turned less predictable along the coast, and communities found it difficult to rely on the bounty of the ocean, the temperatures of which now fluctuated, particularly during the eleventh and twelfth centuries.[7] Consequently, a golden era of shell-mound building around the San Francisco Bay area came to an end. There, coastal mounds propitiously sited along the ocean front every mile or so, each topped with scores of bent-pole houses, were abandoned. Nearby, the Central Valley became drought-stricken. Violence increased, with evidence of scalping, arrow wounds, and forearm fractures indicative of hand-to-hand combat. Inequalities increased, as seen in the treatment of the dead. Increasingly, settlements moved into the interior, at least for part of the year, onto the foothills of the Sierra Nevada, where acorn gathering remained a viable, peaceful economic pursuit.

Farther north along the Northwest Coast, from Oregon and Washington to Alaska, village size first peaked and then crashed as an indirect result of the Medieval Climate Anomaly, commensurate with climate-induced oscillations of salmon populations. In the 1000s, coastal plank house settlements and interior pithouse villages shrank or even disappeared altogether, rebounding only after the fourteenth century.[8]

By contrast, the warmer average medieval temperatures even farther to the north, in the Arctic, facilitated the expansion of the ancestors of the modern-day Inuit or Eskimo, known to archaeologists as the Thule. At least some of this expansion was afforded by the Thule's familial approach to hunting and fishing. Teams of relatives and in-laws pursued bowhead whales across open water in large boats, called umiaks. The open water was itself a function of the warmer temperatures, which melted passages along the northern Canadian coastline that formerly had been frozen shut. After 900 CE, the Thule way of life, if not groups of Thule themselves, moved eastward across the Canadian Arctic.

To the south and east in North America, positive and negative changes are evident as new religions, pilgrimages, migrations, and urban complexes from the Yucatan Peninsula of southern Mexico across Central and North Mexico and into the American Southwest, Mississippi valley, and Southeast. The religions, we will see, were centered around wind and rain gods, all part of one widespread movement not dissimilar to the spread of Christianity, Islam, and Hinduism in the Old World. The most important of the New World gods were variants of one or more Wind-That-Brings-Rain gods. North of the Rio Grande, the Wind-That-Brings-Rain gods were called Thunder Beings or, simply, Thunderers, across the Plains and into the Eastern Woodlands of the continent. Of course, the Native names for these gods were not the same everywhere, which can be confusing. And archaeologists in every region have their own regional designations for the time periods and cultural developments involved, which can be difficult to sort out.

In the Mississippi valley, this was the era of the Mississippian civilization. In North Mexico and the American Southwest, it encompassed the Pueblo, Hohokam, Mogollon, and early Casas Grandes cultures. In Mesoamerica, which is to say from about Culiacan, Mexico, on the Pacific coast to Tampico, Mexico, on the Gulf Coast and south to Nicaragua, the era encompassed the Epiclassic, Terminal Classic, and early Postclassic periods and included the so-called Toltec, Huastec, and Maya civilizations, among others. Whatever the names, and whoever the people, all appear to have been part of a phenomenon—a cult or cults of Thunderers or Wind-That-Bring-Rain gods—that swept the continent over the course of two to three hundred years.

The effects of this phenomenon were profound, leaving lasting imprints on diverse peoples and their civilizations and establishing ways of life that were to last through the arrival of Europeans. These effects were observed by the earliest European conquistadors and colonists in the 1500s—though they did not recognize the cause—long after the world had moved past the medieval era. Indeed, we base some of what we think happened in the medieval era on later Spanish observations. That said, some of these earliest European intruders make poor guides. They include Hernán Cortés, Francisco Vázquez de Coronado, Hernando de Soto, and Juan de Oñate. These men cared little about the Native history and heritage they were assaulting.

But other European explorers, especially the four men who survived the failed Pánfilo de Narváez expedition of 1528–1536, are quite good guides. These four men, the most notable of whom was Álvar Núñez Cabeza de Vaca, crisscrossed much of the same territory covered in this book, meeting colonial-era descendants of medieval peoples who had caused many of the historic changes that gave shape to the provinces that the Spaniards later called La Florida, Nuevo Galicia, Nuevo España, and the Yucatan.

In the chapters that follow, we return repeatedly to the journeys of one or another of these Spaniards to introduce the ancient Indigenes in each chapter. Doing so allows the reader to properly gauge what appears to have happened in the earlier medieval era. We will meet a few archaeologists, anthropologists, and other historical characters along the way as well, including the Lakota holy man Black Elk, the English author Charles Dickens, and a series of twentieth- and twenty-first-century scholars.

Chapter 1 points to some intriguing archaeological parallels across the continent, and sets up a framework for understanding how the parallels might have come about. In Chapter 2, we follow the survivors of the Narváez expedition on a journey from modern-day Florida to Mexico City. From there, we begin our primary journey through the archaeological complexes that emerged from the medieval era, moving amid the remains of millennium-old circular pyramids and monumental landscapes and sharpening our understanding of what Black Elk called the "power of circles." In Chapter 3, we enter the world of the Maya, tacking between the preceding Classic period and the subsequent early colonial era before immersing ourselves in the medieval world in between. In Chapter 4, we move northward into Central Mexico, backtracking via the footsteps of the four survivors of the Pánfilo de Narváez expedition. That chapter begins where the four survivors ended, in the heartland of successive Mesoamerican empires and the birthplace of the Thunderers. After that, in Chapters 5 through 10, we continue up into the borderlands north of Mesoamerica through the realms of the Hohokam, Anasazi, Caddo, Cahokia, and more. The cults of thunder gods and the healing powers of wind and rain here—from North Mexico into the American Southwest, Southern Plains, and middle Mississippi valley—affected human history in dramatic ways. Chapters 11 and 12 tackle the question of *why* this history unfolded the way that it did.

Admittedly, the human events and climatological processes reconstructed on our journey into the past become a little murky once we get off the beaten paths of written records to follow traces of material culture. It is most definitely true that we don't and can't know the names of most who lived and died in ancient North America, and we don't and may never know the precise dates for many important, history-changing events. Yet, thanks to a few recent discoveries, we will come close enough to those events to know that we need to significantly revise our general understanding of Indigenous North American history.

The new narrative is about more than people. It includes the stories of wind and water, upright poles, and dagger-wielding, shell-pendant-wearing, thundering creator gods. As you will see, archaeological evidence suggests that circular water shrines and their associated gods from Mesoamerica were carried into the north in ways that might even encourage us to rethink humanity itself. What is humanity, and does it change through time? More to the point, *how* were history, humanity, and climate related?

The tour of precolonial North America you are about to begin will lead you to answer these questions for yourself by tacking between the ancient past, colonial-era conquistadors, and more recent observers and archaeologists. You will see that there were a series of interconnected politico-religious movements or cults of a beneficent Wind-That-Brings-Rain deity and that being's stormy, diabolical counterpart. These probably first developed two millennia ago near volcanos in particularly thunderstorm-prone regions of Central and West Mexico. Then, in an era of desperation that began around the year 800 CE, the Maya built temples to their own version of the Wind-That-Brings-Rain god, who, for its part, was busily converting many more people across North Mexico and Huasteca and, beyond that, the American Southwest, the Plains, and the Mississippi valley.

Such gods were historically linked to one another, much the way that human beings were, and are, intimately entangled in a global evapotranspiration cycle: clouds produce rain and snow that lead to both groundwater and water bodies that relentlessly evaporate, condense in the atmosphere, and appear as clouds once again. The storms that punctuate this cycle are sometimes fearsome. Hurricanes can destroy. Lightning can kill. So can the freezing cold. The Medieval Climate Anomaly only exacerbated such potentialities.

So perhaps it is unsurprising that something profound happened across precolonial America a thousand years ago. The lives of hundreds of thousands of people were pulled into the global whirlpool of the gods. A wave of change washed over the continent, with eddies swirling in spots and water pooling in others. Few of us have thought about the happenings of medieval America in such big-historical and climatic terms. After all, written narratives are rare to nonexistent from the period, and some people might even wonder how archaeologists can know the past without the aid of written words. Happily, history is and has always been material, lived out in the past and strewn on the ground as bits and pieces of things in the present. You'll see this material along your own walks through the great ruins in this book. You won't be the first to see and walk through them. A hundred thousand human beings have already left their footprints there. Rodents and insects still root around in them. The rains of fifty thousand thunderstorms have washed over them. Yet our understanding of the big history that they tell us is surprisingly fresh.

I

Temples of Wind and Rain

> Quetzalcoatl—he was the wind; he was the guide, the roadsweeper of the rain gods, of the masters of the water, of those who brought rain. And when the wind increased, . . . the dust swirled up, it roared, howled, became dark, blew in all directions; there was lightning; [then it was said that he] . . . grew wrathful.
>
> —Fray Bernardino de Sahagún (1540–1585), Franciscan priest and historian[1]

You can see it today when you switch lines in Mexico City at the Pino Suárez metro station; it's shrouded in leafy greenery in the middle of a semi-subterranean room, open to the sky and the streets above. It's a small Aztec temple that dates to the 1400s, when the city used to be called Tenochtitlan.[2] Before Christopher Columbus landed in Hispaniola, before Pánfilo de Narváez and Álvar Núñez Cabeza de Vaca began their journey into La Florida, and before Hernán Cortés marched into this great urban center, the Aztecs (aka Mexica) built this perfect little stone temple (Figure 1.1).

It is not an ordinary rectangular pyramid to some god or ruler, but a circular platform a little more than 15 feet in diameter and 10 feet high. It once supported a windowless round house of worship with a conical thatched roof. Discovered in 1968 by workers building Mexico City's metro, the temple was buried 6 feet down in the colonial-era rubble left behind when the Spanish razed and buried the Indigenous city. The workers were instructed to build the odd little platform into Pino Suárez station, rather than remove it.

Figure 1.1. Aztec pyramid of Ehecatl in the Pino Suárez metro station, Mexico City. Wikimedia: ProtoplasmaKid, 2011. Creative Commons Attribution-Share Alike 4.0 International License.

Ancient rectangular steps still lead to its circular summit. Looking around and under its stone base carefully, you see that the circular platform was actually built atop an earlier rectangular base, nearly hidden beneath it. That rectangular base was, you notice, also built atop an even earlier circular base. There may be one or two more circular or rectangular foundations hidden underneath. Here, in other words, was an alternating pairing of squares and circles that reached into the Aztec past, a kind of geometric two-step that danced its way through history as the temple was periodically rededicated to a god and rebuilt in place. The specific god who inhabited this temple was the Aztec god of wind, more precisely the Wind-That-Brings-Rain. The Aztecs knew the god as Ehecatl, sometimes in combination with an old storm god, Quetzalcoatl, as in Ehecatl-Quetzalcoatl. An even larger such temple still stands west of Mexico City at Calixtlahuaca, in the Toluca Valley (Figure 1.2). There are similar temples from the land of the Maya to North Mexico, even in Chaco Canyon in the

Figure 1.2. Aztec-era pyramid of Ehecatl-Quetzalcoatl, Calixtlahuaca, Toluca Valley, Mexico, view to south. Wikimedia: Gumr51, 2010. Creative Commons Attribution-Share Alike 4.0 International License.

American Southwest and Cahokia in the Mississippi valley, testaments to the most important religious movement the Western Hemisphere ever witnessed, at least before Christianity arrived in the colonial era.

Ehecatl, Quetzalcoatl, and the other gods in the ancient American world were not necessarily immutable or static; gods could be celebrated, deemphasized, or even combined with others to create new gods, depending on the forces at work in that particular historical moment. Yet Ehecatl and Quetzalcoatl, separately or in combination, were most definitely powerful primeval spirits, known even more intimately to Central Mexican farmers centuries ago. So, too, was this beneficent spirit's alter egos or antithetical twins, one of which was a supernatural anthropomorphized canine god of death and lord of the underworld known as Xolotl, shown often as a skeleton with canine features. Another brother or alter ego of Quetzalcoatl, with characteristics that overlapped both with him and with Xolotl, was a dark underworld lord of nighttime winds known as Tezcatlipoca. Sometimes Tezcatlipoca's name was used in combination with Ehecatl as well: Ehecatl-Tezcatlipoca, the night-wind spirit.

To these creator brothers we must add a few more gods—as old and revered as Ehecatl, Quetzalcoatl, Xolotl, and Tezcatlipoca. The Aztec names for them were Xipe Totec, Tlaloc, Chalchiuhtilcue, Tlaltecuhtli, Coatlicue, and Coyolxauhqui. Xipe Totec was another creator brother of Quetzalcoatl and Xolotl or Tezcatlipoca. He was associated with rebirth and often depicted by the Aztecs as wearing the flayed skin of a sacrificial victim. Tlaloc was the god of water and rain itself. A masculine creator god, he worked in tandem with other gods. In his humanoid form, he appeared with sharp teeth, a twisted nose, and circular, goggle-shaped eyes reminiscent of a fish or a frog. Tlaloc's feminine counterpart was the goddess of groundwater, Chalchiuhtilcue.

Other goddesses, Tlaltecuhtli and Coatlicue, were of the earth itself. Tlaltecuhtli was a monstrous being present at the very beginning, torn in half by creator gods Quetzalcoatl and Tezcatlipoca in order to produce the earth, mountains, trees, rivers, and more. Coatlicue, on the other hand, was a more proper grandmother goddess, believed to be the source of all life, associated with snakes and agricultural fertility, and often depicted with large breasts and wearing a skirt made of serpents. Her eldest daughter, Coyolxauhqui, was the Moon.

The names of all these gods were written down by the Aztecs and then by the earliest Spanish explorers and priests during the colonial era.[3] But the gods themselves were much older, at least as old as the Medieval Climate Anomaly of 800–1300 CE. And there were other names for all of them, separately or in combination.[4] As we will see, these same gods, or their cognates and avatars, were known to many more precolonial people across a vast swath of North America.

Even today, Mexican schoolchildren take annual elementary school-bus trips to the ruins where the gods are carved in stone. They sit and listen to myths from the past told by their teachers at places such as Teotihuacan, one of the ancient world's greatest cities, located just to the north of modern-day Mexico City. They visit the preserved open-air ruins in Mexico City's Zócalo, the center of the Aztec capital, Tenochtitlan.

New Aztec temples are still being discovered from time to time. One of the most important discoveries was made in 2017 "on a nondescript side street just behind the city's colonial-era Roman Catholic cathedral off the main Zócalo on the grounds of a 1950s-era hotel."[5] Buried in a way similar to the temple at Pino Suárez station, the Zócalo pyramid was larger and possessed stepped sides. Originally it may have resembled a coiled snake. On its summit had been a circular temple with a conical thatched roof. By 2017, of course, the temple was long gone, torn down at the direction of the Spaniards who conquered the Aztecs during the reign of Moctezuma II. According to the first Spanish accounts, Aztec priests entered the conical-roofed temple through a doorway made to look like a great serpent's open mouth. Nearby were a ballcourt and a deposit of neck vertebrae from thirty-two Aztec men who had been sacrificed in the late 1400s.

Other circular stone pyramids with rectangular staircases and human sacrifices have been discovered elsewhere in Mexico City, including under the rubble of destroyed temples in a suburb of ancient Tenochtitlan called Tlatelolco. On October 2, 1968, months after the Tet Offensive and the murders of Martin Luther King Jr. and Bobby Kennedy, Tlatelolco was the site of the Mexican army's slaughter of hundreds who were protesting against the Mexico City Olympics and for the rights of workers and farmers. Here, in the same plaza as this modern tragedy, archaeologists found dozens of offerings and burials around the base of a small circular temple. Among them were the remains of forty-one human beings, thirty of whom were infants. Along with these around the base of the pyramid were hundreds of other animal, vegetal, mineral, ceramic, stone, and mollusk-shell offerings, many elaborately shaped into finely made ornaments, utensils, and ceremonial weaponry.[6] They included 6- to 10-inch-long chipped-stone daggers made in a distinctive shape, elongate and doubled-edged in form and wide at the top, with a needle-like tip.

Nearly identical flint daggers, as if made from a tracing, are found at another location 1,400 miles to the north of Mexico City. This is the precolonial site of Cahokia, scarcely known to Americans though it covers a huge chunk of real estate east of modern-day St. Louis, Missouri. In 1922, a team of archaeologists uncovered the remains of a series of circular "wall-trench" buildings on and beneath a circular earthen platform among the ruins of this American Indian city (Figure 1.3). These were dirt-floored structures with central puddled hearths, built by setting vertical posts into a narrow, circular hand-excavated channel or trench.[7] Next to one such building was found a local replica of a chipped-stone, Mexican-style dagger.

Figure 1.3. Two superimposed circular water shrines beneath Mound 33 in 1922. Courtesy of the Illinois State Archaeological Survey.

In association with the buried floors of these buildings were layers of marine mollusk shells imported by the canoe-load from the Gulf of Mexico off the shores of today's Alabama and Florida coastlines. These, too, had been buried at Cahokia as offerings to whatever spirit being or god had been worshiped around and atop the circular pyramid, two or three centuries before the Aztecs came to power in Mexico and a century or two before the twelfth-century appearance of post-Cahokian people that archaeologists generically call Mississippians. The Mississippians inhabited most of the Mississippi valley into the American Southeast. They were ancestors of the Choctaw, Chickasaw, Cherokee, Muskogee, Quapaw, Tunica, and other Indigenous tribal nations today.

At Cahokia, archaeologists have discovered human sacrifices, mostly female, buried in association with great upright poles, the latter up to 3 feet in diameter and, by one guesstimate, 100 feet tall. In all likelihood, the Cahokians dedicated these sacrifices to powerful spirits of creation and thunderstorms called by later Plains Indians Thunder Beings or, simply, Thunderers. Modest versions of the poles are known out into the Plains among the Omaha, Lakota, Hidatsa, and others, sometimes set in the ground by themselves, sometimes located next to sweat lodges, and sometimes emplaced at the center of large ceremonial circles of poles. Inside the circles, people held important dances and rituals in which these same Thunderers were invoked. The powers of the Thunder Beings, the people knew, were quite real. In fact, the Hidatsa people of modern-day North Dakota held the skulls of the original Thunderers-Who-Became-Men inside a sacred medicine bundle, a packet of powerful things and materials wrapped up in a hide like a scroll. The winged Thunder Beings, apparently, had long ago come down to earth and were changed into the first men as they descended.[8]

By the eleventh century CE, similar connections between circular religious buildings, marine shells, and gods of wind and rain are apparent in the American Southwest. This was the time when the Chaco phenomenon expanded across the Four Corners region of the Ancestral Pueblo or Anasazi peoples. The dozen great houses of Chaco Canyon proper did not constitute a city in and of themselves, at least not as most would define that term (Figure 1.4). Most of the human population, in fact, lived not in the canyon but in scattered small pueblos on the slopes of the Chuska Mountains 50 miles to the northwest—a good two days' walk for farmers carrying baskets of corn or workers lugging construction timbers and ceramic pots into the canyon.

Like their forebearers, Chaco's descendants conducted rituals in kivas—stand-alone buildings that were originally circular, often involving the Horned Serpent god. The god was connected to lightning, thunder, wind, and rain, and ensured good corn crops. One could call forth the god by blowing one's own wind through a conch shell, specially cut into a trumpet. The practice can be traced back to Chaco via Paquime (aka Casas Grandes), a great four- or

Figure 1.4. Reconstructed colonial-era kiva at Pecos Pueblo, with a Spanish mission church in the background, Pecos National Historical Park, New Mexico. T. Pauketat, 2021.

five-story-tall Mogollon-culture pueblo in the northwestern part of the modern Mexican state of Chihuahua that dates to the thirteenth through fifteenth centuries CE. The Horned Serpent figured prominently on the thousands of beautifully painted Ramos Polychrome pots buried on the floors of Paquime, this most urban of Mogollon complexes (Figure 1.5). There's a stone-faced rubble mound in the shape of a horned serpent pointing north toward a major spring from which Paquime's people obtained water. There are canals that bring water into the city. There is a two-tiered, 10-foot-tall circular masonry building on a nearby mountaintop, Cerro de Moctezuma, apparently dedicated to the local water, rain, and Wind-That-Brings-Rain gods. And there are four circular masonry platforms, one at the end of each

Figure 1.5. Horned Serpent image on a Ramos Polychrome jar from Paquime, Chihuahua, Mexico. Courtesy of The Amerind Foundation, Inc., Dragoon, Arizona. T. Pauketat, 2012.

arm of a cross-shaped platform, down in Paquime proper. These may have elevated temples to the four directions or winds.[9]

After they moved out of Chaco Canyon in the twelfth century, various Puebloan clans would have spent time around Casas Grandes before leaving again. Eventually, the Puebloan clans went back north, perhaps driven out by enemies. Other Paquime residents presumably stayed in the south. Both groups, in departing, left behind offerings for the gods, including thousands of beautiful whole pots and almost four million mollusk shells or pieces of shells that had been imported from the sea. Most of these shells covered the floors of two rooms or were found in a series of offertory deposits associated with water. That's an astonishing number of mollusk-shell artifacts for a place in the middle of a desert 250 miles from the ocean waters of the Gulf of California. Many were imported whole, strung on ropes, simply to be left as offerings. Some are the remains of the cutting and shaping of whole shells into trumpets, smaller ornaments, and fetishes.[10]

The imagery of the Horned Serpent, as seen on Paquime's pots, also extended eastward into the Plains and Southeast, no doubt in part because the serpent being was quite real. That is, the idea of the Horned Serpent was based on the sidewinder rattlesnake, a southern desert and prairie reptile that possesses the unusual feature of having projections over its eyes that look like horns. In some parts of precolonial North America, from the Mississippians south into Mesoamerica, Horned Serpents were depicted with wings or feathers, probably meaning that these were mythical creatures that could fly between the sky, earth, and underworld.

The earliest agreed-upon Mesoamerican appearance of the great serpent god, with horns and feathers, was at the imperial mega-city of Teotihuacan during Central Mexico's Classic period (ca. 300–600 CE). Officially called Quetzalcoatl, this serpent god wraps around each level on the façade of an early construction of the Temple of Quetzalcoatl in bas relief, the tails shown with carved rattles and the heads protruding outward as sculptures with open, fanged mouths. One might reach into the mouths with one's hand and leave offerings.

In between serpent carvings are repeated depictions of Tlaloc, the goggle-eyed god of water, and carved and painted portrayals of marine gastropod and bivalve shells (Figure 1.6).

Teotihuacan was a truly impressive urban complex, inhabited by more than 100,000 souls and covering more than 8 square miles.

Figure 1.6. Carved-stone façade of the Temple of Quetzalcoatl, Teotihuacan, Mexico. Top: Feathered Serpent and Tlaloc; bottom, close-up of marine shell carvings. T. Pauketat, 1995.

That city's pyramids include the second-largest in the Americas, the Pyramid of the Sun, and its notable lesser counterpart, the Pyramid of the Moon. Hundreds more pyramids, plazas, and neighborhoods are arranged around the wide, formal Avenue of the Dead. Walking it is awe-inspiring. It takes almost an hour for any inquisitive visitor just to stroll along it before climbing the summits of the great pyramids.

More than likely, the Teotihuacanos spoke a very different language than their imperial successors in the Valley of Mexico, first the Toltecs (after 600 CE) and then the Aztecs (after 1325 CE). Some suspect that many of the residents of the earlier imperial city of Teotihuacan spoke a language called Totonac, although there is also ample archaeological evidence to argue that Teotihuacan—like any modern-day cosmopolitan urban district—encompassed several different languages as well as multiple ethnicities. Many of its people were immigrants, merchants, or seasonal visitors coming to see the most fabulous city that the New World had ever known up to that point.

Whatever it was, Teotihuacan came crashing down in the 600s, probably for geopolitical reasons if not for environmental ones as well. Afterward, Teotihuacanos moved away and founded a series of newer, smaller burgs, many modeled on the principles and gods of the old imperial capital. In the aftermath, usually called the Epiclassic period (600–900 CE), a new political ideology took hold in Mesoamerica that built on the population reshuffling and the new interethnic confederations of the time. According to the Mexican historian-archaeologist team of Alfredo López Austin and Leonardo López Luján, this was the time of a nascent pre-Toltec horizon, when leaders ruled a series of lesser diasporic communities populated by diverse citizens in which the old Teotihuacan god, Quetzalcoatl, was reimagined in many localities across Mexico.[11]

Perhaps the god was primarily an elite god, at least initially. Or possibly Quetzalcoatl was so popular and pervasive because he was visible to everybody, sensed in the winds and rains that, in the centuries after Teotihuacan, were so obviously critical to the livelihood of the people living under the fickle climatic conditions of the time.

The Spanish priest and historian who documented the Aztec gods, Fray Bernardino de Sahagún, said that Quetzalcoatl *was* the wind. He guided the rain gods and spoke with thunder.

Besides being seen in storms and heard through thunder, Quetzalcoatl was also seen in the stars. He was identified with the morning star, Venus, by the Aztecs, if not also by Mississippians and their Caddo cousins along the Arkansas and Red Rivers.[12] In Central Mexico, Quetzalcoatl's underworld brother, Xolotl, was understood to be Venus when visible as the evening star. In another guise, Quetzalcoatl or his cognate was seen as a constellation. According to various Plains Indians, the great serpent in the sky was identified with Scorpio. The brilliant red eye of that serpentine constellation was the red supergiant star Antares.[13] After battling the gods of darkness, one of Quetzalcoatl's hands was cut off, and could be seen as a hand-shaped constellation, the lower portion of Orion. Come daybreak, the hand constellation and the rest of the underworld stars would rotate back down below the earth.

By the early 1000s CE, monumental feathered serpent effigies, some doubling as balustrades on great stone staircases or railings in walled ballcourts, were built into the Toltec-inspired Maya city of Chichen Itza, in the Yucatan Peninsula of Mexico. These were massive, dead-eyed, snarling-mouthed beasts with prominent fangs and forked tongues. In their orientations and affects, they referenced the Sun and stars. Walking down the stairs or running one's hand along a railing was a reenactment of a cosmic narrative. In 1000 CE, they would have been painted with gaudy reds, greens, and blacks. Backlit by torches on dark nights, the stone serpents would have seemed to move in the flickering shadows of the firelight. At Chichen Itza, as at Teotihuacan and Tenochtitlan before and after, the open mouths were dark niches for devotees to leave offerings. A devotee might place his or her hand between the exposed fangs and onto the tongue, hoping that the mouth would not clamp shut.

The spirits of thunder, rainstorms, and the Wind-That-Brings-Rain gods Ehecatl-Quetzalcoatl and Ehecatl-Tezcatlipoca had not always been as synonymous as they seem to have been among the Toltecs and Aztecs. In fact, these and other gods were quite distinct among the Maya at least up until about 900 CE. A hundred years earlier, the Maya version of Tlaloc, their own goggle-eyed rain god called Chahk, was the predominant spirit with which human beings were obsessed. The Maya worshiped it within rounded steam baths and made offerings to it deep inside mysterious caves, where they pleaded for rain during droughts. Unfortunately for the Maya, the rains didn't come, and a new god grew in prominence—one that might bring rain and one whose powers could be heard as thunder and seen as hurricanes. It was Ehecatl-Quetzalcoatl, worshiped in small circular buildings atop modest circular stone platforms.

Climate change seems to have both started and ended the cults of this Maya wind god. It began as a shift in the location of the rain belt formed by the convergence of moist air masses in the tropics that, in turn, governs monsoonal cycles around the world. Unfortunately for the Maya, the result were droughts, the first in the 700s but most in the 800s. These seem to have forced segments of Maya society to migrate northward, ultimately to the lands drained by the Moctezuma and Pánuco Rivers and known as Huasteca, in and around the modern-day Mexican state of San Luis Potosí. Jack Kerouac drove through here on the Pan-American Highway when making his own journey into Mexico, reporting the environs as a "jungle" and the Indigenes as part of "a *nation* in itself."[14] In this land, centuries earlier, elevated circular shrines to Ehecatl-Quetzalcoatl became de rigueur, the height of fashion in the tenth through thirteenth centuries. And from here, the strange cult of the Wind-That-Brings-Rain hopscotched northward, carried by visitors from the north themselves driven by a changing climate.

There might even have been a more proactive missionizing process behind such hopscotching. Zealots may have sought to spread the word of their gods to others, or they may have simply intended to travel to far-off places for their own religious purposes, with the secondary or unintended effect of attracting local converts. Such was the case, centuries later, with Álvar Núñez Cabeza de Vaca and his three comrades, the only survivors of the ill-fated Pánfilo de Narváez expedition of 1527. They would travel unmolested for hundreds of miles throughout North Mexico and the American Southwest, a good example of a common Indigenous pattern—pilgrims and healers who traveled cross-country on religious missions were almost always allowed to pass unharmed in Native North America.

Through such journeys and migrations, it now seems, deep historical connections were forged between the ancient Aztecs, Toltecs, and Maya of modern-day Mexico, Guatemala, and Belize, on the one hand, and the Cahokians, Caddos, Puebloans, Mogollons, Hohokam farmers, and other Mississippians of the precolonial Eastern Woodlands, Plains, Southwest, and North Mexico, on the other. The medieval period in North America, that is, had far-reaching historical consequences similar to Europe, North Africa, and Asia. Even more than the people of those other continents, however, Indigenous North Americans journeyed for spiritual reasons, and migrated as part of religious movements.

★★★

Precolonial history in North America itself unfolded in non-modern ways, as has been argued by anthropologists going all the way back to the beginning of anthropology. Franz Boas, Marcel Mauss, and Margaret Mead, to name three famous scholars of the late nineteenth and early twentieth centuries, argued that people in earlier eras did not rigidly divide the world into the categories of "animate" and "inanimate." Earlier peoples did not believe that human beings were exceptional. They did not see human beings as self-contained, autonomous individuals who moved through the world seeking to better themselves at the expense of others. There was no single kind of "human nature."

Indeed, human nature in every historical epoch, Boas, Mauss, and Mead insisted, was what the people of the time made it out to be, across the generations and between cultures, constrained but not determined by biology and psychology. Over the millennia, there have been multiple human natures—though the concept became increasingly homogenized after the mercantilism, industrialism, and globalism of the last few centuries. In contrast to our modern condition, for instance, most people in the past had very different sensibilities about what it meant to be human, if not also what it meant to be individuals. It's true that many people in the past believed that various inanimate things were alive or might possess souls. For most of these people, being human was not something disconnected from the world around them. Instead, humanity encompassed a variety of other-than-human forces and beings, seen and unseen, such that no one person—as we might identify him, her, or them today—could be conceived as being *an* autonomous individual. Today's self-possessed, strategizing, rational human being who makes his or her own decisions and confronts the world alone, in other words, is by and large a modern phenomenon.[15]

Ancient civilizations, on the other hand, began when people's movements through a day or across a landscape were coordinated with the movements of other things, phenomena, and beings on earth or in the atmosphere and heavens above. Civilizations began to take shape, in fact, as people down on earth mimicked the movements of the sky world above. They generally seemed to have done this in the hopes of mitigating some of the disorder in their everyday lives through appeals to the strict order of the celestial realm. Temples to the Sun and Moon or wind and rain were, in this way, anchors to the rhythmic, predictable, awesome order of the cosmos.

Such anchoring is precisely what cities and infrastructures did, according to the latest theories of urbanism.[16] Just look at the greatest cities in Mesoamerica: Tenochtitlan, Tikal, Chichen Itza, Tula, Tamtoc, and Teotihuacan, among others. Archaeologists and astronomers have discovered that the central monumental features of Mesoamerican cities are oriented with respect to various landmarks (mountains or rivers) and celestial events (especially sunrise, moonrise, and the rising of particular stars).[17] Or look to ancient Old World cities: Ur, Harappa, Hierakonpolis, and Angkor. These were the abode of pantheons of gods closely connected to the spiritual powers of rivers, soil, Sun, and Moon. The ziggurats of Mesopotamia's earliest cities elevated temples where people left offerings to supernatural beings, not high-status people.

Cities were never just the domain of human beings, and the history of these cities was never simply human, strictly defined. There were other-than-human forces and beings, in addition to celestial events, whose histories also mattered with respect to people. Such forces and beings of history—the most important of which are the most elemental—also help to explain how and why peoples living far to the north of the great Mesoamerican cities came to build their own centers of civilization drawing on some of the very same religious and architectonic principles as their southern counterparts. This is because fundamental substances, as essential as air and water, are intimately linked to the ground beneath us and the sky above us.

For us, today, air and water are part of the earth's atmosphere and transpiration cycle, which is to say the weather. What we call climate are the patterns and periodicities of rains, droughts, storms, and more. Thus, human history and climate were intimately linked in ancient America, particularly during the Medieval Climate Anomaly. Starting around the year 800 CE and lasting until about 1300, the earth's Northern Hemisphere passed through multiple centuries of anomalous weather patterns. For much of the north, this was a warm, wet period. In parts of North America and Europe, the conditions enabled people to expand agricultural production and, with that, the territories under the control of "states."[18] By the 900s and 1000s, average northern temperatures had climbed 1 degree Celsius or more. For other parts of the globe, Central Asia and Antarctica for instance, things got colder and drier. And, not coincidentally, in the Yucatan Peninsula of southeastern Mexico, Guatemala, and Honduras, the land dried up. Whatever the local conditions, the timing was the same. The earth was receiving increased solar radiation owing to reduced volcanism, and changes in atmospheric temperatures, the intertropical convergence zone, the jet stream, and ocean current flows were the results.

What happened in the atmosphere during this era was, of course, experienced as weather by people on the ground, and for most people in that era, weather—or rather its substantial, palpable aspects such as rain, thunder, wind, and more—was the result of powerful *spiritual* forces. Farmers paid attention. Their maize crops were surprisingly sensitive to temperature, altitude, and water, or the lack thereof. Floods or droughts might lead to crop failures, to which people would respond with special prayers, shrines, and rites that, from time to time, could snowball into full-blown religious movements. Thus, the boundaries between climate, crops, spirits, and human societies, or between climate history and human history, were difficult to see.

Word of crop successes or failures spread because, to paraphrase Chaco archaeologist Stephen Lekson, human beings in the ancient world were more aware of distant happenings than we are today. "Everyone knew everything!" says Lekson, even over distances that span the continent.[19] That may sound counterintuitive, but if so, it's because of our unreasonably high and very modern opinion of ourselves. We have been educated to think of modernity as superior in every way to other times, other places, and other peoples. But Lekson's point that distance was no great obstacle in the past is verifiable through archaeology and history. People in the past did travel extensively in order to gain knowledge of distant phenomena.[20] They returned with pieces of distant places and exotic raw materials. It didn't matter that they lacked planes, trains, and automobiles.

As far back as the Paleoindian period nine thousand years ago, families would engage in annual foraging expeditions across territories that stretched hundreds of miles in any direction. By the so-called Late Archaic era fifty-five hundred years later, pilgrims from across the American South would journey to a place in northeastern Louisiana today known as Poverty Point. A millennium after that, spiritually motivated travelers canoed 2,000 miles down the Ohio River and up the Mississippi and Missouri Rivers to obtain black obsidian glass, grizzly bear teeth, and the horns of bighorn sheep in Yellowstone National Park. Throughout much of that time, itinerant traders moved *Olivella* shells from the Pacific Ocean overland across the Northern Plains into the Midwest.

But the medieval climate intensified the practice of long-distance travel and material acquisition. Knowing what was happening in far-off lands or connecting to the gods of exotic places enabled one to shore up one's family and social position back home. And so shells were transported into North Mexico and the American Southwest from the Gulf of California; Ancestral Puebloan or Anasazi priests and leaders almost certainly made pilgrimages south into Mesoamerica from Chaco Canyon, bringing back macaws and chocolate from tropical Mexico. At about the same time, journeying north and south on the mighty Mississippi, would-be elites from the city of Cahokia traveled the "father of waters" to found religious shrines and to collect the valuable conch shells of the Gulf of Mexico.

The earliest encounters between Native peoples and Spanish explorers echoed this earlier medieval phenomenon. Spaniards crisscrossed the continent and met Indigenous people who had been doing the same. There were entire groups—the Jumanos and Coahuiltecans in Texas or the fabled Chichimecs in North Mexico, for instance—whose raison d'être was to move and trade between other groups. Neither the Spanish nor their Indigenous counterparts were as restricted in their everyday movements as we are today, even though their travel was done on foot, on horseback, or by dugout. What they possessed that we lack is the motivation to do so. Today, it takes a million-dollar prize from the producers of the TV show *The Amazing Race* to motivate people to journey across one or more continents. And these days, such journeys *on foot* are complete novelties covered by the BBC and CNN the few times in a decade that they happen. Perhaps our modern modes of travel and communication are part of the problem.

The motivating factors in the past that led ancient people to explore, acquire, and return home educated about the world around them involved a desire to understand the powers that caused things to happen. Ancient people understood that there really is raw power or energy in rainstorms, rainbows, volcanos, tidal waves, blowing winds, and the daily and nightly movements of the Sun and Moon. Anybody, in fact, can reach similar conclusions by observing the movements and flows of substances and materials around those beings or things. They would correctly reason that something—some invisible force or spirit—caused such movements to happen. Some power, that is, caused plant life to grow from the ground up, with the aid of water. Putting two and two together would lead anyone to ask what exists underground that enables life, and from there to think about how life relates to the burial of the deceased in the dark, damp earth.

Today, we rely on science to explain such power and energy, and we take a lot for granted. In the past, ancient people pondered questions and then sought proofs: What exists where the heavens touch the earth? Why does some water trickle out of caves and other water fall from the sky? Why do the winds typically blow from west to east, while the Sun moves east to west? Why do migratory birds travel north or south? Ancient people knew one simple way to discover the answers to such questions—go and look for oneself. And so they traveled, across the continent, into the earth, and into their own minds. Their journeys were both scientific and spiritual.

To answer our own questions about how and why, we too must travel—into the past, in search of evidence. Yet the motivational factors and alternative cultural orders of the past will require us to change our evidentiary standards a little, at least to appreciate that the evidence we do find supports our search for big-historical explanations based on the spirituality of people in the past. Changing where we look and what we look for—thinking about the past in more spiritual terms—will lead us to see parallels between Mesoamericans and peoples farther to the north, parallels too coincidental to be denied. These were synchronous; they happened at about the same time. Circular temples appeared thousands of miles apart during the Medieval Warm Period, seemingly attesting that climatic shifts were affecting peoples across the Northern Hemisphere. And so the earth itself was underwriting the big history of precolonial North America, much as it had in the other parts of the globe between 800 and 1300 CE.

The evidence lies strewn about the landscape, or sits tucked away in the musty archives of museums and university storerooms. That evidence tells of a series of religious movements or cults rooted in a period of climate change in the Northern Hemisphere. Those cults facilitated the spread of North American civilization, which had long-lasting effects still seen today on either side of today's seemingly intractable US-Mexico border.[21] Those effects were evident at the very intersection of modern history and ancient history along that border in the years 1527–1536. Indigenous North American peoples in those years—Mississippians, Coahuiltecans, Chichimecans, Mogollons, and more—encountered a few Spaniards who were traversing the ocean waters and borderlands of North America. We find them leaving the Caribbean, about to enter the North American mainland on a remarkable journey (Figure 1.7).

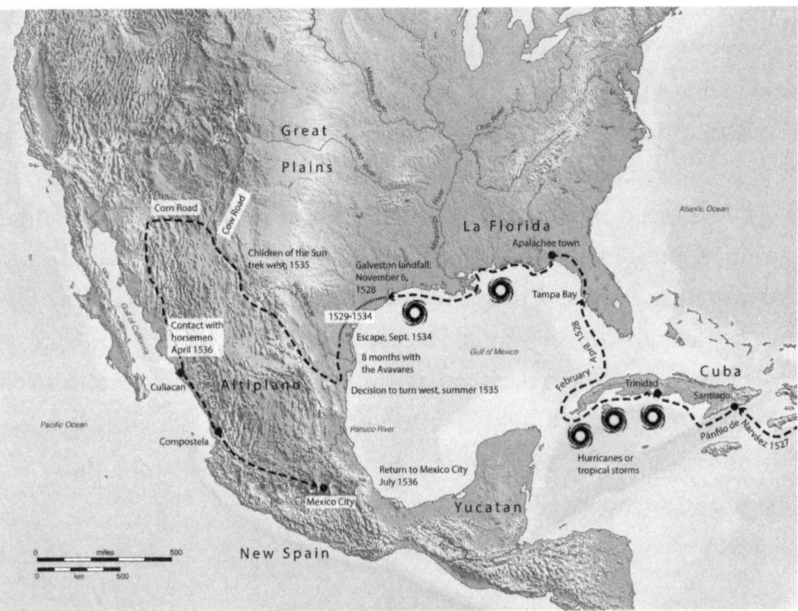

Figure 1.7. Map showing route of the survivors of the Pánfilo de Narváez expedition, 1527–1536, according to David Carson, *The Account of Cabeza de Vaca: A Literal Translation with Analysis and Commentary* (Friendswood, TX: Living Water Specialties, 2018).

Places to Visit

Zócalo, Mexico City (Tenochtitlan), Mexico

For Jack Kerouac in his 1955 classic *On the Road*, Mexico City was the "end of the road" and the "roof of the world." Mexico City's central Plaza de la Constitución, also called the Zócalo, is the cultural, political, and historic heart of the Mexican capital. It covers 14 acres, or about ten football fields, and was laid out quite intentionally by the Spanish to superimpose a colonial structure over the sacred core of the original Aztec city, razed by the Spaniards following the conquest. Any tour of North America that presumes to have as its mission an understanding of the continent's history should start here. Archaeologists have uncovered the basal portions of the Aztec Templo Mayor (main temple) and other lesser pyramids, courtyards, and buildings, which you can walk through today on your way to an impressive museum. As you pass through the exposed portions of the old Aztec epicenter, notice that the ground surface is bulging and bowed, a result of the weight of modern buildings everywhere but the excavated grounds.

The Zócalo has a rich history, and there are any number of sights to see. Consider looking around the Metropolitan Cathedral of the Assumption of the Most Blessed Virgin Mary into Heaven. Then walk through the National Palace, south of the Aztec ruins, to see the Diego Rivera murals on its interior walls. Stay in one of the great hotels in the blocks surrounding the plaza, which range from the ultra-modern to El Gran Hotel Ciudad de México, an Art Nouveau wonder.

Tlatelolco, Mexico

Less than a mile and a half north of the Zócalo is the old heart of Tlatelolco, the sister city of Tenochtitlan. Tlatelolco was officially absorbed by Tenochtitlan in 1473. If you take the metro, walk down into the Zócalo metro station, on line 2, take the train to the Hidalgo station, and then switch to line 3 north to the Tlatelolco station. Walk east to the ruins. Today, they have been excavated and preserved as the Plaza de las Tres Culturas.

Located on the northern end of the island in the middle of Lake Texcoco, Tlatelolco was famous for its great public market. It was here that the Aztec emperor Cuauhtemoc, who succeeded Moctezuma II after his death at Spanish hands, made his last stand in August 1521. After that, the Spanish leveled Tlatelolco's monuments, although the process by which they did so—knocking down the highest pyramids and filling in the spaces between the foundations—actually preserved the original surface of the city core. A walk through it today reveals the base of the main temple and a series of smaller surrounding temples, including the Ehecatl pyramid. A Catholic cathedral was built atop the ruins, the effect being to replace an Indigenous political-religious institution with a colonial one. Close inspection of its walls reveals a patchwork of building materials derived from the old Aztec monuments, mined by Indigenous work crews laboring to build the European-Aztec hybrid. Recent excavations uncovered the remains of features that date to the conquest itself—a painted cistern used by Cuauhtemoc, a group of sacrificed natives, and more.

Calixtlahuaca, Mexico

About 40 miles west of Mexico City, a day trip via bus, is the modern city of Toluca and, at its northern edge just off Mexico Highway 55, the remains of the Aztec city of Calixtlahuaca. Still standing, and in remarkable condition, is the pyramid of Ehecatl-Quetzalcoatl, a 20-foot-high stepped circular pyramid with a prominent rectangular staircase up the east side. Climb to the top and overlook the rolling hills of the modern city, less densely settled than nearby Mexico City, with its scattered gardens and fields, modern streets and houses, and standing Aztec monuments. Visit the museum just a few hundred feet to the west, and then walk to the half-dozen other pyramids, platforms, and partially excavated apartment complexes within a half mile of the museum in all directions. A lunch in the city center and a bus ride back to Mexico City make for a perfect day.

Xochimilco, Mexico

Ancient Tenochtitlan fed itself in part by an agricultural system that relied on chinampas, artificially enriched gardens of earth between the canals that crisscrossed the southern part of the island. Some remain today in Xochimilco, a borough of Mexico City 14 miles south of the Zócalo. The trip is well worth the hour or two that it will take you to travel here. If you don't take a taxi, enter the Zócalo metro station and find line 2 south to Tasqueña. From Tasqueña, hop on the Tren Liguro to Xochimilco, which was a distinct city in Aztec times. From the Xochimilco station, you walk fifteen minutes to the canal boats, where you pay up to $20 to ride a trajinera, a flat-bottomed gondala of sorts. There are music, food, and flowers aboard the trajineras, and you can float blissfully along 100 miles of historical canals for hours, past chinampas growing flowers. The Aztec flower was the marigold, and Aztecs (and other Mesoamerican and Southwestern language speakers) believed in a Flower World afterlife. Today, marigolds are grown in great numbers on the chinampas.

Teotihuacan, Mexico

No archaeological site in the Americas, possibly the entire world, is greater in ruins than the Classic-period city of Teotihuacan, north of Mexico City. Buses leave from any number of bus stations and hotels daily to take tourists to the great center, with the largest pyramid in the New World—the Pyramid of the Sun. Teotihuacan developed as an urban complex beginning around 100 BCE, when the nearby Formative or Preclassic city of Cuicuilco, with its unusual circular pyramid, was buried by 20 feet of volcanic lava. Cuicuilco's residents, and tens of thousands of others from across central Mexico and the

Maya lowlands, moved to Teotihuacan. Although some conservative archaeologists often avoid calling it an imperial capital, the sheer scale of Teotihuacan—8 square miles, 100,000 people, ethnic neighborhoods, the largest and most stone pyramids (five hundred) in Mesoamerica—almost screams empire to the visitor today. Archaeologists across the Americas, from the United States in the north to the Andes in the south, probably underestimate the historical impact of this one supreme Mesoamerican city. Stroll through the inner city along its Avenue of the Dead, from the Temple of Quetzalcoatl northeast, through some of the ruins of painted palaces and perfect little pyramids past the giant Pyramid of the Sun to the impressive Pyramid of the Moon. Soak it in. The walk takes an hour or two.

Paquime (Casas Grandes), Mexico

On the edge of the modern city of Nuevo Casas Grandes, in Chihuahua, Mexico, lie the ruins of ancient Casas Grandes, also known as Paquime. What you see today are the lower portions of what was originally a four- to five-story-high adobe city. Its T-shaped exterior doorways reveal its Puebloan inspirations.

Paquime is listed on UNESCO's World Heritage List and sits at the heart of a cultural region that was developing in the 1100s–1200s, just as Puebloan and Mogollon-culture migrants from today's New Mexico to the north were filtering south thanks to climate change. The pueblo that resulted was remodeled and enlarged in the mid-1300s, when it became the largest urban complex in the greater Southwest and North Mexico. The human population of the city itself reached some three thousand people, and the place was known for its elaborate painted murals and large caged macaw and turkey populations—hundreds of squawking and talking birds. But it was abandoned around 1450, just a few generations before Cabeza de Vaca passed within miles of the city's ruins in 1535.

Today, visitors see Paquime's Mesoamerican-style I-shaped ball-courts, a walk-in well, a number of cisterns, and several stone-faced effigy mounds in the shapes of a horned serpent and headless bird, along with circular platforms. The Ramos Polychrome pottery of Casas Grandes is world famous, having inspired a modern artistic pottery-making tradition centered in the town of Mata Ortiz. Casas Grandes pottery is known for its imagery of horned serpents, anthropomorphized macaw beings, and male and female shamans shown smoking tobacco cigars potent enough to induce trances.[22] The ancient pottery is on display at the site's visitor's center, as well as at the Amerind Museum in Dragoon, Arizona, the institution that conducted the major excavations at the site in the late 1950s.

2

Lost in Ancient America

> I stood looking at it, and thought that no land like it would ever be discovered in the whole world. . . . But today all that I then saw is overthrown and destroyed; nothing is left standing.
>
> —Bernal Díaz del Castillo, Spanish conquistador, reflecting on fallen Tenochtitlan (aka Mexico City) in 1519[1]

Thirteen people walked out of the world-as-it-had-been and into the world-as-it-was-becoming. Álvar Núñez Cabeza de Vaca and Estevanico the Moor stepped out of the bush first. It was April 1536. They were haggard, dressed in deerskins, and trailed by eleven Indigenous escorts.

Across the clearing, four Spanish soldiers on horseback turned to look, and were astonished. Approaching them was a white man, a black man, and an entourage of Indians. The Spaniard and the Moor had been lost in ancient America and were now walking into the America of the future. In the ancient continent, there were no boundaries or border walls between nations. People moved freely through the deserts and scrublands of what is today North Mexico and the American Southwest. Earlier in their journey, Cabeza de Vaca and his company had moved between Indigenous groups through parts of Texas, Nuevo Leon, Coahuila, Chihuahua, Sonora, and southern New Mexico and Arizona with relative ease. No one in those lands was completely isolated. Most knew what was happening in distant territories. To a large extent, their fates and futures depended on knowing.

They paid attention, and not just to people, but to other beings and lands, and to the spiritual forces that infused them both. These forces were in the wind, in the rain, and even in the ocean shells that Cabeza de Vaca discovered were treasured by Indians.

This is partly why the Spanish had been able to conquer the lands that they now proclaimed to be New Spain. In 1519, the Aztec king Moctezuma II (aka Motecuhzoma Xocoyotzin) had been indecisive in his political dealings with the god-like character of Hernán Cortés, who was leading an army of Spaniards and Indian allies into the Aztec capital, Tenochtitlan. Moctezuma had received news of Cortés's movements for well over a year. Perhaps, Moctezuma might have thought, Cortés was a god, and his armored Spanish men were *teules*, lesser gods or demons. Possibly Cortés was even the embodiment of a legendary bearded god-man, Topiltzin-Quetzalcoatl, whose namesake in turn was a great storm god, Quetzalcoatl.

It is said that the god-man Topiltzin-Quetzalcoatl and his Quetzalcoatl priests had been driven out of their kingdom, centered on the city of Tula, some centuries earlier, and had promised to return one day from across the Gulf of Mexico. And here was Cortés in 1519, a bearded leader, alternately fighting and negotiating his way into the heart of Tenochtitlan, insufficiently confronted by the uncertain Moctezuma. After some setbacks, the Cortés coalition, through their bravado, with the aid of horses and superior armaments, and with an Indian army of tens of thousands of Aztec enemies, succeeded in conquering the great central Mexican empire in 1521. The feat astounded the world (Figure 2.1).

Now, just fifteen years later on the northern frontier of New Spain, near the modern-day city of Culiacan in the state of Sinaloa, Cabeza de Vaca was asking four soldiers to take him to their commander. They took him to a local leader who was carrying out a brutal campaign of enslavement initiated by the colonial governor Nuño Beltrán de Guzmán in this part of New Spain, also known as Nuevo Galicia. Cabeza de Vaca and Estevanico the Moor, along with Alonso del Castillo Maldonado and Andrés Dorantes, had survived

Figure 2.1. Tenochtitlan, as imagined by Diego Rivera, 1929–1935, National Palace mural, Mexico City. Wikimedia: public domain.

eight years—some ninety-nine full moons—along the coast and in the arid backcountry of Texas, the American Southwest, and North Mexico. The time had educated the four men about what motivated Indigenous people. In the end, greeting the soldiers on horseback, Cabeza de Vaca was a changed man. He had begun to appreciate the Native, non-Western ways of life and the connections the Indigenous peoples made between life and death, good and bad, earth and sky, and friend and foe. He had gone native, so to speak. Watching the soldiers, he worried over the fate of the world out of which he had just walked.

Of course, Cabeza de Vaca and the other three men's worldly education had come at a high price. Some sixty of the Narváez expedition's men had drowned at sea before ever reaching their initial destination, Florida. After that, raiders from Indian towns on the subtropical peninsula had killed dozens, aiming their arrows at the neck gaps in the Spanish armor. And nearly three hundred members of the original expedition had drowned, starved to death, died of infections or disease, or been executed or otherwise lost somewhere along the way to where Cabeza de Vaca stood now, in this clearing of history, his eyes fixed on the mounted soldiers.

Commander Pánfilo de Narváez had led them into this nightmare. Narváez had been commissioned by the Spanish Crown to take six hundred men from Spain to the New World in order to "conquer" La Florida—the southern portion of the North American mainland that stretched from modern-day peninsular Florida across coastal Georgia, Alabama, Mississippi, and Louisiana to east Texas. He had expected to find gold in La Florida, similar to what Hernán Cortés had taken from the Aztecs just a few years earlier. Narváez must have been sorely disappointed to find no gold, and then he was lost at sea.

Rumors of gold in North America had already brought Juan Ponce de León into the "flowery land" of La Florida in 1513. By that time, some twenty years after Christopher Columbus had landed in Hispaniola, Narváez already had a reputation for brutality, thanks to his activities in the military campaign to conquer Cuba. Cortés had been part of that campaign as well and knew Narváez. Neither was a gentleman, as one might define that category of person today. Narváez's reputation in particular might help to explain why in April 1520 the governor of Cuba, Diego Velázquez de Cuéllar, sent him to stop Hernán Cortés from completing his conquest of the Aztecs, which Cortés had initiated in 1519. All of that Aztec gold meant that Cortés had become a huge political threat to the governor, and politics in the New World was extremely personal. Cortés had married a sister-in-law of Velázquez. She died just three years later at the Cortés home, under mysterious circumstances.

As it turned out, Narváez would fail to stop Cortés, and after the battle between the two Spanish armies Cortés imprisoned Narváez. Outwitted and outmaneuvered, the men who had just fought for Narváez "passed with greater or lesser willingness to Cortés' side" and marched with him and his army back to the great Aztec imperial city of Tenochtitlan.[2] They would tell the story of the conquest that followed to their grandchildren, and those grandchildren told the story to their grandchildren.

At the end of June 1520, a few months after their arrival, the Spaniards killed the Aztec emperor, Moctezuma II, and then battled their way out of the city, losing more than eight hundred men on the night of June 30 (known to this day as La Noche Triste, the Night of Sorrows) or shortly thereafter, taken captive and then sacrificed atop an Aztec temple. Cortés himself was almost slain, but he was saved by his loyal subcommanders Pedro de Alvarado and Cristóbal de Olid. Later, they would all return to lay siege to Tenochtitlan, having rallied a non-Aztec Indian army of many tens of thousands along the way. Including the Indigenous cooks and laborers who traveled with the army, upward of a hundred thousand natives allied to Cortés converged on Tenochtitlan. The Aztecs, now faced with an overwhelming force of all of their enemies at once, would lose that fight and, soon thereafter, their empire. Tenochtitlan fell in August 1521. Meanwhile, Narváez convalesced, having lost an eye to the business end of a pike in the fight against Cortés's army. A little deeper—another inch, a little more thrust—and the pike would have been jammed into Narváez's brain.

As they traversed the continent, Cabeza de Vaca, Estevanico, Castillo, and Dorantes must have rerun this fact in their minds time and time again, imagining themselves in some alternative universe where the Narváez expedition had never materialized in 1527 and where they had never needed to endure their arrogant, one-eyed, red-haired commander. "Where would I be now?" Cabeza de Vaca—treasurer and second-in-command of the expedition—might have thought, over and over and over. He had ample time to ponder the question, lying on his back looking up at the night sky, night after night, year after year. Up to this moment, stepping out into the open daylight, Cabeza de Vaca and his comrade Estevanico were unsure that they would ever make it out of this northern wilderness, back to Mexico City and then back to their homelands—Spain and Morocco, respectively.

Released by Cortés in 1523, Narváez returned to Spain, where he successfully petitioned King Charles V to be allowed to settle La Florida. Leaving Spain again in June 1527, Narváez might have seemed to the Spanish Crown like the ideal candidate—brutal, committed, and expendable—to lead a rather risky and open-ended expedition to take La Florida.[3] To Narváez, the assignment might have seemed an opportunity for redemption—another chance at fame and fortune. It would not play out that way.

Narváez departed with five ships and six hundred men and sailed to Santo Domingo, in the present-day Dominican Republic. Once he set sail for La Florida, he would never see Cuba, Hispaniola, or Spain again. From the time they arrived, Narváez and his group were beset with problems, some beyond their control and some of Narváez's own making. The first problem happened upon the expedition's arrival in Santo Domingo, when 140 members of the crew ditched the whole enterprise, deciding that the opportunities of the Caribbean island were too good to pass up, too good to risk it all on whatever lay in wait for them in La Florida. Perhaps they also had worried about what might happen if they continued with the overzealous Narváez. They chose wisely.

The expedition added a ship, but then lost both it and another to a hurricane along the southern coast of Cuba. The storms were a tremendous problem for the Spanish: relentless winds, waves that could overturn a frigate, the respite of the storm's eye, and then more of the same. In this one hurricane off Cuba's coast, sixty expedition members perished.

Narváez pushed onward. A brigantine from Cuba was added to the expedition, and after wintering on the western end of that great island, the force of four hundred soldiers, settlers, wives, children, priests, servants, and slaves—and forty-two horses—crossed the Straits of Florida and sailed up the western coast of the Florida peninsula, landing near modern-day Tampa Bay. The landing went fine, and initial explorations inland were made. But within days, Narváez made a fatal error in judgment. Against all advice, Narváez ordered the ships and a hundred of the men, women, and children to sail away in the direction of the Pánuco River, directing them to seek a suitable bay for them all to meet up later. Meanwhile, he, three hundred men, and the forty-two horses would march overland into the dark, dank, and dangerous new land. From there, Narváez apparently thought, they would march along the coast and meet up again with the ships.

Ultimately, only four of the three hundred would survive: Cabeza de Vaca, Estevanico, Castillo, and Dorantes. It seems unlikely that Narváez fully appreciated how unprepared his expedition was. It is unlikely that he even appreciated the distance from present-day Tampa Bay, Florida, to the Pánuco River: 1,000 straight-line miles across the expanse of the Gulf of Mexico, and more if by land. Narváez led on horseback, followed by mounted officers and foot soldiers.

Instead of gold in the interior, Narváez and company marched toward the native province of Apalachee. Fighting skirmishes along the way, finding no gold, unimpressed with Apalachee, and eventually starving, Narváez and second-in-command Cabeza de Vaca withdrew the men and horses back down the coast, holing up at a small Native settlement called Aute. The ships, of course, were long gone. Increasingly desperate, the expedition's men fabricated log barges—big rafts that could each hold fifty men. Weeks into the venture, they were barely able to muster the energy to do so until they killed and ate their horses.

The expedition was already a disaster, but it would get worse for the Spaniards. Had they been asked, however, the Indigenous Floridians would not have seen it the same way. Forcing out of your country an army of invaders wearing metal armor, riding great four-legged beasts, and carrying deadly weaponry never before seen by them—pikes, lances, halberds, swords, and firearms—was surely understood by Indigenous leaders to be a great victory. It was the summer of 1528. The native Floridians had killed forty-some invaders and a few of the beasts, the latter doubtless viewed with wonderment by the Indians for whom, up to that point, a deer was the largest quadruped known. The people of Apalachee and Aute used bows and arrows, wooden shields, and war clubs in battle. With those weapons in hand, they conducted a hit-and-run campaign against the Spaniards from the protective cover of swampy forests and underbrush.

Their tactics were entirely understandable. The Indians had no domestic animals besides dogs, and none of them had ever contemplated the likes of a snorting and charging Andalusian covered in armor plating, sporting a similarly armored human rider who, advancing, would drop a sharp iron-tipped halberd low to impale any native warrior in the way. "Horses," concluded Cabeza de Vaca years later, "are what the Indians dread most, and the means by which they will be overcome."[4]

In Florida, the Indians hid in the underbrush and swamps, releasing their deadly arrows into the Spanish lines. Traditionally, the primary targets of native Floridian armies were not people, such as the Spaniards in front of them now, so much as the enemy towns themselves, especially the town's sacred temples (Figure 2.2). These

Figure 2.2. Mississippian method of setting fire to an enemy village at night. Theodor de Bry, 1591. Wikimedia: public domain.

held the bones of powerful ancestors and the relics of each town's religion. For an enemy to defile one of them was more powerful than killing a hundred warriors. Destroying the supernatural powers of the temple undercut the legitimate claims of elites to the lands and produce of entire districts. The best defense to such threats was to distract and deflect the enemy away from one's hometown and toward the next town.

***

Indian tactics in La Florida were not so apparent to Narváez and Cabeza de Vaca, since their force had proceeded no farther into this southeastern North American world than Apalachee. But they were encountered by later Spanish expeditions, especially that of Hernando de Soto, who penetrated deep into southeastern North America. Landing in Tampa Bay eleven years after Narváez and Cabeza de Vaca, in 1539, Soto seems to have learned from the earlier expedition's mistakes, possibly via accounts told to him before leaving Spain, perhaps even by Cabeza de Vaca himself. Listening closely, Soto would have decided to bring more men, more horses, and more food. As it was, he arrived with 600 soldiers and African slaves, 220 mounts, and, importantly, a herd of 200 pigs—a moveable feast that would sustain his army. From Apalachee north into the Carolinas, west into the Deep South, across the Mississippi, and into Arkansas and east Texas, Soto and his Spanish, Portuguese, and North African men saw firsthand Native southeastern American society as it was before it was decimated by European and African diseases, and before the depopulation and reorganization of Mississippian society in the later 1500s.

In the interior, Soto's men noted, there were scattered towns, each centered on a large pole-and-thatch temple. In the largest towns, the temple sat atop a flat-topped, four-sided earthen pyramid. Sometimes it was accompanied by a great upright pole standing 50 or more feet in the air, occasionally with an effigy of a falcon or thunderbird perched at the top. Sturdy upright-log palisade walls protected these temples and, sometimes, the central grounds and homes of local elites.

The non-elite farmers, on the other hand, those thousands of commoners who did most of the living and dying in each region, usually resided outside town walls in scattered houses and hamlets. They grew maize, squash, and other native crops in fields tilled by adult men and women with handheld hoes. It was hard work. In the heat of the ancient South's summers, everyone would have sweated profusely.

The largest Native towns entered by Soto in the summers of 1539, 1540, and 1541 were in modern-day northern Georgia, southeastern Tennessee, north-central Alabama, and northeastern Arkansas (Figure 2.3). The human populations of these burgs ranged from hundreds to a couple of thousand. Ruling families conducted most of the business within each province, vying with the rulers of neighboring provinces, who lived as close as two or three days' walk away. Warfare was endemic and especially bad in the vicinity of modern-day Memphis, Tennessee. Soto used the enmities of neighboring

Figure 2.3. Hernando de Soto's force burns Mississippian town of Mabila, in modern-day Alabama, 1540. Wikimedia: Herb Roe, 2008. Creative Commons Attribution-Share Alike 3.0 Unported License.

towns in that region to his advantage, much the way Cortés had used armies of the Aztec's enemies to defeat the Aztec.[5]

Archaeologists call all such contact-era Native southeasterners "Mississippians," after a way of life founded around the year 1050 CE along the middle stretch of the Mississippi River near modern-day St. Louis. It was around that year—in the middle of the Medieval Climate Anomaly—that construction began on an American Indian city today known as Cahokia. The founding families of this precontact urban center had previously led sedentary lives, residing in small pole-and-thatch homes in a series of large villages, growing maize and squash (and, later, beans), making pots using clays mixed with crushed mussel shell, and being led by town councils and influential families. The lifestyle they led before 1050 is what archaeologists call the Woodland culture. But after their city of wood, earth, and thatch was built, radical change was introduced, and archaeologists call that change Mississippian culture.

A veritable Mississippian civilization would ultimately stretch from Cahokia northward up the Illinois River toward modern-day Peoria, Illinois, hopscotching all the way up to western Wisconsin and eastward into Indiana. From Indiana, Mississippian peoples stretched out to the south and southeast, over to the Carolina coast and down into peninsular Florida to Apalachee. Other Mississippians lived across the Deep South to the west along the Gulf of Mexico. One distinct group of Mississippian people resided in the deciduous forests of eastern Texas, northwestern Louisiana, southwestern Arkansas, and southeastern Oklahoma. They spoke the Caddo language and lived in dispersed farming hamlets around open ceremonial centers that dotted the Red River and adjacent valleys. Aspects of their culture remind one of Mesoamerica: populations farming maize aggregated around flat-topped pyramids, public plazas, and upright poles. One of the Caddo-Mississippian pottery decorations, which were distinctively local otherwise, was a spiral volute virtually identical to those of the Huastecs and Toltecs to their south.

★★★

Of course, Narváez, unlike Soto, would never make it into the Deep South, much less across the Mississippi. And he would never understand, had he even cared to try, the connections between Caddo peoples and Mesoamericans. In fact, Narváez had only entered a little piece of the Mississippian world before being driven back by the Indian archers of northwestern Florida. Starving, the 250 surviving intruders slaughtered their remaining horses for meat. They melted down whatever iron they had and made brackets and nails. With them and a good deal of expediently handmade rope they built the five barges, each with a ragtag sail made, literally, of the shirts off their backs. Once the barges had been constructed, the Spaniards boarded the crafts and floated into St. Marks Bay, in northwest Florida, and after a few days headed out into the stormy Gulf of Mexico to an unknown future.[6]

Initially the open water must have seemed a relief to the men of the Narváez expedition, but it turned into a nightmare. For a month they drifted westward along the Gulf's shoreline, seeking the ships that Narváez had sent off to some unknown bay in the direction of the Pánuco River. Today, the Pánuco's mouth is the location of the city of Tampico, Mexico. Tampico sits way down the southern Gulf Coast, straddling the present-day Mexican states of Tamaulipas and Veracruz. Narváez and his men had only a general sense of its location and distance. After just a few days afloat, all were famished, water-starved, and desperate. The Mississippians around the inlets and coves along the coast of Florida's panhandle and southern Alabama and Mississippi watched. They lured at least a couple of the men off the barges. These men were never seen again.

Hurricanes battered the flotilla out in the Gulf. The barges drifted apart. A few men died from the convulsions that come with drinking salt water. Others were presumably washed overboard in storms. Only eighty men and four widely separated watercraft were blown by an autumn hurricane onto the barrier islands near present-day Galveston, Texas, in early November 1528 (Figure 2.4). Narváez's barge was among them, but he refused to leave it to come

Figure 2.4. Cumulonimbus calvus cloud over the Gulf of Mexico in Galveston, Texas. Wikimedia: Matthew T. Rader, 2012. Creative Commons Attribution-Share Alike 4.0 International License.

ashore. That first night, he was blown back out to sea, never to be seen again.

Back on the barrier islands, most of the others in their separate groups were starving. That first winter, some survived by cannibalizing the recently dead. Others may have committed murder for the meat. The local Indigenous foragers, whom the Spanish stragglers begged for food, were likely horrified. Within a few months, the expedition survivors attached themselves to local Indian camps, who soon tired of the ugly, hairy, smelly beggars. The lost Europeans were abused and made to work like pack animals. They were practically enslaved. Some were killed by the locals for their perceived offenses. After a year, Cabeza de Vaca escaped alone to the mainland, where he acted as a trader, passing off goods that he acquired in one place to the people of another: ocean shells from the Gulf Coast into the interior, and flint, paint-stones, and animal hides from the interior back toward the coast. He lost track of time.

Some four years later, he met up with Estevanico, Castillo, and Dorantes. By then, the four of them were the only survivors of the initial three hundred who had marched into the Florida swamplands. Through some hurried communications, the men escaped in late 1534, naked and afraid, through a stark, cold landscape of prickly pears. Spending eight months with the Avavares people in that south Texas or northern Tamaulipas countryside in 1534–1535, the four men began to relax. In their written accounts, they describe how they laughed at their Avavares hosts for believing in a mythical killer who emerged from below the earth, known as Bad Thing. This monstrous being, who sounded to Cabeza de Vaca as if he might have visited just "fifteen or sixteen years ago," was said to inflict wounds with a large flint knife "as broad as a hand and two palms in length."[7]

As it turns out, such elongated, double-edged, lanceolate-shaped knives are known to have been imported to the region from the Edwards Plateau of central Texas.[8] Moreover, these were possibly modeled on Postclassic-period Toltec and Aztec daggers, known as *tecpatl*. The Texan forms were quite conceivably part of a widespread cult of a dagger god, in Mesoamerica sometimes called Flint or Flint Knife and more formally known as the devilish god Tezcatlipoca (aka Smoking Mirror, a reference to the shiny, chippable volcanic glass known as obsidian). Tezcatlipoca, in turn, was an evil counterpart of the age-old Mesoamerican lord Quetzalcoatl.[9]

Having experienced firsthand the captivity and treatment afforded strangers in coastal Texas and Tamaulipas, the men turned west to avoid the coast, and ended up traveling through the thinly scattered mobile foraging bands of today's backcountry Texas, Coahuila, Chihuahua, southern New Mexico, Arizona, and Sonora. It was a long detour, but taking it exposed them to people who looked upon their bearded black and white faces with wonder. As the lost men moved among the dispersed populations, they were asked to use their "medicine," a combination of magic and the healing properties of salves and remedies, to heal the sick and injured. Their healing powers amazed even themselves. Besides applying their practical medicinal knowledge, the three Spaniards and the Moor waved the sign of the cross in the air, perhaps hoping to convert people along the way. It worked.

In return, Cabeza de Vaca, Estevanico, Castillo, and Dorantes were given assistance, sometimes even porters and guides who would pass along information about the travelers to the next group. The men's reputation and following grew, and they were dubbed the "Children of the Sun" by the Indians.[10] Little did the four wanderers know the mythical and historical significance of that name or their number, four. The Indigenous cosmos, it turns out, was made up of four directions. Four worlds had preceded the present world. There were four Children of the Sun, who were the gods of creation. And the direction of their journey—east to west—coincidentally recapitulated the mythical return of the Children of the Sun according to stories of various North American peoples. To Mesoamericans and, probably, these native Texans, the bearded god Quetzalcoatl himself was one of these gods, one of a band of supernatural brothers. So, too, was the god Tezcatlipoca, who was associated with night winds, black volcanic glass known as obsidian, and darkness. Perhaps Cabeza de Vaca or one of the others was perceived by locals in Texas and North Mexico to be Quetzalcoatl. It is equally likely that Estevanico, the earliest explorer of African descent in the Americas and the onetime enslaved manservant of Dorantes, may have been thought to be Tezcatlipoca. In apparent recognition of his supernatural abilities, one Indigenous group in the interior gifted Estevanico with a shaman's rattle decorated with the feathers of an owl, a bird of the night.

The locals were accustomed to such healers and their accoutrements. They relied on their own healers, men and women with magical curative abilities. After all, simple sicknesses and wounds—an infected molar or a broken limb—could lead to serious complications and death. Illness and injury were grave affairs. Lacking a healthcare system or social security network beyond family and community, the people relied on medicine men's and women's knowledge of remedies and spiritual powers. Knowledge, religion, and health went hand in hand. It was not so different for the four wayfarers, and being lost in ancient America began to convince them that they shared a humanity with the Indigenous people in the lands through which they journeyed.

The year 1535 found Cabeza de Vaca and the others cutting through southern Texas, perhaps into Nuevo León and Coahuila, and then across northern Chihuahua (Figure 2.5). Soon thereafter, they missed

Figure 2.5. Big Bend National Park, Chihuahua Desert, Texas, as Cabeza de Vaca, Estevanico, Castillo, and Dorantes may have seen it. Wikimedia: John Cummings, 2012. Creative Commons Attribution-Share Alike 3.0 Unported License.

the ruins of Paquime, the great pueblo-style Mogollon city, which had probably just been abandoned some fifty or sixty years earlier. The men cut through the middle of what had earlier been Mogollon and Hohokam territory. There, Cabeza de Vaca rejoiced at finding "permanent houses" with people who ate maize, beans, and squash, just like the inhabitants of Mesoamerica. In his later account, he noted the fine appearance and manners of these people, who wove cotton blankets "better than those of New Spain." Had the four men ventured a little farther north, they would have entered the Anasazi world, where a host of Puebloan farmers lived in the "big houses" that constituted towns, or pueblos.

Just a few years later in 1539, Estevanico would return to the Puebloan Southwest, serving as the lead guide for a Franciscan missionary, Fray Marcos de Niza, in turn an advance party of the Coronado expedition. Marcos desired to travel into the heart of Pueblo country. Estevanico led the way, moving northward a day or two out in front of the friar. Marcos hung back and would receive signals from the Moor in the form of variably sized Christian crosses, each indicating the size of the settlement ahead. Upon reaching the largest Zuni pueblo, Hawikuh, Estevanico sent a very large cross back to Marcos. That was the last that Marcos heard from the Moor. Reading this dark-skinned man's appearance and owl rattle as an existential threat, the elders of Hawikuh had him killed. That fateful morning, the Zuni elders sent a group of young warriors into the room where Estevanico slept. As quick and silent as an owl in the night, they murdered the Moor.

The elders reasoned that doing so would keep the people safe from evil. In the long run, it did not pan out as they had hoped, of course. Hearing of Estevanico's murder, Marcos fled back to Culiacan, by then the northwesternmost Spanish outpost, where his embellished account of "seven cities of gold" inspired Francisco Vázquez de Coronado to mount his expedition to Zuni the very next year. Coronado marched his three hundred or so mounted Spaniards, some number of African and Indian slaves, a thousand Mesoamerican warriors, and a herd of cattle north from Culiacan, formerly a traditional native town on the

Gulf of California. He would find the seven cities—the pueblos along the Rio Grande and Zuni—that Marcos had glimpsed and for which Estevanico had died.

Coronado realized fairly soon after entering Zuni in July 1540 that these cities were, in fact, pueblos made of adobe, not gold—unless one considered as gold the yellow maize then growing in the fields all around. There was little wealth of the sort Coronado had imagined. So Coronado next broke the expedition into a series of smaller companies, one of which entered the country of the Hopi to the north and, from there, the Grand Canyon. Another traveled to the east and encountered the Rio Grande pueblos, catching a glimpse of one mesa-top town known as Acoma.

Coronado's men couldn't get into Acoma, but they had forced their way into Zuni and the other Rio Grande pueblos, killing hundreds of people. Not finding what they expected, Coronado next turned to a Pawnee man, a displaced Caddoan-speaking Plains Indian trader or captive from the east who had somehow ended up in the pueblos.[11] This man, whom they called "the Turk," told Coronado of another city to the east across the great open expanse that we know today as the Great Plains. Here, near his own homeland, said the Turk, lived a lord of a great domain who prayed to a goddess while sitting beneath a tree from which hung golden trinkets. At the mention of gold, Coronado's interest was piqued again.

Following the Turk's directions, Coronado struck out to find the fabled city that the Turk called Quivira. They traveled by way of north-central Texas. There he happened upon an old blind Indian man who recalled meeting Cabeza de Vaca and his comrades just a few years earlier. There, possibly based on what he learned from the man, Coronado began to realize that the Turk might be leading him away from, not toward, Quivira. Coronado decided to turn northward, crossing modern-day Oklahoma into Kansas. Had he continued eastward, Coronado might have joined forces with what remained of the army of Hernando de Soto. One can only imagine the havoc that a joint Coronado-Soto force might have wreaked upon the peoples of

Arkansas, Oklahoma, eastern Texas, and northern Louisiana. But this was not to be.

By the autumn of 1541, Coronado was on his way back to the Puebloan Southwest. Soto, in the meantime, was in western Arkansas confronting the warriors of a Caddo-speaking nation. These were some of the most populous and organized people his army had seen, and additional encounters with the Caddo would follow, though not with Soto in the lead. En route back to the Mississippi River, Soto became ill with a fever. He died on the banks of the river.

The rest of his men went west once again, back into Caddo country, hoping to find a land route to Mexico City. They headed southwestward through Arkansas and crossed into the Great Bend region of the Red River. From there they continued into modern-day Texas and the heartland of the Caddo nation. Here they seem to have decided that they would not be able to make it to Mexico this way, possibly advised by the Caddos that the water route was better. So they backtracked to the Mississippi and, from there, rafted down the great river and out into the Gulf. Coronado, still unaware of the near convergence, continued northward, having passed within 300 miles of the Soto expedition.

Out in the Great Plains, Coronado gave up the quest to find Quivira. Perhaps he tired of the Turk's deceptions. Perhaps he doubted the existence of anything remotely like what he had imagined Quivira to be. Frustrated, the arrogant conquistador had the Pawnee guide garroted, and turned his men around. The expedition returned to Zuni and the pueblos late in 1541.

By this time, Alonso del Castillo Maldonado and Andrés Dorantes were living in Mexico. Cabeza de Vaca was returning from three years in Spain, headed to South America, where he would act as a regional governor. Estevanico's ghost, one might suspect, haunted Zuni. All four had lived to see the beginning of the end of Native cultural and historical patterns that had been set into place six and seven centuries earlier, at the beginning of the Medieval Warm Period. In that earlier era, spurred by hemisphere-wide climatic shifts, spiritual journeys and long-distance travels had facilitated the creation of a series of historical interconnected civilizations. To understand the connections, we must look back to a place and time where rainwater and rain gods had enabled great cities of stone in the jungle, seven hundred years before Castillo, Dorantes, Cabeza de Vaca, and Estevanico. We begin with the Maya.

Places to Visit

Apalachee, Florida

The Florida Department of State manages Mission San Luis, near the site of the original Apalachee town, in Tallahassee, Florida. Visited by Cabeza de Vaca and Hernando do Soto in 1527 and 1539, respectively, the Catholic Church established the original mission town of San Luis de Anhayca on the site of the town in 1633, followed a few years later by a small garrison of Spanish soldiers, converting the Native capital town into a center of European ideology and global economy. Today, the park includes a reconstruction of a great circular council house at the second site of Mission San Luis, where it moved in 1655. This supersized but traditional building held up to two thousand Apalachee on special occasions. In 1527, Cabeza de Vaca described Apalachee town as comprising just forty houses, probably overlooking the fact that those houses were at the center of a sprawling low-density concentration of the Apalachee people for miles around.

The Bryan Museum, Galveston, Texas

Directions to the Bryan Museum, on 21st Street, can be found on its website. The museum is home to a large collection of Texas and western US historical artifacts and exhibits, including Cabeza de Vaca's original memoir and a miniature reconstruction of the raft aboard which Cabeza de Vaca washed ashore. The beach is just ten blocks' walk away, and a relaxing 25-mile drive southwest along Highway

3005 leads one to the San Luis Pass, where Cabeza de Vaca's raft is believed to have landed.

Coronado State Park, Kuaua Ruins, New Mexico

Francisco Vásquez de Coronado's expedition stopped at the town of Kuaua when it entered the Rio Grande valley near modern-day Bernalillo, New Mexico, along US Route 550 north of Albuquerque. Kuaua was the northernmost of a dozen such pueblos that Coronado entered, some by force. Built of adobe, the Kuaua pueblo featured two plazas surrounded by rectilinear patterns of apartment rooms. Some twelve hundred Tiwa-speaking people lived here when Coronado arrived, and the residents were compelled to provide food and shelter for his men. Today, the park is open to the public with a modest admission price. Standing amid the ruins, look east across the Rio Grande. This is where most of Kuaua's agricultural fields would have been located. Then look west toward a distant escarpment. Rock art is found amid the volcanic boulders along the ridge and can be visited to the south in Albuquerque at Petroglyph National Monument. Visitors to Kuaua can also enter a rectangular kiva in the southern plaza, built before 1541. On display inside are elaborate polychrome murals showing Katsina gods bringing lightning and rain to the people.

Inscription Rock at El Morro National Monument, New Mexico

Located on the Native trace between the Zuni and Acoma pueblos (today's Highway 53), the Zuni called the prominent sandstone bluff the Place of Writings on the Rock. The first inscriptions date to the thirteenth century and are associated with a large pueblo atop the 200-foot-tall prominence. Declared a national monument in 1906 by President Theodore Roosevelt, the rock entered written history in March 1583, when the chronicler of Antonio de Espejo's expedition noted a "Place of the Great Rock." All travelers stopped here because of the natural pool of potable spring water at its base. Indeed, we know from the archaeological remains of a campsite that the rock was a stop on the Coronado expedition in 1540, 1541, and 1542. Juan de Oñate, brutal conquistador of the Southwest and Southern Plains in the late 1500s, was the first non-Native visitor to leave behind an inscription. "Passed by here, the expedition leader Don Juan de Oñate, from the discovery of the Sea of the South the 16th of April of 1605," he wrote. The following year, Oñate returned to Mexico City to face charges of massacring hundreds at Acoma in 1599.

3

Dark Secrets of the Crystal Maiden

The long walk through the jungle to the cave entrance had been followed by a slow procession through waist-deep running water into the cool, dark underworld that she had only dreamed about up to now. In the dark silence of the sacred cave, sometime in the mid- to late 800s CE, the maiden stood in torchlight awaiting her fate. She knew what was coming, and understood, here at the end, that her life in this world was to end for the good of the people. She longed to see her grandparents again. The sound of trickling water calmed her. Behind her a priest quietly repeated some words.

Outside the cave today, the jungles of southern Mexico, Belize, and Guatemala have largely disappeared. Pockets remain around the ruins of some ancient Maya cities thanks to federal parks in those countries. One can experience what's left around Calakmul, Caracol, Copan, and Xunantunich, but the city and jungle to visit, if you must choose just one, is Tikal, Guatemala. Standing atop its tallest pyramid, Temple IV, you overlook the treetops. At 212 feet, it is but a foot shy of the tallest ancient monument in the Americas: Teotihuacan's Pyramid of the Sun, north of Mexico City.

The jungle steam rises from below the summit of Temple IV at Tikal (Figure 3.1). Green parrots wing their way above the uppermost limbs. Toucans perch on a few of the high branches. Tree frogs cling to tree trunks somewhere below, croaking in the background. Leafcutter

Figure 3.1. Temples I and II as viewed from Temple IV, Tikal, Guatemala. T. Pauketat, 2015.

ants stream across the jungle floor, slowly deconstructing the entire scene and returning it back to the earth.

From some distance away, howler monkeys call through the leafy canopy that covers all but the highest temples. The calls reverberate through the jungle, gradually moving from right to left over the course of twenty minutes. Sitting there, you realize that families of the lanky anthropoids are roving through the overgrown ruins of the central city, and it takes time. In the past, the Maya revered the monkeys. For them, the howlers and spider monkeys were another order of human being. Monkeys, they assumed, had souls. Today, they chatter disrespectfully down at any visitor who gets too close, throwing feces with amazing accuracy at perceived threats. Jaguars are just such threats, and the coatimundis and turkeys roaming the forest floor remain ever vigilant.

In 1956, a team of Guatemalan and American archaeologists began working at Tikal, the city at the center of the most expansive of the Classic Maya kingdoms. At the time, they ran one of the largest archaeological projects in the world, and it would lead to the establishment of Guatemala's first national park and a cultural and scientific exchange of sorts that included Latin American and Anglo-American scholars and workers. The dig team would go on to produce reams of archaeological reportage, initially abridged and published as a series of some twenty volumes out of the University of Pennsylvania. If you stack them up, they measure two feet thick.

Of course, before the Pennsylvania team could publish results, they had to dig, and before they could excavate, they needed to arrive with all of the tools, surveying instruments, and supplies needed by a twentieth-century archaeological team. A successful archaeological project, of course, necessarily starts with sound logistics, and in the Guatemalan jungle, this meant transporting all of the goods in by air. After landing on a newly built airstrip, the archaeologists and local laborers cleared the jungle vegetation from the North and Central Acropolises. Potable water would always be a problem; attempts at digging and drilling wells proved difficult.

Few Spaniards in 1524 would have understood, nor could they have imagined anyone wanting to study Indigenous ruins. Fewer still could have envisioned airstrips and archaeologists. In that year, Hernán Cortés, now governor of New Spain, left Mexico City—previously known as Tenochtitlan—and marched an army of 3,000 Central Mexican warriors and 140 mounted Spaniards south through the Guatemalan jungle and past the ruins of the ancient Maya city of Tikal to crush an attempted breakaway republic in Honduras. Cortés had sent his most trusted subordinate, Pedro de Alvarado, east to take the Maya highlands the previous year. And he sent another trusted commander, Cristóbal de Olid, age thirty-six, to Honduras to shore up control there. But Olid rebelled, wanting to rule this distant land—too distant, he reasoned incorrectly, to be controlled by Mexico City. Cortés, enraged, marched past the breathtakingly tall white limestone temples—featured in George Lucas's *Star Wars: A New Hope*—and took no notice of them.

Seeing the great ancient city for what it was took the archaeologists of the Tikal project. For over two decades, from 1956 through the 1970s, the men and women of the Tikal project cleared, trenched, and tunneled their way through the basic cultural and political history of the great ruins. They were confident—one must be to jump into the middle of a large-scale jungle archaeology project—but they had reason to be. Maya archaeologists and epigraphers were on their way to decoding Maya writing at the time. Expanding on work done in the 1950s, an epigraphical breakthrough followed in the 1970s and early 1980s. The primary glyphs, the epigraphers recognized, were numbers, places, and people. Other Maya glyphs were syllables, a discovery that led epigraphers in the 1980s to reinterpret the historical events commemorated by the Maya scribes at various cities across the Yucatan lowlands and southern highlands of Mexico, Belize, and Guatemala.[1]

Combining their discoveries with the extensive trenching of the Tikal Project has led us to understand how Tikal's political and monumental history fits in with the rest of the Mesoamerican world. It all began long before the Medieval Climate Anomaly, way back in the Preclassic period, almost fifteen hundred years ago. Tikal's North Acropolis, according to project excavators, was primarily a Preclassic construction that was initiated around 600 BCE with the burial of a human skull and pottery. The buildings elevated atop the acropolis in the years that followed were successively burned and razed before the platform was enlarged a number of times, most enlargements commemorated with human offerings—adults and children. In cross section, the acropolis appears like a huge stone-and-rubble layer cake, with the final Late Classic temples and palaces being the icing and ornamentation on top.

The reasons the location developed as the site of a Preclassic ceremonial center and destination for pilgrims far and wide stemmed from the Tikal area's geological and hydrological properties. Tikal, which is the modern name for the ancient city, refers to the ancient reservoirs that figured prominently in the rise and fall of the Maya.

This is not only because people need water to drink but also because water itself is a spiritual entity among the Maya that separates this world from one below, a dark land of the dead beneath one's feet. Tikal might even have been the mythical Place of Reeds—the site of Maya origins, the place from which Preclassic people thought they had emerged from under the ground. Much later in time, using the Nahuatl language of the Aztec, such a place was called Tollan. Other Mesoamericans, of course, would have identified additional locations as other Places of Reeds or other Tollans.

Teotihuacan, as already noted, was one of them. But at 630 miles to the west-northwest, Teotihuacan, in Central Mexico, was a long way from Tikal, in the Yucatan's interior lowlands. And, as opposed to the imperial capital of Teotihuacan, the great Maya city of Tikal sat in an area known for its eroded basement rocks, pockmarked landscape, and standing water during the rainy season. That is, at Tikal, most surface water doesn't even drain laterally into streams or rivers; it simply seeps down into the porous bedrock, a topography known to geologists as karst. Hundreds of small depressions, or *bajos*, are scattered across the karst landscape around Tikal, just a few miles north of the 40-square-mile Lake Peten Itza, a water-filled depression into which excess surface water collects before the earth and its permeable limestone foundation soak it up. Many of the *bajos* also hold water during the May-December rainy season, drying up in January through April. Then again, at least one natural spring—later enlarged by Tikal citizens—would have provided potable water year-round. Given the array of watery features and seasons, the entire effect would have been an annual, if not spiritual, convergence of land, stone, water, and people punctuated by the sights and sounds of both wet- and dry-season plants and animals.

Building a city out of stone that soaks up water in the midst of a landscape covered in scattered waterholes might seem ideal to a people who revere water. But Tikal's location in its natural state could not have sustained a Classic-period human population into the many tens of thousands between the years 100 and 800 CE. There were no rivers that might be diverted to irrigate the fields or supply a city's water storage tanks. The Maya in this region were almost entirely rainfall dependent, and the great urban complex could only have developed in this location following decisions by leaders to build a complex water management infrastructure that, for the most part, might capture and hold rainwater.[2] Alongside the stone pyramids, plazas, and palatial buildings of the central acropolises are reservoirs, cofferdams, cisterns, canals, and retention basins with sluice and switching gates to allow water to move and be moved into and out of holding ponds. There may even have been a sand filtration system connected to these reservoirs, used to purify drinking water.

There are a dozen primary reservoirs at Tikal, the largest of which sit smack dab in the middle of the central complex and were fed by the original spring. Around that spring and the central three or four reservoirs are three elevated, rectangular acropolises crowded with rectangular temples, halls, homes, and administrative edifices built entirely of limestone. The builders scraped, leveled, elevated, and terraformed the landscape on which these monumental constructions sit before the acropolises were built, all without draft animals and using only wooden and stone tools. The dedication that it took for the city planners, engineers, and tens of thousands of laborers to design and construct this kind of place during the several centuries of the Classic period is unimaginable today. People in the twenty-first century simply wouldn't do it.

That the Maya did, and not ancient aliens or wandering Atlanteans or Phoenicians, is patently evident in the construction techniques and decorative flourishes used. Buildings are covered with carved stone façades depicting aspects of Maya spiritual beings associated with earth, water, and sky. Imposing monstrous faces with full lips, goggle eyes, fangs, and bifurcated tongues greet any who would enter. Carved upright stone slabs, known as stelae, line Tikal's plazas, each of them covered both with the images of historical personages and mythical supernatural waters, trees, and other beings and with Maya writing that described and dated construction events, wars, and other singular achievements of the characters.

Of course, this was a city occupied by real people, too, both aristocrats and commoners. With respect to the former, the central city's palatial, four-sided buildings most often come in groups of four, each set arranged around an interior quadrilateral courtyard. The most important royal households had their domestic buildings and courtyard atop one of Tikal's primary acropolises. The elite buildings are impressive even today. They are long, tall, and dark inside when viewed from the front. But they are also narrow, a characteristic that results from the use by the Maya of the false or corbelled arch to support the heavy stone roofs. The false arch, appearing as an upside-down V, simply can't span much interior floor space. To construct a wide building, the Maya simply set one narrow room up against another, and another, and another.

Given such architectural limitations, even the buildings on the summits of the pyramidal temples might seem modest in their horizontal dimensions. Of course, what they lack horizontally they make up for vertically. The temple summit buildings have exaggerated roof combs—elaborate corbelled extensions of limestone masonry with complicated carved exteriors that poke skyward another 20 or so feet above the roof. From a distance, these roof combs can make Tikal's temples appear to be the greatest works of the ancient world (Figure 3.2).

The Maya emphasis on the exteriors of otherwise narrow and relatively small monumental interiors may be partially explained by the intended uses to which the buildings, and indeed the entire central city, were put. On the one hand, many tens to hundreds of thousands of common laborers must have built Tikal. However, after the fact, it is likely that only a few hundred people could have fit comfortably into any of Tikal's great spaces at any one time. The crowded central city's monumental landscape was simply not intended for ceremonial gatherings of thousands of commoners. Rather, the elites were the

Figure 3.2. Temple I, adjacent palatial buildings, courtyard, and stelae, Tikal, Guatemala. T. Pauketat, 2015.

main users of inner Tikal, and they were the primary occupants of the narrow, corbelled palaces and temples of downtown Tikal.

This observation seems obvious given the size of Tikal's ballcourts. As played across much of Mesoamerica, the ballgame was a team sport, much like basketball. In the Mesoamerican game, the ballcourt was shaped like a capital letter I, the ball was small and rubber, the players couldn't use their hands, and the hoops (when present; they weren't at Tikal) were set vertically along the sides of the court. There are two or three Late Classic ballcourts next to palaces and temples at Tikal. But the Tikal ballcourts are petite compared to those in Central Mexico or northern Yucatan. Only a couple of elite men must have faced each other in any one game, much as described among the Aztecs when a young king Moctezuma played against an elderly neighboring king and lost.

That a few elites were the main audiences of the theatrical rituals and games of inner Tikal is also exemplified by another fact: there were no great spacious vistas built into Tikal at ground level. To the contrary, the most stunning vistas built into the city were treetop views only possible from the summits of the tallest temples. Doubtless, these were viewing locations reserved for kings, queens, and priests. Back down at ground level, even the central plazas were but the size of a modern football field, and these are surrounded by vertical walls, roofs, and staircases such that one cannot see far outside the plaza in any direction. All around, palatial buildings and temples were crammed into the central city, some literally sitting atop others, creating an impressive, multistory, multidimensional, and richly sensorial arena to be experienced by but a few special people.

Maya commoners by the scores or hundreds may have ceremonially processed into the core of Tikal for ceremonies, perhaps amazed at the entire complex, but they didn't gather by the thousands and they didn't stay long. And more than likely they had to be content with looking on from outside the cordoned-off inner sanctum of Tikal. Indeed, only a few hundred to a thousand or so might have fit comfortably into any one of the plazas—and archaeologists are in no way certain that commoners were ever invited in.

The experience of the common Maya visitor to Tikal in the late Classic period would have been similar to that of a visitor nowadays, up to the point of entering the city's inner sanctum. Today, you follow one of four major earthen and stone causeways into the inner city's elevated plazas, temples, and palaces. Walking in from the southeast along what archaeologists have dubbed the Mendez Causeway, you pass through a half mile of jungle that obscures scores of scattered house platforms in every direction, some palatial in their proportions and others more ordinary. These were spaced out several hundred feet apart as far as the eye could see. In the jungle, they are effectively hidden, and the scene feels natural, even though it is not.

Tikal was an instance of "low-density urbanism."[3] Rather than being crammed into multistory apartments in a central city, some one hundred thousand people were spread out across miles of clearings amid a managed jungle environment. Each family had its own house, outbuildings, courtyards, backyards, refuse heaps, and gardens.

One can imagine them off to your left and right as you walk along the Mendez Causeway. They lived here centuries ago, before the fall of the Maya, just a few steps into this very jungle. How much time did they spend building the great monuments? Who of them labored in their fields of maize, beans, and squash? How were they treated by the lords of Tikal? Were any of their kin sacrificed in the inner city?

At a point, your daydreaming ceases, because your gaze is captured by the sudden verticality of a great white stone pyramid. This is Temple I. Its weathered limestone backside has no staircase. Even in ruins twelve hundred years later, its 170-foot height, steep sides, and roof-combed summit building, up near the sun, astonish. Beyond this point few of Tikal's commoners would have passed. The central acropolises, temples, impounded waters, and god-like aristocrats were simply too powerful to be observed up close by ordinary people.

Quite possibly, the primary destination for many of Tikal's ordinary class was not the central city anyway, but one of the hundreds of extended families whose domiciles and courtyards were scattered in every direction. The higher-status families were the core "houses"—high-ranking kin groups similar to those of early medieval Europe—to which many Maya farmers might have been related by blood, marriage, or debt. Through such houses, they would have donated their labor for the periodic large-scale construction projects in and around central Tikal. Here, they would have left their offerings of food, drink, or valuables to be subsequently carried to the appropriate temple by the male or female heads of the family.

Visiting family members would see their kinfolk's homes as they walked in. Many would have detoured off the causeway well before they reached sight of Temple I, following one or another informal trail to their destination somewhere on the outskirts of Tikal. We can imagine that upon arrival they experienced smiles, greetings, and other polite familial protocols that determined who sat where, spoke to whom, drank from which cups, and rose at the appropriate times to help with the cooking or cleanup. Later, relatives and in-laws would have eaten together, shared stories, played games, and laughed. An alcoholic maize ale would have been served to adults, lubricating the conversation into the night. The echoes of children playing in the backyards would have eventually given way to the sounds of frogs and crickets as the day dimmed.

Such scenes would have played out over many thousands of gatherings a year, time and time again, during the Classic-period pinnacle of Tikal's power and population, from the year 100 to at least 796 CE. This was the era of grand political rituals that elevated the heads of Tikal's ruling families as absolute, god-like rulers, feared for their power over life and death. That power, in turn, was rooted in the ruling families' control of time, history, and the cosmos. They could influence the very stars in the night sky, or so it seemed to commoners. No one would have remembered a time when this way of life, a complete merger of church and state, was not the way of the world. After all, centuries—dozens of human generations—had passed since the first Preclassic monument had been built at this mysteriously spiritual Place of Reeds.

By the third and early fourth centuries CE, elite houses were able to mobilize the lion's share of the fruits and labors of many thousands of farmers for their own purposes. In that way, Tikal had grown strong—so strong, in fact, that the people of another powerful city took notice. That city, of course, was Teotihuacan, the great urban behemoth around which all of Mesoamerican history hinges. Teotihuacan and Teotihuacanos: the place and the people were the sine qua non of ancient America.

In the year 378 CE, a series of stelae at Tikal and nearby sites were carved to depict the "arrival" of a new personage: Sihyaj K'ahk, or Fire Born.[4] Sihyaj K'ahk is shown in non-Maya garb carrying non-Maya-style weaponry. He was almost certainly a conqueror from Teotihuacan, for a couple of reasons. First, the previous king is said to have died—the Maya use the euphemism "entered the water" to describe one's passage into the afterlife—on the day of Sihyaj K'ahk's arrival.[5] That's suspicious. Then, Fire Born is said to have installed a vassal lord at Tikal the very next year, 379. The new vassal king was named Yax Nuun Ahiin, or Curl Snout, and he seems to have been the son of another lord who hailed from Teotihuacan, as both are shown in Central Mexican garb.

Whatever the identities of the players, the effects of the apparent imperial removal of Tikal's old king, followed by the installation of a new one, are clear. Valuable green obsidian and pottery vases from Teotihuacan were funneled into the Maya lowlands from Central Mexico. The symbolism of Tlaloc—the Central Mexican version of the Maya god Chahk—was added to Tikal's artwork and handicrafts. A new, uniquely stepped pyramid style from Teotihuacan, called talud-tablero by archaeologists, was built in Tikal. Materials and goods were extracted from the Yucatan lowlands around Tikal and sent back to Central Mexico. This included people. One of Teotihuacan's most prominent barrios was inhabited by Maya residents, no doubt many of whom had moved to Central Mexico from Tikal.

Teotihuacan's power and influence were exerted through Tikal into other quarters of the Maya world, including to the lowland cities of Uaxactun, Bejucal, and Río Azul. Later, it would be felt at the great city of Copan, situated in the highlands of western Honduras 160 miles south of Tikal. However, it took almost two human generations for the Central Mexican influences to reach Copan, and when they did finally arrive, they were conveyed in the form of a ruler who hailed from Tikal. This ruler, a Maya man named Yax Ku'k Mó, nevertheless identified closely with Central Mexico and founded a new dynasty at Copan, commemorated by a central carved altar stone in the heart of the city.

The lag between the arrival of an actual Teotihuacano at Tikal, on the one hand, and the appearance of Teotihuacan's influences at Copan in the person of a Tikal lord, on the other, probably means that the distances and political and linguistic boundaries between Teotihuacan, the Maya lowlands, and the southern highlands imposed serious limitations on anybody with political or military ambitions. Such limitations were precisely what the Spanish realized centuries later, when Pedro de Alvarado attempted to conquer the Maya for

New Spain and Hernán Cortés in 1523. The ruthless Alvarado wanted to achieve the goals that Cortés had set before him, but it took time. For years, there remained a series of semi-independent Maya provinces that warred with the Spanish and with each other, everyone with its own political history and its own capital town (and all lacking the grandeur of the preceding Classic-period cities).[6]

That said, the Maya were unified in another way. Maya cultures and languages are distinctive compared to those of peoples west and east. There are certain philosophies or ways of being that still seem to characterize the Maya today. Anthropologists have labeled such regionally distinctive ways of being "ontologies," thereby breaking ontology—the philosophical study of the nature of being—into a series of culture-specific modes.[7] Minimally, we can see Maya ontologies through the lifestyles of people. The Maya farm maize, beans, and squash in the Yucatan Peninsula south into the highlands of Mexico, Guatemala, and western Honduras. They live in cities, of course, and always have, but many reside in rural thatched-roof farmhouses, in turn built on simple platforms of earth and stone. So did their ancestors going back to the Preclassic period at Tikal and elsewhere.

Maya peasant dress was simple, with shirts and skirts made from hand-woven cotton. Color was important, and contributed to the sense that the Maya had, and still have, that the landscape and many of the things in it are vibrant and alive. In the past, many Maya saw the world as filled with animate forces, many non-human beings and things having souls or filled with a life-force that matters in their lives.

Anthropologists use the word "animistic"—the root word being "animate"—to describe the distinctive Maya ontology, which is to say their particular theory of the world and people's place within that world. Although the distinction is easily overdrawn, we might contrast their animistic ontology with those of their Teotihuacan contemporaries, the colonial Spanish, or today's modern people. The ancient Maya, similar to the Teotihuacanos, would have understood their history to be part of a much larger history of human and other-than-human persons, places, and things. Like most if not all ancient Americans and other traditional peoples around the world, they understood that plants, animals, pots, stones, mountains, lightning, water, and more affected the livelihood and well-being of human beings in a very direct way. Thus, a person might call upon or leave offerings to the spirits of birds, snakes, jaguars, storms, water, or even pottery clay during any one of the many rituals that people regularly conducted. Maya community extended to many living and non-living, and past and present, entities in the jungle.

By contrast, the Teotihuacan community was probably more human oriented, though not as much as the Spanish. The Spanish, similar to most Europeans, were actively separating their humanity from the non-human realm in the sixteenth century, with the conquistadors embodying a new kind of individualism—evident in the signatures on New Mexico's Inscription Rock—not previously seen in the world up to that time. Today's Westernized people are even more anthropocentric and disconnected from their non-human surroundings. We tend to see non-human beings as lacking souls and think of the landscape as the inanimate surface of the earth. We see people as history-makers, with the rest of the natural world consisting of inert resources to be used, if not used up. Not so with the Maya.

As evident in the founding and infrastructure of Tikal, the most important substance to the Maya, the one that links earth and sky, was the substance necessary for the life of both people and their maize crops: water. Not only was the maize plant itself reliant on rainfall in the right amounts at the right time, but an important way the Maya ate their corn was as hominy, which involved a process using lye water in order to remove the husks, make the kernels palatable, and produce a mash that might be used to make dough. This is possible because lye water, a strong alkaline solution that itself can be made from wood ash or burned limestone, reacts with corn kernels to remove their indigestible exterior skin and plump up and soften the kernels. For the Maya, at least until the Postclassic period, that was enough.

Both growing and processing maize involved intimate associations with water, and the Maya people prayed for it to arrive at the right times, called it down from the sky, poured it out in ritual cleansings, and, especially at the end of the Classic period, atomized it inside special religious steam baths. Most of them would have learned that the god of rain was a frightening spirit named Chahk. With his open, snarling mouth, curled nose, and dead goggle-shaped eyes, Chahk was terrifying, yet carved hundreds of times on the façades of Maya-style buildings (Figure 3.3). At a site such as Tikal, slightly less gaudy than, say, Uxmal's Palace of the Governors, Chahk's rains would have been understood to be what maintained a cosmic balance. After all, rain falls from clouds, pools up and sustains life, makes the corn grow, quenches human thirst, and soaks back into the earth. For human beings, water's cultural meaning was thoroughly entangled in how people lived their lives with and through it.

Now, imagine if the rains stopped. Contemplate the effects of a drought, or a series of droughts lasting years. What sort of maize

Figure 3.3. Stone faces of long-nosed, goggle-eyed god Chahk on the façade of Kabah's Codz Poop palace, Yucatan, Mexico. T. Pauketat, 2003.

production shortfalls would people experience over the course of that time, and would people go hungry? That was what happened historically, as noted by an early traveler among the Maya in 1843: "The distress occasioned in this country by the failure of the corn crop cannot well be imagined. . . . Famine ensued, and the poor Indians died of starvation."[8] How long would the city's reservoirs hold out when the only water source was a spring? What might happen to the daily routines of Tikal's citizens when the city management became stingier with the gods' waters? What might happen to the management if conditions worsened?

What happened has been imagined by Maya archaeologists to explain the ninth century's Terminal Classic period, when the Maya world went into a tailspin. It began around the year 796, and had its roots in a water crisis and an attendant loss of faith by commoners in elites. The Maya collapse that followed was not a sudden catastrophic event. Rather, it was like a giant who stumbles while running in slow motion and tries to regain his footing. The scene will end with the giant facedown in the dirt, arms and legs splayed. "It is possible," says archaeologist Lisa Lucero, "that changing seasonal patterns set in motion a series of events, including conflict over water, or exacerbated existing problems that eventually resulted in the demise of rulership. Thus, it is not surprising that there was a 'mosaic' pattern of political failure during the Terminal Classic."[9]

The year 796, according to the deciphered carved-stone glyphs at Tikal, was the end of the twenty-ninth ruler's reign and the beginning of a period of warfare and turmoil across the lowlands of the central Yucatan Peninsula. The leaders of the Maya city of Calakmul, 60 miles to the north, were rivals with those of Tikal, and the relationship degenerated into all-out warfare. The nobility of yet another city, Dos Pilas, joined with Calakmul to fight Tikal. The disintegration of the elaborate structure whereby the nobility supported artisans and scribes and maintained reservoirs full of water was hastened.

After 800 CE, across much of the Mexican, Guatemalan, and Belizean lowlands, Classic Maya regimes began falling like dominos, or at least they became unable to support the scribes and stoneworkers whose efforts would otherwise be mobilized to carve dates and events onto stelae. The last monument at Copan records the date 822. The final one at Tikal is translated to read 869. The last such monument with a long-count date of any kind in Maya country records the year as 909. A century of stumbling, and the giant had fallen. With that final carving, the Terminal Classic period was over. Everything had hinged on a delicate balance between the cities, their commoner populations, and the ruling elite, and that balance was gone.

Lucero and other Mayanists believe that the Maya, in their increasing desperation, turned to prayer and magic. Great pilgrimages to places of water began: rivers, natural pools, water-filled sinkholes, springs, and caves. In one of the most famous, Actun Tunichil Muknal (the Cave of the Stone Sepulcher) in central Belize, are a series of offerings that range from shattered water jars to human sacrifices. These were left in the cave until 900 CE. The entrance is itself marked by the crumbled stone ruins and disintegrated thatched roofs of Maya water temples that probably date to the 800s CE. Here, Maya priests would have begun their ceremonial processions into the cave, dressed in high ceremonial garb, followed by attendants packing powerful medicine bundles. If you were unfortunate enough to follow, then you might be about to have the most notable experience of your life—a ceremonial death.

Today, led by a guide, another archaeologist enters Actun Tunichil Muknal. It is Susan Alt, a veteran Mississippi Valley researcher who is visiting Lucero. Water, in Alt's ontological view of the past, is less a resource to be used and more a substance to be experienced. At the opening of the cave, she removes her outer clothing beside the temple ruins. Initially stepping into the edge of the cold, clear pool at the mouth, she then plunges headlong into the water and swims through the cave's opening. The water is deep, over her head. Ten or twelve yards inside, her feet find a rocky purchase and she walks up out of the pool into a waist-deep stream flowing from the earth's underworld. Already here, near the opening, there are Maya offerings that seem to begin a story, told as Alt walks farther into the cave. There are two upright slate stelae shaped to look like stone knives. Several bends and pools later, there are Maya pots, some ceremonially killed by punching a hole in the bottom, some smashed outright, all dating to the Terminal Classic period—the 800s (Figure 3.4).

The entourages that accompanied the Maya priests would have lit their way with torches. Alt and her guide use flashlights, shining their beams into the depths of large antechambers where a million water droplets glisten on the flowstones and speleothems all around. What's more, what the Maya left behind has become covered in a fine crystalline layer of calcium carbonate, stone that reconstitutes itself after having been dissolved from the bedrock above as rainwater passes through it.

Here, and farther into the cavernous depths, the silence is pierced only by the gurgling water of the underground stream. In the depths

Figure 3.4. Maya water jar offerings in Actun Tunichil Muknal, Belize. Wikimedia: photo by Jkolecki, 2010. Creative Commons Attribution-Share Alike 3.0 Unported License.

of a cave such as this, time slows down. One loses track of it because, lacking the constant sensory stimulation of the outside world, the human brain experiences less time passing than actually does pass out in the sunshine. The effect is awesome, a feeling only sharpened by one's ritual procession through the cold water and into the darkness. Maya prayers, liturgical pronouncements, and offerings here must have been powerful indeed. They included the blood of the priests themselves, who cut themselves with sharp obsidian blades inside the cave.

About that time, Alt's flashlight catches a crystal-coated object lying in the water nearby. It is a human skull, a piece of scattered human remains near yet another pot, one of many. Next, she climbs vertically up some great chunks of roof fall to a hidden side chamber. There, in the dark upper passage, is the skeleton of an eighteen-year-old female, glistening with microcrystals, with legs and arms splayed out. Some eleven hundred years ago, in torchlight, with time slowed to an eternity inside the cave, a priest dispatched her with a quick stroke of a chipped-stone knife, leaving her fully articulated skeleton to be rediscovered in the beam of a flashlight.

The effect on any first-time visitor into Actun Tunichil Muknal is emotional. Lucero believes that such victims were likely witches—people blamed perhaps for the environmental failures then apparent in the outside world of the Maya.[10] Others would characterize them as human offerings or sacrifices, meant to bring back the rains. Whoever they were, they were not alone. Human beings were offered up to the waters of the deep at other locations during this time and into the subsequent Postclassic era across the Maya world. These included cenotes, water-filled sinkholes. One of the best known is at the unusual Maya city Chichen Itza, in the northern Yucatan. There, at the end of a 30-foot-wide constructed avenue, or *sacbe*, is a temple overlooking an 1,800-foot-wide, 90-foot-deep cenote. It is informally called the Well of Sacrifices because hundreds of golden idols and human remains from sacrifices were dropped into the water from above.

Why sacrifice? Not everyone across the continent made human offerings to the gods in same way during the eighth through twelfth centuries CE, but offerings during the medieval era were common nonetheless, and such practices seem to define the core values of various cultures in similar ways. With the fall of Teotihuacan and the onset of the medieval climate, central Mexicans did make frequent offerings to an invigorated Wind-That-Brings-Rain deity, among other gods. In the Altiplano of North and West Mexico, ancestral bones were venerated in the monumental and ceremonial centers of farmers seeking the assistance of a rain god. Farther north into New Mexico, magical wands and carved wooden figures were buried with a prominent pair of ancestors, whose spirits may have haunted a great house also linked to rain. And in the middle of the Mississippi valley during the eleventh and twelfth centuries, young females were most definitely sacrificed to water, the Moon, and the Wind-That-Brings-Rain.

For the Maya, the answer to the question of human sacrifice is to be found partly in their distinctive ontology, or spirituality, and partly in climate change. Unhappy spirits need to be propitiated. Dissatisfied gods need to be made content. Severe crises call for drastic measures. The prolonged droughts of the ninth-century Maya crisis, for instance, would have driven many to seek answers to seemingly insurmountable questions. There were simply too many people, too much political and ceremonial infrastructure, and too little water to go around. Something had to be done. Cosmic ills needed to be healed, a process that will take us from Chichen Itza and its Central Mexican counterpart, Tula, and into the lands of Huasteca.

Places to Visit

Actun Tunichil Muknal, Belize

A trip to Actun Tunichil Muknal is not for the casual visitor, but access to the cave is possible by means of a limited number of tourist agencies in Belize City or the town of San Ignacio. A hike back to the cave entrance from a parking area involves walking over occasional scatters of stone and pottery sherds that the attentive visitor will recognize as Maya house foundations. This is followed by a total immersion in water and, for much of the passage, walking in water. Cameras and various other articles are prohibited in the cave, and you will of course want to take nothing with you that can't get wet. Wear light clothing, including canvas sneakers—no socks. Expect the extraordinary, the most sacred of sacred locations at a time when the Classic Maya world was falling apart.

Tikal, Guatemala

Only three or four places in the Western Hemisphere awe a visitor the way that Tikal does. To see it with the least amount of hassle, hire a tour company in Belize City to take you from Belize into Guatemala and stay in the island town of Flores or elsewhere along Lake Peten Itza. Traveling in by car, you will most likely arrive at the end of the Mendez Causeway. On it, you will walk into the ancient city center. The walk in is quiet. The dense packing of stone buildings, plazas, and stelae in the Central and North Acropolises is impressive, and there are many paths to follow.

Like many Maya cities, there is a series of precincts, acropolises, and distinctive areas revealing a complicated, deep history, with factions of elites or rulers responsible for the construction of the various parts through time. Over the generations, the rulers and their rules, along with their favorite gods, changed. This is evident in part by the multiple alignments of buildings and *sacbes* evident in different parts of the sites, revealing, in turn, the altered cosmic and terrestrial benchmarks or referents used in subsequent design plans. You can detect these from below and above. While various temples are now off-limits to tourists, climb to the summit of Temple IV and overlook the city from the treetops.

4

Mesoamerican Cults and Cities

> Round structures in Middle America were dedicated principally to the God Quetzalcoatl . . . and there is some evidence for both having originated in the Huasteca.
>
> —Gordon F. Ekholm, archaeologist-curator, American Museum of Natural History, 1944[1]

In crisis situations throughout human history, people turn to visionaries and new religions. A "small group of committed citizens can change the world," the eminent cultural anthropologist Margaret Mead is thought to have said. "Indeed," she continued, "it's the only thing that ever has."[2]

In the recent Indigenous North and Middle (or Meso-) American past, such world-changing citizens included visionaries or prophets who sought to return their people to traditional paths in order to drive out unwanted intruders and evil influences. The man called the "Shawnee Prophet" had a vision in 1806 somewhere in today's Ohio, and he used politics and religion to promote his cult-like following, building a new town—Prophetstown—in the process. A Piute visionary named Wovoka foresaw a Ghost Dance in 1889 that would bring back depleted herds of bison and drive out the whites across the American West. A rebel leader among the Maya, in 1848, discovered a talking crucifix near a cenote, or sacred sinkhole, and built a shrine on the spot, giving life to Yucatan's mid-nineteenth-century attempts to secede from Mexico. There were many other such movements.

One swept through the same territories crossed by the survivors of the Narváez expedition not long after them. The men who had met Cabeza de Vaca and Estevanico north of Culiacan had continued their brutal campaign of killing, raping, and enslaving thousands under colonial governor Nuño Beltrán de Guzmán through the 1530s. With the removal of troops from Culiacan to accompany Coronado's march north in 1539, an opportunity presented itself. With the help of a god that the Spanish believed to be the devil, Chichimec shamans from the mountains of the Mexican Altiplano are credited with inventing in 1541 a millenarian movement to rid the country of the Spanish. So began what was known as the Mixtón War—a spiritually motivated campaign waged by an alliance of so-called Chichimec peoples of the Altiplano.[3] There were some Indigenous successes—Pedro de Alvarado was killed—but the victims were primarily Native. Untold thousands died and hundreds of villages were burned. In the end, at the fortified cliff of El Mixtón in southern Zacatecas, Indians jumped to their deaths rather than give up the cause and submit to Spanish rule.

The common ingredients in such politico-religious movements include a vision of a spiritual force or god and a set of material things or practices that connect people emotionally with that supernatural power. Depending on the charisma of the visionary and the demonstrable veracity of the vision, these movements might last, growing rapidly with a fervor akin to a tidal wave, or they might quickly dissipate, like ripples in a small pond. They might even lead to military actions that bring about profound historical change very fast.

So, we must wonder: what forces might have been behind the introduction and spread of a new religion beginning with the ninth-century Maya? Around the year 800, a distinctive sort of Maya water shrine or temple was spreading along the coasts of the Yucatan. It was circular in outline, consisting of a low platform topped by a small circular house with a conical roof made of thatch (Figure 4.1). Some were built to

Figure 4.1. Artist's reconstruction of a Terminal Classic–period Maya water shrine. Patricia A. McAnany, "Terminal Classic Maya Heterodoxy and Shrine Vernacularism in the Sibun Valley, Belize," *Cambridge Archaeological Journal* 22, no. 1 (2012): 115–134, fig. 2. Courtesy of the Xibun Archaeological Research Project Archives.

overlook a spring, a natural pool, or a stream. Others were integral components of ceremonial centers near a river, cave, or seep.

There were also rounded Maya steam baths. These vapor or sweat houses had precedents going all the way back to the first millennium BCE.[4] The earliest examples were domestic facilities in the backyards of homes. In the Classic era, these became incorporated into the official religions and rectilinear spaces of Maya cities. In fact, up until the Terminal Classic period, these were all rectangular in plan. Great Maya rulers sometimes even elevated them atop their pyramids. Only much later, during the ninth century CE, did steam baths assume circular or rounded shapes, at which time they became part of a pancultural movement.

The dark interiors of the steam baths and other circular water shrines evoked the interiors of caves, the dark bottoms of pools, the interiors of pottery jars, the night sky, and the underworld, all associated with water. Some steam baths were even set at or below the surface outside and were small, with just enough space inside for a few people to sit together (Figure 4.2). No doubt, their size was largely a result of their intended function—these were ceremonial rooms in which water would be poured over hot rocks to produce steam. This association with water, via steam, was a way of enabling human bodies, on which sweat would quickly accumulate, to become one with the transpiration cycle of water. Such mergers were palpable and, for that reason, powerful. When ceremonially terminated, some water shrines

Figure 4.2. Nude man and woman inside precolonial Mixtec steam bath, with attendants pouring water from bowls to create steam. Codex Nuttall. Public domain.

were filled with offerings to the great Wind-That-Brings-Rain god Ehecatl-Quetzalcoatl, called Kukulkan among the Maya.[5]

The circular water shrine association with the Feathered Serpent in parts of the Yucatan lowlands is said to have constituted an "alternative" or "transcendent" ideology, or a new religion, that began among the non-elite members of society and spread along the northern and eastern coast of the peninsula in the early 800s.[6] As a movement, it "existed in tension with prevailing Classic Maya ideology of divine and hereditary rulership" in its "waning" years, says Maya archaeologist Patricia McAnany. It may have flourished as local Maya communities turned away from their Classic Maya cities, with their overly demanding royal houses, and toward other mythical Tollans, or places of origins. Chichen Itza may have been one such legendary city that became the basis of a new pan-Maya identity.

The evidence of this bottom-up movement takes the form of unofficial or vernacular temples sprinkled around the Yucatan that reference the major shrines, as we will see at Chichen Itza. There was some variation in these temples, though one thing they apparently had in common was a reference to Kukulkan. Apparently, with the collapse of the royal houses at Classic Maya cities, this pan-Yucatan cult to the Wind-That-Brings-Rain unified people's beliefs but did not result in a common pan-Maya empire.

Certain pilgrimages or regional movements of the water-starved Maya might have begun as walks to a local water hole to leave offerings. Some may have entailed treks to Chichen Itza. Either way, the resulting religious movement soon undercut the authority of Classic Maya rulers across the Yucatan and, ultimately, led to migrations out of the Yucatan lowlands to the coast. Some Maya commoners migrated even farther afield. The latest linguistic models, in fact, suggest that certain Maya factions hopped in boats and sailed away to new homes in a region known as Huasteca, hundreds of miles north of the Yucatan. And from there, the mysterious alternative ideologies seem to have gained an even more distant North American foothold.

To understand all of this, we must first locate the river that the men of the Narváez expedition never did, the Pánuco. Along that river today live diverse multilingual groups of people who include the Mayan-speaking Téenek—oddly out of place in the nearly 20,000 square miles of dissected hilly lands and coastal plain in northern Hidalgo, eastern San Luis Potosí, southern Tamaulipas, and northern Veracruz. The Téenek are known for their distinctive language, colorful dress, and an acrobatic pole ritual performed by *voladores*, or flyers.

The flyers, usually five men, parade out to a vertical, freestanding pole, traditionally planted in a hole (or post pit) in the ground, extending 100 feet or more into the air. Then, in front of the gathered community, blowing conch-shell trumpets and playing the flutes of the Wind-That-Brings-Rain god, the flyers climb to the top of the pole, around which four ropes, attached to the pole, are then wound. The opposite ends of these ropes are attached to four flyers and draped across a rotating, four-sided, wooden framework on which the men sit. The fifth man, high above the crowd, with a breeze in the air, stands on the tiptop of the pole and, risking his life, plays a flute and dances. When ready, the other four men—often costumed as birds—lean back and drop their bodies off the top of the pole, from which the ropes begin to unwind. From that point, centrifugal force flings the bird-men outward as their upside-down bodies spin and rotate around the pole clockwise and slowly descend back down to the ground. In their spiral motion, the *voladores* reenact the circulatory motions of winds and storms, if not the body of the feathered serpent, Ehecatl-Quetzalcoatl. The crowd cheers (Figure 4.3).

But what are these ethnic Maya doing here, 400 miles to the north of the Maya homeland in the Yucatan? At one time, it was supposed that an ancestral population of Mayan-speaking Téenek had migrated north three thousand years ago, away from their cousins who remained in the Yucatan Peninsula. But today, archaeologists and linguists are coming to understand that the Téenek migrated more recently, blending their Maya culture with preexisting non-Maya

Figure 4.3. *Voladores* at the Church of the Assumption, Papantla, Veracruz. Wikimedia: AlejandroLinaresGarcia, 2010. Creative Commons Attribution-Share Alike 4.0 International License.

Huastecs upon their arrival. As proof, scholars point to the fact that Maya symbols and material attributes are virtually unknown in the Huastec region until about 900 CE.[7] The upshot is a whole new scientific narrative: the ancestors of the Téenek arrived from the Gulf Coast and traveled up along the Yucatan to the Pánuco River during the Maya Terminal Classic and early Postclassic eras, during the centuries-long medieval climate crisis, most just before or just after 900 CE.[8]

Whoever they were, the Huastecs found themselves on the front lines of the Spanish invasion, beginning with the 1518 exploration of the coast by Juan de Grijalva, who sailed from Cuba across to the Yucatan Peninsula and, from there, westward up the Gulf Coast to the Pánuco River, in the middle of Huastec territory. The Pánuco is the fourth-largest river in Mexico, in terms of volume of water, and where it debouches into the Gulf of Mexico, it is wide and deep enough to allow wooden ships to sail right up it. The modern city of Tampico overlooks the mouth today. Flowing from the southwest, the Pánuco and its tributaries, the Tula and Moctezuma Rivers, lead directly up into the highlands to the Valley of Mexico and the Aztec capital.

Staying at Grijalva's house in Cuba later in 1518, Hernán Cortés might have been told of the existence of a river at the northern end of the New Spain coastline. However, in 1519, Cortés may not have connected the Huastecs' Pánuco River with Grijalva's. He also wouldn't have understood the potential of the Pánuco as a port. This would take another year, Cortés learning of it from a Huastec leader and relaying the same in a letter to Charles V, king of Spain and Holy Roman Emperor, in 1520. Being ignorant of the potential of the Pánuco in 1519, Cortés had anchored his ships in a wide bay much farther south along the Gulf Coast, at Veracruz. There he offloaded his army, horses, and supplies, and marched overland to Tenochtitlan. The Aztec island capital, Cortés and his men would see firsthand, was as impressive as Teotihuacan likely had been eight or nine hundred years earlier. Tenochtitlan's human population between the years 1325 and 1520 was at least two hundred thousand, not counting the hundreds of thousands more who lived in other cities of greater Tenochtitlan along the shores of old Lake Texcoco—all of which is covered by modern-day Mexico City today.

The access to both the Aztec and the Gulf, of course, was part of the reason the Pánuco River was so important, and why the Huastecs became the Huastecs vis-à-vis their bigger imperial neighbors—first Teotihuacan, then Tula, and finally Tenochtitlan. That access also made them especially susceptible to being enslaved and exported by the Spanish in later years to Cuba, Hispaniola, and Puerto Rico by Nuño Beltrán de Guzmán. In these far-off lands, they would labor and die working in the mines and on the cattle ranches of early Caribbean encomiendas. In the sixteenth century, thousands would be removed from their homeland in this way, forever altering Huastec-Téenek history.

Yet, in their role as gateway to Mesoamerica, the Huastecs also had a disproportionately large influence on other Indigenous peoples to the north. While Narváez, Cabeza de Vaca, and their men didn't make it to the Pánuco on their desperately built barges, one might presume that plenty of precontact-era Indians, paddling down the Gulf Coast over the centuries, did. Certainly, it seems unlikely that Narváez's men were the first explorers or traders, whether European or Indigene, that coastal Mississippians and Texan foragers had ever encountered.[9] In fact, there are Huastecan artifacts—a few broken earthenware pots, stone tools, and stone beads—among the ancestors of those foragers who later captured the survivors of the Narváez expedition along the Rio Grande in Texas.[10] Doubtless, like the coastal and inland Indigenous Texans described by Cabeza de Vaca, these people also sought exotic objects for both their practical uses and their special qualities.

★★★

Unfortunately for us, Huasteca has never received the archaeological and historical attention paid to other regions in Mesoamerica by scholars, says Ross Hassig, one of the foremost authorities on preconquest and early colonial Mexican history and a retired professor of anthropology. This is no doubt because, he notes, Huastecans didn't build the biggest cities or dominate their neighbors like, say, the Teotihuacanos, Toltecs, or Aztecs farther south. "They were a pissant little society at the northeastern edge of Mesoamerica," says Hassig, sitting in his living room in Santa Fe, New Mexico.

Even Hassig remains committed to an older anthropological view where the people of the big Central Mexican empires—the Teotihuacanos, the Toltecs, and the Aztecs (aka Mexica)—were the primary movers and shakers of history. Surely, his logic goes, the emperors and administrators of large-scale, highly organized empires would have controlled commerce and managed migration, production, and identity far more extensively and effectively than the less-powerful leaders or councils who ran Huastec or southern Maya cities.

Generally speaking, the Maya were organized on a smaller scale than the Central Mexicans, just a few hundred miles to the west. They built small-scale city-states, not imperial realms. Not that Mayanists like hearing this, because, in Hassig's view, almost all Mayanists—the archaeologists, epigraphers, and art historians who study the ancient Maya—are "Maya exceptionalists." They consider the Maya forms of urbanism, monumentality, art, astronomy, and writing or counting systems to be major cultural achievements that originated with the Maya, not in Central Mexico.

Hassig scoffs at such arguments, including one that holds the Postclassic city of Chichen Itza, in northeastern Yucatan, to be a Maya achievement, first and foremost, and not a result of Toltec influences from Central Mexico. This idea goes back to the early 1960s, when art historians came up with the notion that the Toltec-style features at this 2-square-mile city must have originated among the Maya living at that site, later to be transplanted into Central Mexico.[11] The reasoning was based on Chichen Itza's exceptional size and hybrid appearance. Many of its architectural features are way out of place in the Maya world, but they are still bigger and better than their Central Mexican (which is to say Toltecan) counterparts in Tula (Figure 4.4).

Certainly, concedes Hassig, Chichen Itza's initial construction started as a Classic Maya city around 600 CE. The architecture of that early era covers part of Chichen Itza's monumental core. However, later Toltec-style architecture sits astride the early Maya buildings. At the center is the stunning Temple of Kukulkan, also called El Castillo, as well as other major stepped pyramids, stone platforms, ballcourts,

Figure 4.4. Kukulkan or Quetzalcoatl head (foreground) and Temple of Kukulkan (aka El Castillo, background), Chichen Itza, Mexico. Wikimedia: ZuyuaT, 2015. Creative Commons Attribution-Share Alike 4.0 International License.

and great colonnaded halls. The pyramids include a mix of Maya- and Toltec-style temples, while the thirteen ballcourts include the largest ever built in Mesoamerica. At 550 feet long by 230 feet wide, it puts Tikal's small courts to shame. A feathered serpent deity carved in stone slithers down along its outer railings. Another snakes its way down the balustrades of the Temple of Kukulkan's staircase, punctuated by a carved serpent head at the base of each. Even the colonnaded halls in the central city are carved with Kukulkan imagery.

The tops of some pyramids, including the Temple of Kukulkan, are associated with carved stone chacmools, which are sacrificial altars in the shapes of reclining human figures. The figures seem to showcase masculine warriors, perhaps ancestral or historical figures, dressed in simple attire, outfitted with protective cotton armor (wrist, arm, leg, and head bands) and wearing classic Central Mexican butterfly-shaped pendants around their necks. A Toltec-style dagger, or *tecpatl*, is usually shown strapped underneath one armband. It looks to be about 6 to 10 inches long and is made in a distinctive shape: elongate and double-edged in form, and wide at the top, with a needle-like tip (Figure 4.5).

The feathered serpents, colonnaded halls, and chacmools aren't the only Central Mexican attributes. There is also a tzompantli, a low and flat stone platform with façades carved to show rows of human skulls. This was presumably originally topped with wooden racks of actual human skulls similar to those observed by Cortés and his men in the Aztec capital in 1519 and recently rediscovered by archaeologists. Even today a carved stone tzompantli can yet be seen alongside the ruins of the central pyramids in Mexico City's Zocalo. Finally, there

Figure 4.5. Chacmool (life-size humanoid stone sacrificial altar) showing *tecpatl* strapped to upper forearm of the figure, Tula, Hidalgo, Mexico. T. Pauketat, 2014.

is one other singular building, a two-terraced tower, described in the 1840s as circular in plan and called the Caracol (meaning "seashell"). A balustrade made up of "the entwined bodies of two gigantic serpents, three feet wide," lined the twenty winding steps to the first platform.[12] "The platform of the second terrace is reached by another staircase," and on this "platform stands the building." Inside were "four small doorways facing the cardinal points" giving access to a circular corridor, the walls of which had been painted with brightly colored scenes. From that corridor, one accessed four more doors, at intercardinal positions, through which was yet another corridor and, at the center, a circular stone mass.[13]

This circular tower may be the inspiration for the lowly vernacular water shrines of the Terminal Classic Maya lowlands far to the east and south. It may also be an archetype for a few similar towers as far north as modern-day Colorado, in the United States. Like the latter, the Caracol was meant to let the light of celestial objects in at dusk, night, and daybreak, if not also to elevate human priests into the wind. Its staircases spiraled upward, perhaps to meet the great coiled feathered serpent and storm god in the sky.

Such similar architectural attributes in widely scattered locations have confounded archaeologists for years, even when those locations aren't separated by that much space, as with Chichen Itza and Tula (back in Hidalgo). On this point, Ross Hassig practically bursts a vein: "Quetzalcoatl imagery everywhere, a tzompantli platform, colonnaded halls, chacmools—and you tell me that it came from the Yucatan? It's just like archaeologists to miss the forest for the trees."

The forest, for Hassig, seems obvious enough. He and others have studied Aztec folklore that tells of a factional dispute at Tollan between the followers of a dark lord from the north, called Tezcatlipoca, and the followers of the old Central Mexican creator god, Quetzalcoatl. Generally speaking, Quetzalcoatl was a creator god of the sky, and a supernatural heroic figure who helped bring human beings into this world. Tezcatlipoca was his evil counterpart, who brought death and trouble from the underworld.[14] These two gods were each other's antithesis, and they are sometimes understood to have been brothers. A supposed Aztec legend holds that while they were at the ancient city of Tollan (i.e., Tula), their disputes culminated in a separation, and Quetzalcoatl and his priests were driven out. The legend also tells of a king, Topiltzin (who assumed the full name Topiltzin-Quetzalcoatl), leaving Tollan and heading east across the Gulf of Mexico, promising one day to return.[15]

Archaeologically, we now know that many of the Toltec attributes precede the actual Postclassic-era Toltecs in the north-central interior of Mexico. These can be seen out in the Epiclassic world of the Chichimecs, in the Altiplano of West and North Mexico, where climatic change was already having effects not unlike those in the Yucatan far to the east. Out in the Altiplano, at places today named Alta Vista and La Quemada, were the earliest known colonnaded halls, warrior imagery, and oversized ballcourts.[16] Some of people who built and frequented such places may themselves have been forced to relocate later, owing to droughts or political upheavals, and a popular destination in the early years of the Medieval Climate Anomaly, or the eighth and ninth centuries CE, was Tula.[17] The historical connections between the Tula, the Altiplano, and West Mexico remained strong and extended well into the subsequent Postclassic period, or the late medieval era.[18]

The ruins of Tula sit 40 miles north of modern-day Mexico City and the Valley of Mexico, about the same distance from the truly ancient city of Teotihuacan to the southeast. Walking through Tula today, visitors see that water, wind, and serpentine symbolism abounds. Coiled or scroll motifs evocative of swirling air and liquid or snakes pervade the painted designs on the sherds of dishware used and broken by Toltec households, strewn on the ground in between prickly pear cactuses. A great stone wall showing a monstrous serpent is carved in bas-relief around one of the larger city pyramids, Pyramid B. The great snake is shown alongside images of human skulls and bones.

On this second-largest pyramid of the core of the city, dubbed Tula Grande, was a massive roofed building supported by large basalt Atlantean columns carved to look like Toltec warrior gods or great ancestral men, each 13 feet high and wearing a feathered headdress. They are depicted holding short fletched darts, curved wooden swords, and atl-atls, which are hooked sticks used to throw the darts (Figure 4.6). All were Toltec weapons of choice.

The stone men's dead eyes are open and stare out into the midday sunlight across a great plaza, mute witnesses to a momentous past. Their afternoon shadows grow long until they disappear into the darkness of night. Other stone platforms surround the plaza, each topped with prominent carved-rock columns that once supported additional flat-roofed palaces and administrative complexes. To the west and north are two great I-shaped ballcourts, the largest almost as large and impressive as the one at Chichen Itza. All three are larger than anything at Tikal or other Classic Maya sites in Yucatan's lowlands, revealing the

Figure 4.6. Atlantean columns atop Pyramid B at Tula, Hidalgo, Mexico. T. Pauketat, 2014.

game, if not society in general, to have been less individualistic and more group-oriented.

Beyond this monumental core and covering an area of 6 square miles are the cobblestone foundations of single-story, multiroom apartment houses that constituted neighborhoods sprinkled across rolling hills adjacent to the Tula River. The human population of this Postclassic city once reached sixty thousand or more.[19] But Tula didn't start out that large.

Both Aztec legend and archaeological discoveries suggest that Tula was founded around 650 CE by newly arrived "Chichimecs" from the northwest. When they settled just north of the Valley of Mexico, these immigrants constructed an early monumental core to the city, dubbed Tula Chico by archaeologists. It includes a prominent circular pyramid with a massive staircase, attached on its backside to an equally large rectangular pyramid. The monument was enlarged at least once, ending up being more than 20 feet tall. A few thousand people lived there in those days, and Hassig and others still argue that Tula Chico was the heart of the mythical Tollan vacated by the legendary leader Topiltzin-Quetzalcoatl.

Archaeologically, we know that the lesser, early complex ceased being the city center in the late 800s CE, at or just before the beginning of the so-called Tollan phase and the upswing in medieval warming. At that time, Tula Chico was burned, and the destroyed old monuments were left to sit there as memories of an old order. In its place, a newer, grander city center, Tula Grande, was built three-quarters of a mile to the southwest, and the city grew to its maximum proportions. This was after the Classic Maya cities had dissolved, some ancestral Maya had moved to Huasteca, and Chichen Itza in the Yucatan became the Mexicanized giant that we know today, even though some archaeologists and historians still argue over which came first.

There are no arguments over what happened later. Sometime shortly after 1150 CE, at the crest of the medieval climatic wave, Tula collapsed, and shortly thereafter so did Chichen Itza. The extent to which Tula's end was a result of regional geopolitics is unknown, but the great city was but two or three days' walk south of a land later known to the Aztec and colonial Spanish to be less civilized and more politically unstable. That's how they characterized Huasteca, conquered by the Aztecs around 1450. From Tula, one could have climbed into a boat on the Tula River and drifted all the way down to a series of Huastec towns.

★★★

If one begins a journey to Huasteca from any other point, then the easiest access into that country is through Tampico, at the mouth of the Pánuco River. A Huastec village and port of entry since before Pánfilo de Narváez sailed for La Florida, Tampico became a Spanish mission in 1532, and an official town, San Luis de Tampico, in 1554. From there, the Spanish—especially the ruthless Nuño Beltrán de Guzmán—exported Indian slaves and produce out into the Caribbean and beyond. The location and those goods, however, made Tampico a target for pirates in the 1600s. The most significant pirate raid came in April 1684, when ethnic English and English American buccaneers, led by a New Yorker, descended on the "impoverished fishing village."[20] The pirates raped, pillaged, and stole what they could. The villagers not taken captive could take it no more. They dispersed, ending the Spanish occupation at Tampico for a century and a half.

Today, one flies into Tampico International Airport and taxis 3 miles south into the old city. Modern Tampico's antique appearance reminds one of New Orleans's French Quarter, at the mouth of the Mississippi River. So do Tampico's summer heat and humidity. On the banks of an ancient lagoon north of the Pánuco River lies the old Huastecan town of Las Flores, occupied mostly between 900 and 1250 CE, coeval with Tula's heyday. Concrete block and stucco homes and paved streets hem in the last of the more than two dozen circular mounds, all built of earth, that once comprised the Huastec burg. All that is visible today is a single 18-foot-high plastered and flat-topped earthen mound with a staircase on one side. Formerly, a circular building of wood and thatch stood on the summit, with evidence that this building consisted of a wooden framework set into "wall channels" built around an interior hearth.[21] The building's elevated circularity and likely conical roof are reminiscent of both Terminal Classic and early Postclassic Maya water shrines as well as the circular observatory—the Caracol—at Chichen Itza. In their verticality and stepped profiles, they seem to appeal for rain to the winds and clouds themselves.

If one continues up the Pánuco and its tributary, the Moctezuma River, one comes to Tamtoc (Figure 4.7). Tamtoc sits just 8 miles off the Pan-American Highway, as the crow flies, resting in the floodplain of a tributary to the Moctezuma River before that river meets the Pánuco and flows into the Gulf Coast. Near here, Jack Kerouac and his mid-twentieth-century traveling companions spent a memorable night sleeping outdoors. In the distant past, this setting would have been ideal for farming corn, beans, and squash, and the region receives more precipitation per annum than all other Mesoamerican zones this far north.[22] A walk through the manicured grass of Tamtoc today reveals it to be a great sprawling monumental complex laid out to align with the cardinal directions. Tamtoc's pyramids are actually mounds of earth with stone facing arranged in rows around plazas and borrow pits, locations where earth was dug (or "borrowed") to build

Figure 4.7. Tamtoc's circular and rectangular pyramids, San Luis Potosí, Mexico. Wikimedia: Panza.rayada, 2015. Creative Commons Attribution-Share Alike 3.0 Unported License.

the pyramids. Some may have been constructed long ago, as early as the Classic or even Preclassic period, according to its most recent excavators.[23] But most of the mounds probably date to the Postclassic urban phase of the site.

Some are massive, including a voluminous, 112-foot-tall earthen mound currently covered in brush and small trees. In outline, this great mound consists of a large upper circular tumulus sitting on an eroded lower rectangular terrace. The effect is not unlike the complementary and alternating circular and rectangular stages of the later Aztec temple to Ehecatl-Quetzalcoatl in the Pino Suárez metro station or the linked circular and rectangular pyramids at Tula Chico. But Tamtoc's central pyramid was huge, volcanic in its proportions. It measures over 800 feet across at its base.

A second great pyramid at Tamtoc is even taller, if smaller overall. It is a nearly perfect truncated cone rising 118 feet in the air. Also circular in outline, this mound has a base that measures 550 feet in diameter but a narrow flat summit just 20 or 30 feet across—big enough for a modest circular water shrine or a vertical pole.

From either summit, a human being can look out over the floodplain of the Tampaon River, where the rest of Tamtoc's sixty-plus pyramids sit—surrounded, we suppose, by the remains of hundreds of pole-and thatch homes. Most of the pyramids are small, no more than stone-faced earthen mounds a few feet in height. About half are rectangular in shape. A few have linear or loaf shapes, as if they were built like a causeway for people to process along. The rest are circular in outline, an unusual characteristic for a site this size in Mesoamerica.

Equally important to these mounds and plazas are the city's water features. There are three major depressions or artificial lagoons that hold water in the city's central precinct. Each was also a borrow pit, or location where earth was dug to build the pyramids, and the overall effect is similar to the *bajos* and reservoirs of places in the Yucatan, such as Tikal. Of course, also similar to those Maya water holes, Tamtoc's lagoons would have hosted the sights and sounds of aquatic life, at least during the monsoon season, with wading birds and waterfowl being common visitors and frogs, salamanders, dragonflies, and mosquitos more permanent residents. More than likely, such locations were understood back in the day to be access points or portals into the invisible world beneath our feet, the underworld—a place of both feminine life-giving spirits and the dead. Indeed, the most famous water feature at the site was such an access point.

At the central precinct's northern edge is a spring, a series of carved stone ledges, a canal, and a large lagoon that catches runoff from rain and groundwater. The spring is enclosed by rock walls and a series of large stone slabs before emptying into the canal. It is also overseen by an upright slab of rock, some 13 feet tall and 25 feet wide, known today as Monument 32. The slab itself is a 27-ton piece of sandstone that was quarried from the Tanchipa Mountains and floated on a raft down the Tampaon a dozen miles to the site. On the side of the Monument 32 slab facing the water is a bas-relief carving of three female characters (Figure 4.8).

Figure 4.8. Tamtoc Monument 32. Wikimedia: Javier Carrera, 2013. Creative Commons Attribution-Share Alike 3.0 Unported License.

The characters present what might seem at first a gruesome image. They are shown with legs resting on human skulls and arms in the air. The central female has a skeletonized head and holds in her hands flowing streams of blood that emanate from the necks of the other two and crisscross the entire scene in the shape of giant X's. On either side of her are headless females who yet raise their arms above their bodies to support diadems, apparently to be worn on the missing heads. The diadems are quite literally the pointed crowns of conch shells sectioned through the middle.

Archaeologists suggest that the great stone references the long 18.6-year cycle of the Moon in relation to the Sun, perhaps even indicating an understanding of the periodicity of eclipses. There doubtless were many other meanings to the scene lost to us today, but the skeletonized characters are almost certainly deities sacrificing themselves for the living Huastecans who gathered at the spring. Female supernaturals here, and elsewhere across Huasteca, have always caught the eye of scholars. Blood offerings by both human beings and the gods were very definitely a Mesoamerican thing, but here at Monument 32, marine shells, green fluorite, and pottery vessels were left as offerings to the feminine powers who resided in or below groundwater.

Water, of course, is a special substance to most human beings, especially to the Maya and their Postclassic Huastecan cousins. After all, "agua es vida" (water is life), in the parlance of Indigenous water-rights activists across the continent today.[24] Water is a universal concern. We need it to quench our thirst, to wash our bodies, to cook our foods, to grow our crops, and to make a suite of objects and utensils useful for daily life: ceramic pots, paints, plasters. When seeping from the earth, water is typically connected to the feminine spirits of the earth and underworld in Mesoamerican mythology. Indeed, associations of women with water, earth, agricultural fertility, and birth are widespread across the Americas.

Moreover, our perceptions of water's transcendental power stems from what we see it do: it falls from the sky, soaks into the ground, and makes things grow. It takes shape and changes states, from gas to liquid to solid. It magically evaporates off a surface in the sunshine or boils into steam, on the one hand, and freezes solid in the cold, on the other. As ice, water has crystalline characteristics similar to flint or volcanic glass. In its liquid state, water flows on its own from here to there. It is transparent, yet when it is still we can see our reflection on its surface. Moreover, we can see the other beings that live below its surface, an entire world apart from human beings and apart from the sky world above.

Marine gastropod or conch shells, of course, originally came from water. That a feminine spirit might wear one, as a crown or a necklace, is a way for people to feel that they are part of a bigger cosmic cycle. Never mind that shells derive from oddly locomotive blob-like creatures (snails and bivalves) that live in the mud on the bottom of lakes, streams, and oceans at the interface of the underworld and this world. The creature itself is a study in contrasts: its actual body is soft, but its shell is hard, durable, and white, with a mother-of-pearl interior that glimmers in sunlight. Most shells are symmetrical in one dimension or another, with snail shells often having a spiral form that mimics other animate—often powerful and even violent—things and phenomena: serpents, thunderstorm cells, tornadoes, and hurricanes.

Shells also retain some of the animacy of the original snail. We all know that they have audible, interactive qualities. Hold a conch shell to your ear, they say, and you can hear the ocean. Blow into the same shell, and you can make a trumpet-like sound. Your breath itself animates the shell. And what is your breath but your spirit, visibly emanating from your mouth on cold mornings?

So perhaps it is less than surprising that shells were prized for the manufacture of Huastecan ornaments and offerings. Perhaps it is also less than surprising that shells might be used as offerings to wind, rain, and storm gods, as they were in Terminal Classic Maya water shrines in the Yucatan. Finally, perhaps it is also less than surprising that, just to the north in Texas three or four centuries later, Cabeza de

Vaca might be employed as a trader of shells, moving them from the coast inland, where they were prized. A little farther to the north, in Caddo country, an elaborate shell-ornament tradition that mimicked Huastecan shell art also flourished for a while.

The fact is that most Indigenous people—especially maize agriculturalists in Mesoamerica—sometimes wore a piece of a wind or water spirit to embody that spiritual power on land among their fellow human beings. Among the Aztec, the god Ehecatl-Quetzalcoatl, in human form, is usually depicted wearing a conch shell or "wind jewel" on a necklace.[25] Like their southern Maya counterparts, the Aztecs and Huastecs were linking mollusk shells to water and wind and, from there, to the primary spiritual forces of everyday life.

Apparently, Monument 32 dates early in the history of Tamtoc, possibly either the Preclassic or Classic period, which is to say sometime before the fall of Teotihuacan around 600 CE and the rise of Tula in the 900s. At some time before the Postclassic period, excavators infer, the flooding Tampaon River swept through Tamtoc, knocked over the standing bas-relief carving, and silted over the location. Perhaps the place was abandoned for a while before it was revived after the 900s.

Besides the basic scenario of early construction, hiatus, and later urban renewal, what we know of Tamtoc are the generalities: some pyramids—both circular and rectangular—were built early during the Classic Period, while others were added centuries or even millennia later. We are left to surmise the rest. If Tamtoc was built according to the traditional scenario of Huastec origins by a group of immigrant Maya during the Preclassic or Classic period, then it seems odd that there are no contemporary images evocative or derivative of a Maya water god, such as Chahk, at the spring. There are also no hints of the corbelled arches of Classic Maya cities, though the use of earth and facing stones for construction at Tamtoc might have made such a thing impossible.

There are, instead, many circular pyramids, a feature unknown in the Classic Maya world of the Yucatan Peninsula and the highlands of Chiapas and Guatemala. And these circular pyramids were almost certainly elevated temples to the Wind-That-Brings-Rain or storm god, mostly depicted in the form of the feathered serpent, who wasn't a factor in the Yucatan until an alternative ideology emerged during the Terminal Classic period.

Piecing the facts together, we can infer that the early Postclassic circular temples at Las Flores, if not Tamtoc, were shrines to Ehecatl-Quetzalcoatl, perhaps also associated with a vertical pole. The combination might have constituted another novel politico-religious movement, an extension of the alternative ideology among the Maya to the south. The result may have been a dynamic ninth- or tenth-century amalgamation of Classic Huastecan culture with incoming Mayan-speaking immigrants, those who would become the Téeneks.

Increasingly, such a scenario seems likely because of the joint linguistic and archaeological impression that few to no ethnic Maya were present in Huasteca until the beginning of the Postclassic period, around 900 CE. This was in the heart of the Medieval Warm Period, when both the Yucatan to the southeast and the Mexican Altiplano to the west were experiencing serious droughty periods. We already know, of course, that various groups of Terminal Classic Maya farmers were on the move in the ninth and tenth centuries, as the Yucatan's Classic kingdoms were breaking down, as new "transcendent" religious movements were forming around water shrines, as the Maya were assuming a maritime orientation, and as complicated historical relationships were forming between the "twin Tollans" of the Mexican Postclassic world: Tula (with its West Mexican influences) and Chichen Itza (with its Yucatan influences).[26] Quite possibly, Toltecan-Maya relationships were actually enabled by the people living along the river so desperately sought by Narváez and Cabeza de Vaca a few centuries later—the Pánuco.

In a bit of symbiosis, the new, vibrant mix of people along the Pánuco would have catapulted Postclassic-period Huastecan culture. Starting around the year 900, Maya influences or decorative styles are evident in the distinctive, large sculptures of human beings or anthropomorphic deities, with as many female as male figures depicted.

On their heads are typically tall cone-shaped hats, also common to depictions of Ehecatl-Quetzalcoatl and looking like the roofs of temples to this same god. One can see Maya characteristics in some of their faces. Around their necks are hung pendants of distinctive cut marine shell. Some of these pendants have a star shape, the result of sectioning a particular species of gastropod shell through the middle.

Such pendants have been found by archaeologists at Huastec sites in large numbers, and include other uniquely Huastecan varieties made from single pieces of the outer whorls of individual conch shells from the Gulf of Mexico. Drilled with stone-tipped bow or pump drills, carved with sharp blades of flint or obsidian, these include circular gorgets and trapezoidal pectorals, each several inches wide and up to 6–10 inches in length. The gorgets and pectorals were intended to be suspended vertically around the neck of the wearer. In that position, the inner mother-of-pearl surfaces are exposed to the onlooking world and were used by Huastecan artisans to highlight the imagery of human and superhuman characters, etched into the surface with flint or obsidian gravers and then rubbed with pigment to bring out the design. The characters are most often shown in sacrificial poses, shedding blood from veins, including from their genitalia, in typical Mesoamerican fashion. The primary god depicted is the incarnation of the storm god Ehecatl-Quetzalcoatl.

Locally reimagined versions of that god and a derivative tradition of marine shell engraving are also found more than 600 miles to the north among the Caddo, a people encountered by later Spanish conquistadors beyond a metaphorical "sea" of Chichimec peoples in the Mexican Altiplano that the Aztec considered their uncivilized ancestors.[27] How did the engraving tradition and the reimagined gods get there? How did wind gods Ehecatl-Quetzalcoatl and Ehecatl-Tezcatlipoca—aka the Thunderers—get anywhere? Ordinary people before and after, and near and far from the imperial core of Mesoamerica, will give us some conceptual help with that question, as we see if we journey north.

Places to Visit

Chichen Itza, Mexico

Compared to Tikal and Actun Tunichil Muknal, visiting Chichen is a walk in the park. The site was a working cattle ranch already in the late sixteenth century. Get tickets online or on-site, although you may need to wait in a queue to get in. See all the major buildings, including El Castillo, the Temple of the Warriors, the Great Ball Court and the Tzompantli, the Caracol observatory, and the Sacred Cenote. Observe the cultural influences and robust art style from central Mexico, especially the presence of Kukulkan (aka Quetzalcoatl), the Feathered Serpent god, on many buildings. Contrast it with the ornate decorative flourishes of the Maya styles seen mostly in the older part of the site. Stay locally, or drive in from the colonial city of Merida, easily accessible by air and only 76 miles from Chichen. Other northern Yucatan sites can be seen nearby, including Uxmal and Kabah.

Las Flores, Tampico, Mexico

Some online chatter proclaims disbelief as to why anyone would want to go to such a "nasty, dirty, stinky, unfriendly, corrupt place" such as Tampico. Book a taxi driver to take you to "la Piramide de las Flores" near the old colonial center of Tampico. This mound and others were partially excavated by Gordon Ekholm of the American Museum of Natural History in 1941–1942 as gravel mining operations that preceded the modern city were eating the mounds away. At one time, there were more than twenty-four small plastered pyramids clustered on a natural terrace overlooking a lagoon and the channel of the Rio Pánuco to the south. We have little understanding of what happened at Las Flores, though we know that it was occupied primarily during the Postclassic period. Was it a shrine complex at which visitors might leave offerings in temples? Was it a multiethnic community, with arriving Maya immigrants and traders (the proto-Téenek, as it were) settling here before some moved inland after 900 CE? Is it here that people from far to the north, Mississippians and other foreigners seeking knowledge of Mesoamerica, landed, stayed, were schooled, and departed? Ekholm found no distant North American artifacts, but he did find hints of pottery more like that of the Hopi, in the American Southwest, and he did find the remains of circular wall-trench pole-and-thatch buildings sitting atop circular platform mounds that may have been the inspirations for the circular water shrines and circular platform mounds known from the city of Cahokia, in the American Midwest.

Tamtoc (Tantoc), Mexico

Fly to the site virtually using Google Earth (Ruinas de Tamtoc) before you arrive in the city of Tamuín by car or air. Tamtoc park sits on the inner bend of the Tampaon River, and only the central core of the site is publicly owned. Other portions lie in fields and pastures outside the park boundaries, including the eastern half of the site's largest mound. Monument 32 sits under a pavilion at the northern edge of the park along a walking path. The lower half of a stone statue, showing a nude male figure, rests under another pavilion. Brush and trees cover some of the central mounds, many of which remain uninvestigated.

Tula, Mexico

The air of Tula today smells of the pollutants emitted by oil refineries, thermoelectric plants, and cement mills. The museum at the entrance to the ruins features many good examples of Toltecan art and artifacts, including pottery, stone chacmools, and sections of great Atlantean columns. Walking to either Tula Grande or Chico, one crosses remnant cobble foundations of Tula's apartment complexes scattered with potsherds and chipped stone debitage. Oddly, these habitations cover a number of hillsides around the monumental cores, each of which occupies a hilltop overlooking the Tula River. Tula Grande's ballcourts and pyramids are clearly and abruptly separated from the city's housing. Walk through the impressive colonnaded hall of rooms, called Palacio Quemado, with plastered floors, west of Pyramid B's Atlantean sculptures. The columns here and atop Pyramid B would have given Toltecan monumentality a distinctively open breeziness. The largest ballcourt in the city—the second-largest in Mesoamerica—is so large that it takes up the entire western side of the great plaza. It faces the partially excavated Pyramid A—largest of the complex. If Tula was the governmental seat of a Toltec empire, the realm was likely not as extensive as that recorded for the Aztec.

5

Across the Chichimec Sea

> After two days, we decided to go in search of corn and not to follow the road to the cows [bison], since the latter carried us to the north, which meant a very great circuit, and since we were always sure that by going toward sunset we should reach our desired goal.
>
> —Álvar Núñez Cabeza de Vaca, survivor of the Narváez expedition, 1542[1]

North and west of Huasteca and Central Mexico, and north and east of West Mexico, lie the high and dry lands of the Mexican Altiplano. Royal Spanish roads connecting north and south, and their ancient precursor routes, all ran through here. Subject to extreme heat and droughts, the Altiplano supported only modest populations of people, called Chichimecs by the Aztecs. Perturbations to the climate here during the medieval era had ripple effects on peoples all around—north into the lands of the Hohokam, Mogollon, and Pueblos, south into the traditional culture areas of Mesoamerica, and northeast into the Great Plains.

In early 1536, Cabeza de Vaca, Estevanico the Moor, Alonso del Castillo Maldonado, and Andrés Dorantes were passing through the Chichimecs' arid, desolate region and came to a crossroads, where they had a decision to make: continue west in search of corn-eating villagers, or take a road to the north that skirted the Great Plains, to people who ate bison meat. They chose the "corn road" instead of the "cow road" as they were approaching El Paso, Texas.[2] After another three or four weeks in the desert, the men entered Mogollon and Hohokam country in present-day Chihuahua, southern New Mexico, Arizona, and Sonora.

But they could have gone north, walking along the edge of the thinly populated, windswept Great Plains. Other people probably had, and traversing such cultural and ecological boundaries was not insurmountable, as the four men's journey itself highlights. Indeed, Mesoamerican gods and human narratives diffused across these lands centuries before and after Cabeza de Vaca and his comrades arrived at this point in their journey.

We can recognize the effects of such diffusion as late as the nineteenth century CE in the person of Lakota holy man Heháka Sápa, also known as Black Elk. In 1873, when he was a nine-year-old boy, the Thunderers of the western sky brought him a vision while he was lying ill in a tipi. Three years later, as a twelve-year-old, Heháka Sápa found himself at the Battle of Little Bighorn, where he shot and scalped one of Custer's soldiers. A few years after that, he relayed the vision that he had seen to his father and uncles, also holy men. They were stunned by its singularity. Heháka Sápa had seen a tree of life. That tree's roots and branches stretched out to the earth below and the sky above.

At the age of twenty-three, in search of knowledge, Black Elk joined Buffalo Bill's Wild West show and traveled across the United Kingdom. He met Queen Victoria at her residence in Windsor Castle, and then toured France, Germany, and Italy for the next year. As a twenty-six-year-old, Black Elk would witness the Massacre at Wounded Knee, which he recalled vividly and sadly well into old age. Later in life, Black Elk became disillusioned. He had married twice, fathered two sets of children, and adopted Catholicism. But he had failed to see his great tree-of-life vision realized among his own people. He died in 1950 at the age of eighty-six.

Black Elk transmitted to the wider world some of the sacred knowledge that he had inherited from his forefathers or had been told by the Thunder Beings, via Euro-American scholars in the 1930s and 1940s who transcribed his words.[3] Among the rites described in print today were two involving circular ritual buildings, the Sun Dance and the *inipi* or sweat lodge ceremony.

The Sun Dance had been adopted by Black Elk's Lakota people just a few generations earlier, introduced by another visionary before Black Elk was born. Among the ceremonials studied by anthropologists and featured in popular American and European media, including Hollywood films such as *A Man Called Horse*, the Sun Dance is among the most significant. Among the Lakota, said Black Elk, the dance happened annually over a period of four days, before and after a full moon. It began by constructing a circular ritual space 50 or more feet in diameter. A series of perimeter poles, each up to 10 feet tall and with Y-shaped forks at the top, were set into the ground around a tall central post, 20 or 30 feet tall. It was the sacred tree of Black Elk's vision, and the circle became the space wherein the Great Spirit, called Wakan-Tanka by the Lakota, could commune with people. Lateral stringers were laid between the tops of the perimeter posts. Even longer poles were laid from the same perimeter posts to the top of the central post.

Over the next few days, the participants performed highly scripted, rigidly gendered, and directionally precise dances day and night inside the open space, which sometimes was draped with temporary fabric walls. Songs were sung and shouts of recognition were made at key moments. The climax of the event came when the ritual leader pierced the chests of adult male supplicants using a knife or sharpened bone pin or antler in order to insert wooden pegs through holes in the flesh, one on the left breast and one on the right.

According to Black Elk, seven men usually took part in the ritual, a sacred number among many Indigenous North Americans. For other Plains tribes, four men took part, another sacred number. Whatever the count, the next step involved the pegs—stuck through the muscle and skin of the men's pectorals—being attached to long leather straps.

The other ends of the straps were tethered to the top of the central pole and, once that was done, the supplicants commenced dancing "sunwise," or clockwise, and in the process pulled their bodies away from the post as the tethers tightened (while looking up to the top of the central post at a Thunderbird nest, a bison skull, or the Sun, hence the name).

Years later, another Indigenous man, the archaeologist Robert Hall, would remark on the similarities between this pole-hanging ritual and those of the *voladores* in northeastern Mesoamerica.[4] Along the east coast of Mexico, from Huasteca down into the Yucatan, four human flyers dressed as bird-men hang from their feet and slowly spin clockwise down to the ground as an homage to the Wind-That-Brings-Rain god, Ehecatl-Quetzalcoatl.[5] A fifth bird-man dances atop the pole and oversees the rotating ritual (Figure 5.1).

In the central Great Plains, the proximate goal of hanging from or leaning away from the central pole over the course of a day and night was to endure the pain and rip the pegs out of one's pectoral flesh. Doing so led each of the dancers to achieve a state of mind that afforded a vision. The vision, similar to bloodletting in Mesoamerica, involved a self-sacrifice to the gods—namely, the Thunder Beings—on behalf of the community. In the Lakota case, men offered their flesh and blood for the good of the people in order to restore balance to the world. The circle was a microcosm of the universe and a metaphor of the Lakota nation.

At various points in the Sun Dance, performers were required to go into another circular building, the *inipi* house—a sweat lodge—for purposes of ritual purification. The sweat lodges, unlike the Sun Dance circles, were small, 10 to 15 feet in diameter, big enough only for several people to sit side by side. Pliable saplings or limbs of willow trees were used to create their arched, wigwam-shaped roofs. These roofs were then covered over with hides and mats so that the heat and steam generated could be kept inside. There, human bodies were purified via the heat and steam created by the repetitive sprinkling of water over red-hot rocks.

Figure 5.1. Diego Rivera's reconstruction of a pre-contact *voladores* rite at El Tajín, Veracruz, in the National Palace, Mexico City. T. Pauketat, 2014.

Steam was the "breath" of the Thunder Beings, or Thunderers, the great winged gods of the west—sometimes embodied by cumulonimbus storm clouds—who brought rain and visions. The point of the steam, then, was to enable the breath of the gods to be absorbed by people inside, making them one with the Thunderers, at least momentarily, while also occasionally illuminating the otherwise dark interior with outside light and air. Not venting the interior from time to time, of course, could lead to dangerous and even fatal conditions inside, as realized today by non-Native amateurs attempting to build and use their own sweat lodges. This is why rocks had to be heated outside the lodge. No one could survive a fire inside such a small, air-tight dome for long.

For the Lakota and other Plains peoples, building the fire to heat the rocks, carrying the rocks—pieces of Mother Earth—inside the sweat lodge, and preparing, igniting, and smoking tobacco using a pipe were all parts of the *inipi*. And, like so many aspects of the Sun Dance ceremony, the physical movement between the hearth outside and the steaming rocks and sweating men inside was highly scripted. Even the fire was lit and maintained in strict liturgical fashion.

As Black Elk explained:

> To make this sacred fireplace, we first place four sticks running east and west, and on top of these we place four sticks running north and south, and then around these we lean sticks as in a tipi, first on the west side, and then on the north, east, and south sides; rocks are then placed at these four directions, and then many more are piled on top. But as we build this fire, we should pray. "O Grandfather, *Wakan-Tanka*, You are and always were. I am about to do Thy will on this earth as You have taught us. In placing these sacred rocks at the four quarters, we understand that it is You who are at the center. O sacred rocks, you are helping us to do the will of *Wakan-Tanka*!"[6]

Black Elk further explained that a hole was dug in the center of the sweat lodge to hold the hot rocks. Archaeologists would call this a hearth, though it was not for containing a fire, just red-hot stones. From the hole, earth was dug and then taken out the eastern doorway to be sprinkled along an arrow-straight sacred path some 20 or 30 feet long. Prayers were offered to Grandmother Earth when the hole was dug and earth sprinkled. At the terminus of the sacred path, just before reaching the actual fire where the rocks were heated, the builders piled up a small mound of earth on which would sit a smoking pipe. The ritual leader or holy man moved along this path as part of the sacred rite.

The Plains Indian Sun Dance ceremonialism that Black Elk described is astonishingly similar to the Mesoamerican acrobatic rites. Circular *inipi* lodges were also reminiscent of Wind-That-Brings-Rain temples atop circular pyramids in Mesoamerica. Are both pole ceremonialism and sweat lodges evidence of some common, pan-American belief system that dates back to the very beginning of time in North America? Or is there a more recent, if complicated, history of religious movements and long-distance travels that explains the presence of Mesoamerican-style sacred circular architecture and pole ceremonialism in nineteenth- and twentieth-century North Dakota?

Black Elk was clear that, compared to the Sun Dance, the *inipi* rite was ancient—from the distant past, from some time before memory. Yet he understood it to have a history. It came from somewhere else and was adopted by the people at some point, usually owing to the actions of a local visionary who had returned from some distant place where he or she had learned the secrets and sacred meanings of the rite from a supernatural source. In the case of the more recent Sun Dance, Black Elk even remembered the leader who had brought it to the Lakota. Other Plains peoples adopted the Sun Dance owing to other visionaries, and anthropologists guess that it was spread through social and religious movements into the Great Plains by groups of people formerly occupying Minnesota, Iowa, or Wisconsin in the 1500s–1700s. Indeed, many Siouan-speaking groups—Lakota, Ponca, Mandan, Hidatsa, Crow—say that they obtained the dance from the Algonkian-speaking Cheyenne and Arapaho, both of whom had moved out onto the Great Plains from Minnesota in the late precolonial era, sometime after the 1300s.[7]

The word "obtained" needs to be stressed here. The rights and necessary accoutrements required to correctly perform such ceremonials were held in sacred medicine bundles, wrapped-up sets of things, mnemonics, and powerful materials. Items would be taken out of the bundle one by one and used before being carefully replaced. Among the items found in bundles were feathers, stones, crystals, skins, special tool kits, and star maps. These powerful bundles, wrapped in skins or fabrics, were not touched by ordinary folk but were meticulously held in shrines, tediously tended by human bundle-keepers as living beings. They were opened with considerable ritual care, consulted by priests as oracles, and passed along to heirs or sold to power-seeking visitors at great cost only after lengthy apprenticeships. Most major ceremonials across North America had their own associated bundle that was a necessary part of the ritual. Historically in North America, there were bundles called upon for specific ritual dances, rainmaking, warmaking, soothsaying, and human sacrifice, among many other ritualized practices. There were bundles that told stories of a person, a community, or an entire nation. Even sacred architectural constructions and important architectonic protocols were held in one or more larger ceremonial bundles.

Such bundles might be replicated a limited number of times so that others might keep their own copy and reanimate a ceremony elsewhere. Indeed, for the right price (and after spending a long time learning the secrets of the bundle), such a replication or transfer of a bundle might be made from one bundle-keeper to another, to an apprentice, or to an heir. Sometimes transfer could occur across ethnic lines or between strangers, with travelers and other members of large religious processions passing unharmed through foreign lands. Such processions were recorded in the historical era far out onto the Great Plains to include men traveling cross-country with calumets or "peace pipes."[8] As late as the 1830s, Indigenous missionaries connected to the Shawnee Prophet traveled far out in the Northern Plains of Saskatchewan attempting to convert locals to this new religion.[9]

Presumably, in such ways and as parts of such entourages, new ceremonial practices or newly reinvigorated ones were bundled or rebundled and then moved from one region to another. This is the way the Sun Dance was transferred and, before it, the *inipi*. Perhaps before both, it was the way that the ceremonials associated with a circular pyramid would also have been moved from here to there. With each transfer, of course, the ceremony, its associations, and its ritual architecture may have changed a little or a lot. This is because the ceremony, through performance in a new space with new people and their memories, would have to be superimposed onto preexisting practices and fitted to the extant stories of the people who lived there. Sometimes this superpositioning and fitting meant supplementing the bundle with new objects from new bundle-keepers, who by adding the novel content updated the old stories.

Robert Hall, the Indigenous archaeologist who studied the origins of such ceremonials, suspected that the eleventh- and twelfth-century city of Cahokia, in the middle of the Mississippi valley, was a historical bottleneck in the spread of an early form of the Sun Dance and pole ceremonialism.[10] Perhaps they had adopted an older Mesoamerican practice, reinvigorated it, and then transferred it out into the Plains via such bundles.

Other bottlenecks in other places may have done likewise. Hall recognized a myriad of North American pole-climbing or pole-flying rituals and circular dance grounds that he believed were connected to Plains ceremonialism in some way, through Cahokia or locations other than Cahokia. To the east, the image of a circular pole dance ceremony was painted by an early English artist (and governor of the failed Roanoke colony) in North Carolina in the 1580s. To the west, the people of Taos and Picuris pueblos had their own pole-climbing ceremonies, involving contrarians or clowns, greased poles, and prizes hung up in the cross members at the top.

***

By far the oldest if not clearest instance of pole-flying rituals conducted in circular performance grounds is known from the West Mexican state of Jalisco. There, 300 miles west-northwest of Mexico City and 800 miles south of Arizona and New Mexico, not far off the road followed by Cabeza de Vaca, Estevanico, Castillo, and Dorantes and their Spanish escorts from Culiacan back to Mexico City, a unique experiment in proto-urban living was under way as early as 300 BCE. At sites scattered into the neighboring Mexican states of Nayarit and Colima, mortuary temples of the so-called Teuchitlan tradition were being constructed around contiguous circular plazas and central posts. I-shaped ballcourts sat in between the various temple-and-plaza groups of the larger sites.[11]

The most elaborate Teuchitlan sites, dating to Mesoamerica's Late Preclassic and Classic Periods (300 BCE to 600 CE), consist of groups of eight to twelve rectangular temples built atop stone-faced earthen platforms. Known as *guachimontónes* (i.e., orphaned mounds), these temples were arranged around a prominent circular altar or pyramid (Figure 5.2). Beneath each of the temples, circular shafts were dug 10–20 feet down to a tomb that held the bones of lineage ancestors. Artifacts such as conch shells and beautiful ceramic pots, the latter made to look like the deceased as well as dogs, macaws, dancers, musicians, and ball players, have been looted from such features by treasure seekers over the last two centuries to sell on the global art market.

For our purposes, what matters most is the circular central pyramid. On its flat, altar-like summit was emplaced a great wooden post, and men impersonating birds and seeking to commune with the powers of the sky climbed to the top. Archaeologists presume that the sky powers included an early version of the Mesoamerican Wind-That-Brings-Rain god, Ehecatl, who would later be merged with

Figure 5.2. Los Guachimontónes, Jalisco, Mexico. Wikimedia: Tlatollotl, 2017. Creative Commons Attribution-Share Alike 4.0 International License.

Quetzalcoatl. Archaeologists are reasonably confident about this because the Teuchitlan people were careful to show us through their ceramic sculptures what happened around the *guachimontón* complexes.

Many of them show the thatched-roof *guachimontón* temples sitting on rectangular platforms, with the ancestral tombs and human figures beneath them. Some show the entire circular complex, with colorful macaws sitting atop roofs watching people dancing in the circular plazas who were, in turn, looking up at a bird-man on a pole atop the great stepped circular pyramid. There are even some ceramic sculptures of the great world tree, a feature common to later Mesoamerican myth and strikingly similar to the one envisioned by Black Elk centuries later and thousands of miles away. Birds sit on its limbs, like so many souls about to fly into the heavens.

The largest of the Teuchitlan complexes is the type site, Los Guachimontónes, adjacent to the modern-day town of Teuchitlan, Jalisco. Significantly, Los Guachimontónes sits immediately south of a great volcano. This is the Tequila Volcano, and at 9,500 feet above sea level it dominates the horizon. Looking up at the volcano from the pyramids of Los Guachimontónes, one can see that the large circular mounds perfectly mimic the fiery mountain, at least when viewed from south to north.

Today, the Tequila Volcano is famous for being covered in blue agave plants, from which a well-known distilled alcoholic beverage is made. And while the Tequila Volcano has sat dormant for a few hundred thousand years, it is yet active in another way. It does what all high peaks do—it alters the flow of the winds and materializes clouds. That is, the volcano forces moist air off the Pacific Ocean upward, causing the moisture to condense as clouds immediately above the mountain peak. Viewed from below, it appears as if the volcano, which is circular at its base, is controlling the wind and causing rain clouds to form. That's quite the powerful landmark, never mind the impression one would take away from seeing a volcanic eruption. One might easily look to it and conclude that the volcano is the abode of the wind, rain, thunder, and fire gods, if not a god itself.

Connecting the volcano's natural power to that of a god is a small, logical step for people of the Late Preclassic and Classic periods to have made. During the conquest of Mexico, Cortés's men witnessed the understandably genuine fear of the Native people regarding an active volcano. A group of Spaniards climbed up to the circular crater summit of Popocatepetl, on the rim of the Valley of Mexico (Figure 5.3). They described "earth-tremors" and "great tongues of flame, . . . half-burnt stones of no great weight, and a great deal of ash" during an eruption. Indigenous guides accompanied them partway but were "too scared to make the ascent" and "would not dare to climb further than the *cues* [i.e., shrines] of those idols that are called the *Teules* of Popocatépetl."[12]

Since volcanic peaks are also common across Jalisco and into the highlands of Nayarit, another logical conclusion follows: the pyramids of Los Guachimontónes drew their sacred powers—their ability to connect the world of the dead below to the sky world above—from the circular volcanic mountains. In a manner of

Figure 5.3. Popocatepetl volcano. Wikimedia: Xicotencatl, 2014. Creative Commons Attribution-Share Alike 4.0 International License.

speaking, the circular pyramids were probably miniature volcanos that brought down the powers of the world above into the world of living farmers, all of whom would have been concerned with winds, rains, and storms. What's more, this mountainous region of West Mexico is subject to more thunderstorms than almost all other parts of Mesoamerica.[13]

At some point or points, aspects of the circular pyramid and pole-climbing rituals must have been transferred from Jalisco to other places, or perhaps from some third location to Jalisco and these other places. That is, the stepped, stone-faced circular pyramids of Jalisco are nearly identical to those of Huasteca, 330 miles to the east-northeast across the Sierra Madre. The religious practices surrounding pyramid and pole ceremonialism also moved from one to the other. Some of the circular pyramids at Tamtoc, it will be recalled, may also date to the Preclassic (1500 BCE–300 CE) as well as the Classic (300–600 CE) and Epiclassic (600–900 CE) periods. Their stepped shape and stone facing are identical to the Teuchitlan pyramids, though the Huastecan examples were not built in the middle of circular plazas. But was there yet another, even older circular pyramid and pole complex that may have been the mother of them all—the place from which bundled knowledge of circular building and pole ceremonialism might have been transferred far and wide?

There was. The ancient city of Cuicuilco, just south of Teotihuacan in the Valley of Mexico, is estimated to have had a population of twenty thousand. At its center sits a great stepped circular pyramid that dates to the Preclassic period, as early as 500 BCE. At 60 feet high, the great pyramid sticks out above a 20-foot layer of hardened lava like a sore thumb (Figure 5.4). The flat summit has not been systematically investigated, but archaeologists in the early twentieth century found a small, circular semi-subterranean chamber built of stone.[14]

Unfortunately for our understanding of ancient history, most of Cuicuilco was covered by lava from one or more eruptions of the Xitle volcano between 100 BCE and 400 CE.[15] It remains controversial as to whether or not Xitle lava was the cause of the city's abandonment;

Figure 5.4. Cuicuilco's principal circular pyramid. Wikimedia: Pedro Elias, 2013. Creative Commons Attribution-Share Alike 3.0 Unported License.

Popocatepetl is also nearby. In fact, it seems that if the lava from Xitle didn't force the city's inhabitants to flee, then the adverse effects of ash from Popocatepetl may have.

Either way, we can guess that Cuicuilco's pyramid was a monumental replica of the Xitle volcano. Such an idea is likely rooted deep in the human mind. To connect with the supernatural power resident in the volcano, people need a medium of communication, and that medium was the pyramid itself. The same seems true of all early human monuments: Stonehenge in England was aligned to geological formations and a river as well as the Sun and, perhaps, the Moon. It was the lens through which the powers of earth and sky might be viewed by people. The Old Kingdom pyramids in Egypt mimicked the rays of the Sun god, their four sides referencing the cardinal directions established by watching the Sun over the course of a year. Easter Island's *moai* statues were made of a resilient stone that endured, held spirits of powerful ancestor gods inside them, and watched over the island. Chaco Canyon's masonry great houses were all of the above—they mimicked local geology, were aligned to celestial movements, and were the abodes of ancestral spirits.

Back in West Mexico, circular pyramid rituals returned, or were transferred back into the region, during the Postclassic period. There, in the southern part of modern-day Nayarit, just north of Los Guachimontónes, a slightly later circular pyramid sits in the middle of the Toltec-era ruins of Ixtlan del Río. Although it contains shaft tombs predating the year 500 CE, most of Ixtlan del Río dates to the Epiclassic or early Postclassic, sometime after 600 CE (but before 1100 CE). The architecture of that era is unmistakable even to a casual visitor. It includes a Toltec-style circular stone pyramid, rebuilt several times and only partially restored by Mexico's National Institute of Anthropology and History. The staircases from the various constructions are all exposed today, with each one leading to what would have been successively higher summits. On one of the early summits, two small stone altars remain, facing each other. The pyramid, presumably a Toltec temple to Ehecatl-Quetzalcoatl, was built not at the center of a Teuchitlan-style circular plaza but alongside rectangular structures arranged on a grid pattern, similar to Tamtoc, Tula, or Teotihuacan. The rectangular gridded buildings each had a Toltec-style colonnade on one side.

Despite its late date and Toltec associations, the Ixtlan del Río pyramid also sat in the shadow of a prominent volcano in this region, named Ceboruco. The power of the Ceboruco volcano—similar to the Tequila volcano in Jalisco or Xitle in the state of Mexico—presumably would have attracted pilgrims, if not permanent inhabitants. Unfortunately for the latter, the Ceboruco volcano was also active at the time of the Postclassic occupation, and it erupted around the year 1000 CE. When it did, Ceboruco buried the landscape within an approximately 8-mile radius under a 1- to 2-foot-thick layer of ash and pumice. Fortunately, Ixtlan del Río is 11 miles to the southeast and escaped the worst of the damage. People did return. In fact, the Postclassic occupation of Ixtlan del Río continued into the Aztec era, even though active lava flows continued sporadically up to the time of the Spanish conquest.[16]

★★★

Thinking about both earlier and later sites with circular pyramids, one could conclude that there were at least three regions in north-central Mesoamerica during the early centuries CE where people were living around circular, stone-faced platform mounds with stepped profiles. These include Jalisco's Teuchitlan to the west, San Luis Potosí's Huasteca to the east, and the Valley of Mexico's buried city of Cuicuilco in the middle. And while we are not sure who built the first one, it was probably not the Huastecans. Both Cuicuilco's great pyramid and the Los Guachimontónes pyramids were probably earlier than the Huastecan circular structures. And while we are not sure about Cuicuilco, the Los Guachimontónes pyramids were the bases for *voladores* poles.

Perhaps some of the early (pre-Maya) Huastecan examples at Tamtoc were also built as bases for pole-flying rituals. Certainly, the pole-climbing ceremony is still practiced today by Huastecan descendants, the Téenek, as well as a host of Totonac-speaking peoples to the south in Veracruz. Unfortunately, excavations at Tamtoc have not resolved the question of what sat atop the circular pyramids. The opposite is true of the Postclassic Huastec mounds at nearby Las Flores. These were clearly surmounted by circular temples, large versions of Maya water shrines, instead of a pole. Perhaps both circular shrines and poles occupied Tamtoc's circular pyramid summits. Either way, both circular buildings and poles were ritual constructions dedicated to the wind and storm god Ehecatl-Quetzalcoatl.

In most other ways, the Teuchitlan, Valley of Mexico, and Huastec cultural traditions, material practices, and art styles—each separated by 150–300 miles—are quite unlike each other. They are also, of course, unlike Lakota culture in the Great Plains, a full 1,600 miles to the north of Jalisco or San Luis Potosí. Yet it is difficult to deny the parallels between the circular religious architecture and the pole ceremonialism, if not also the imagery of a sacred tree of life of both Mesoamerica and the Plains. *Something* must explain the nearly identical subset of religious ceremonies and imagery among otherwise unlike people across such great distances and one thousand years of time.

There is no reason, apart from a simplistic view of cultural traditions and religious beliefs, to contend that the ritual practices, priesthoods, and gods connected to circular sweat lodges, water shrines, upright poles, trees of life, and Wind-That-Brings-Rain or Thunderers remained constant across North America through time. Rather, as Black Elk explained, these things had histories—they were bundled and moved quite intentionally from place to place. In fact, the intentionality of such movements and the localized fervor that might grow around them are the very definition of a religious movement or cult. Thus, while we might not fully understand the history of, say, circular, flat-topped platforms in Mesoamerica—did their bundled history begin at Cuicuilco, Teuchitlan, or Huasteca?—we can be sure that one existed, that it mattered, and that it enveloped the Great Plains at some point.

We could also venture a guess that the histories of such religious movements might depend on other histories, even the histories of ceremonies and cultural practices that were avoided, resisted, and flat-out rejected by some people in some places at some times. In ancient North America, the place that mattered most in terms of what it did and didn't do with respect to circular pyramids and pole ceremonialism in Cuicuilco, Teuchitlan, and Huasteca was the Classic-period mega-city Teotihuacan. This great city boomed following the demise of Cuicuilco, the latter's people streaming out of the old burg in advance of falling ash and molten lava. The twenty thousand or more people projected by archaeologists to have lived at Cuicuilco around 100 CE had to go somewhere. More than likely, many went to Teotihuacan, and as a result, this greatest of ancient cities assumed the scale and economy of an imperial capital. It exerted direct control over people and places far away. The Maya city of Tikal was one of them, 630 miles to the east-southeast. Presumably Tamtoc was another, just a week's march by a Teotihuacan army to the north. We aren't sure about the Teuchitlan centers, with their circular *guachimontónes*, just a two-week walk from Teotihuacan via the same overland route used by Cabeza de Vaca to reach Mexico City in 1537.

Let's assume for the sake of argument that Teotihuacan did control, in some ways, what happened in both Huasteca and West Mexico. Let's further assume that there was some considerable overlap between Cuicuilco and Teotihuacan in the early centuries CE. We can even guess that, with the smoke and ash belching out of Xitle or Popocatepetl, the Cuicuilcans left their increasingly unviable city for the bright, burgeoning capital Teotihuacan. Why, then, are key cultural elements from these other places *not* at Teotihuacan? In point of fact, there are no circular pyramids, no upright poles, and no circular plazas or shaft tombs at Teotihuacan. In addition, there are no I-shaped ballcourts like those seen in most of the rest of Mesoamerica—at, say, Tikal, La Quemada, or Los Guachimontónes. The game was painted on a well-known Teotihuacan mural, but it was apparently not played in exclusive ballcourts.

The absence at Teotihuacan of these bits of material culture, religion, and sporting events common to peoples all around Teotihuacan may mean its imperial controls were not so great, despite the evidence of Sihyaj K'ahk and Yax Nuun Ahiin at Tikal or, less directly, Yax Ku'k Mó at Copan.[17] Or perhaps the Teotihuacanos didn't want to appropriate gods and religious practices of people outside their own domain. Maybe the Teotihuacanos had their own new and improved gods, including feathered serpent and goggle-eyed rain deities, and they thought it better to leave the powers of the circular pyramid of Cuicuilco at the ruined city of Cuicuilco. After all, the Cuicuilco pyramid hadn't gone away—it was sticking out of the petrified lava, and any Teotihuacan priest or ruler could go there to make offerings and commune with ancient spirits should they choose.

Likewise, maybe Teotihuacanos did not restrict the play of their ballgame to I-shaped courts because they took a different, more "meritocratic" approach to team sports.[18] Perhaps the ballgame was less politicized, with fewer religious overtones. In any event, the lack of I-shaped courts seems odd, because there were ballcourts 1,100 miles to the north of Teotihuacan among the Hohokam of southern Arizona in the centuries that followed the collapse of the great Classic-period city. Did the collapse of the great city that lacked ballcourts and circular pyramids lead indirectly to the appearance of these attributes elsewhere in the north?

Places to Visit

Los Guachimontónes, Mexico

You reach Los Guachimontónes by flying into Guadalajara, Mexico, and driving a rental car an hour west to the little town of Teuchitlan (6 miles south of the Tequila volcano and 12 miles south of the town by the same name). Be vigilant about travel in Mexico, and check travel advisories before you go. The circular pyramid complex sits on the northern edge of town and requires a walk up to this 19-acre park. It is well worth the small admission price. The largest pyramid is the 30-foot-high La Iguana platform. It can be seen best by climbing a stone path up another circular mound. A small visitors center has a video to watch, modest exhibits, and a gift shop. Listed on UNESCO's World Heritage List, the site has suffered over the years. Some of colonial and modern Teuchitlan's architecture was built using stones from Los Guachimontónes.

Cuicuilco, Mexico

What's exposed of Cuicuilco—the Zona Arqueología Cuicuilco—is a natural oasis in a sea of modernity in Mexico City's suburb Tlalpan. Just off Avenida Insurgentes Sur, the park is reachable via taxi or by metro and bus from anywhere in Mexico City. If you want to overnight in Tlalpan, consider staying at the refurbished colonial-era Hacienda Peña Pobre. At Cuicuilco proper, a small museum awaits the visitor, open most days 9 AM to 5 PM. Originally, the ancient city sat on the alluvial fans that spilled out of the forests to the south and into the Valley of Mexico and Lake Texcoco to the north. As you approach the great pyramid, 75 feet tall, you walk over the rippled lava that buried the pre-Hispanic city some fifteen hundred years ago. It looks like it was laid down just yesterday. Wildflowers poke up between the crevices in the lava, and people stroll through the park in the noontime sunshine. Imagine a circular temple with a conical thatched roof on the summit of the impressive circular, four-terraced mound. One of the greatest early cities in Mesoamerica lies beneath your feet.

Wounded Knee, Pine Ridge Reservation, South Dakota

Including a visit to Wounded Knee at this point in travels across ancient North America might seem odd, and the experience itself, on the Pine Ridge Reservation in South Dakota, may feel even odder. Wounded Knee's history might seem better connected to modern rather than ancient history. Here is where the US cavalry massacred three hundred Lakota men, women, and children at the end of December 1890. Here is where a struggle against tribal corruption in 1973 led to another standoff between two hundred Oglala Lakota and the FBI. When you pull into Pine Ridge Reservation, north of Oglala, South Dakota, read the sign MASSACRE AT WOUNDED KNEE, see the site of the mass grave, and consider how recent history has deep roots, via the corn and cow roads, in Mesoamerica.

6

Ballcourts at Snaketown

At the end of that journey we found some permanent houses with plenty of harvested corn, the meal of which they gave us in great quantities, as well as squash, beans, and cotton blankets. . . . Among the houses there were several made of earth, and others of cane matting. From here we traveled more than a hundred leagues, always coming upon permanent houses and a great stock of corn and beans . . . and cotton blankets better than those of New Spain. They also gave us plenty of beads made of the coral found in the South Sea [i.e., the Gulf of California] and good turquoises, which they get from the north.

—Álvar Núñez Cabeza de Vaca, survivor of the Narváez expedition, 1542[1]

The world of North Mexico and the American Southwest through which the survivors of the Narváez expedition traveled and to which Coronado would return in three short years was the product of some seven centuries of a thick, complicated history. What tribal elders, historians, and archaeologists know today is that North Mexico and the American Southwest were not simply irrelevant backwaters of Mesoamerican empire. Rather, this area, hundreds of miles north of Central Mexico across an arid Altiplano desert, had its own unique cultural history, distinctive qualities, and special developmental twists and turns. This history, for all intents and purposes, owed itself to the auspicious cosmopolitan beginnings among both the so-called Hohokam irrigation farmers of the Sonoran Desert around present-day Phoenix and Tucson, Arizona, and the Puebloan and Mogollon inhabitants farther north and east in today's New Mexico.

It also owed itself to the extraordinary climate dynamics of the lands between the Mexican Altiplano, the Gulf of California, and the California coast to the northwest. While the Medieval Warm Period and its various El Niños adversely affected Native cultures along the coasts, deserts, and interior highlands of the Far West, the monsoons emanating from Pacific waters and blowing to the northeast into the interior Southwest made the Sonoran Desert and Colorado Plateau bloom. In parts of North Mexico and the American Southwest, farming conditions between 800 and 1300 CE might be ideal for decades in between less-ideal periods, encouraging people to invest in the infrastructures and "permanent houses" that produced the "fine appearance and manners" of Hohokam and Puebloan peoples described by Cabeza de Vaca more than two hundred years later.

It is difficult to exaggerate the historical significance of the interplay between global climate, the Hohokam, the Mogollon, and the Puebloans. Indeed, it was the Hohokam's success at irrigation farming and their Mesoamerican-style culture that inspired the constructions of Puebloan or "Anasazi" great houses at a place called Chaco Canyon.[2] The historical relationship between the Hohokam, Mogollon, and Puebloan peoples and rainfall or heat waves was thus symbiotic over the long term. All of these northerners grew Mesoamerican crops—maize, beans, and squash. And, over the centuries, some people did move between these otherwise distinct cultural and linguistic zones: Puebloan farmers sometimes migrated south; Hohokam agriculturalists less often came north, crossing language barriers and a geological wall, known as the Mogollon Rim, that kept them apart. Even the ancestors of the Diné, or Navajo, are implicated in Anasazi cultural history.

Migrations to or from lands farther south in present-day Mexico are likely. After all, the Casas Grandes sites, centered on the adobe city of Paquime, were located in the northern Mexican state of Chihuahua and had clear Puebloan roots. That may have been the place where the late Puebloan Katsina religion emerged, and today the Hopi of northern Arizona claim it as an ancestral site. In addition, an established foot road existed between the Rio Grande and Central Mexico, and certain exotic materials, such as shells and turquoise, likely moved south along it. More than likely, Cabeza de Vaca, Estevanico, Castillo, and Dorantes had decided to travel west from the Gulf Coast because they were told of the existence of just this road and were searching for it before turning south into New Spain.

In late 1535 and early 1536, the four men were cutting west, encountering people in North Mexico and the American Southwest who built houses of earth, ate corn and beans, and possessed good blankets, coral beads, and turquoise from the north. These were almost certainly descendants of the pre-Hispanic Mogollon or Hohokam cultures of modern-day southern New Mexico, Chihuahua, Arizona, and Sonora, who in turn spoke of the Puebloan big houses to the north, still going strong in the mid-1530s. The Pueblos had prospered by adapting to the environmental risks of a heavily dissected, sometimes mountainous high-desert landscape that geologists call the Colorado Plateau, north of the Mexican Altiplano. For Cabeza de Vaca and colleagues, the Mogollon or Hohokam descendants were key to sustaining themselves on their long journey home. For us, they are key to figuring out the problem of how Mesoamerica and the American Southwest were connected.

Those connections have been a subject close to the heart of Randall McGuire, an activist archaeologist who has devoted his career to North Mexico and the role of class and labor in the past. McGuire is particularly intrigued by the paradoxical Hohokam. On the one hand, the Hohokam were markedly different from almost all other southwestern peoples—Puebloan and Mogollon peoples—to the north and east. Try to find a kiva, or any Puebloan or Mogollon circular structure, among the Hohokam. You can't. Then again, you will find clear Mesoamerican stylings among the Hohokam that are unknown among the Pueblos, says McGuire. We "can identify a profound degree of shared cosmology, iconography, metaphor, and ritual" between the Hohokam and Mesoamerica.[3]

These shared religious aspects include Ehecatl-Quetzalcoatl imagery on some pots and in the corners of rectangular schist palettes used in the processing of the cremated ashes of the dead. The latter practice was common between 700 and 1000 CE and might be tied to Mesoamerican myths about Quetzalcoatl, in his creator-god guise, going into the land of the dead to retrieve the ashes of his predecessors for purposes of reincarnation.[4] Such Hohokam practices seem to have developed during the Mesoamerican Epiclassic period, just as the god Wind-That-Brings-Rain was surging in popularity down in Mexico.

On the other hand, Hohokam and Mesoamerican societies remained "qualitatively different" even during this time, says McGuire. Look long and hard for a circular platform mound or shrine to the Wind-That-Brings-Rain, all the rage in portions of Mesoamerica at the time. You won't find it among the Hohokam. The same seems true of the Mesoamerican rain god Tlaloc. Well represented among the Altiplano farmers down in Mexico, there are no clear depictions of this goggle-eyed deity among the early Hohokam.[5]

Today, the descendants of the Hohokam farmers are known as the O'odham, specifically the Akimel, Hia C-ed, and Ak-chim (formerly the Pima and Papago). From about 1300 to 1450 CE, the ancestral O'odham built elaborate poured-adobe or mud great houses in the middle of large towns scattered along the tributaries and channels of the Gila and Salt Rivers as they flowed through the Phoenix, Tonto, and Tucson Basins in southern Arizona.[6] You can still see the standing adobe ruins of one such monumental structure outside Phoenix today at Casa Grande National Monument (Figure 6.1). To archaeologists, Casa Grande is known as the Grewe site. Its standing ruins sit inside what's left of an adobe compound wall, astride other building

Figure 6.1. Casa Grande great house, built of adobe. T. Pauketat, 2006.

and compound wall foundations, near an old ballcourt, and under a modern freestanding roof, a testament to the remarkable Native ingenuity that made the Sonoran Desert into a garden seven centuries ago.

The high-status family who lived in or alongside this great house also managed the construction and maintenance of one of many impressive and extensive irrigation systems that watered Hohokam fields. Miles and miles of canals were dug. Water control gates on these canals were the source of considerable political power. So well delineated were the rights and responsibilities of these powerful families and their irrigation systems that boundaries and locations of towns, fields, and ditches were inscribed in stone. Petroglyphs near major Hohokam towns use simple artistic conventions—dots, circles, lines, and polygons—to map out the irrigation networks of towns. In their final phase of existence, Hohokam settlements were governed by these local elites. Besides managing their town's water supply, they hosted festivals, performed necessary rituals, adjudicated disputes, and acquired exotic materials—coral, shells, and turquoise—for use in ceremonies and ceremonial costumery. Beads of coral and bracelets of shells from the Gulf of California were especially prized.

But significant climatic shifts in the mid-1400s dried out portions of the Sonoran Desert and undercut the authority of these high-status families. The Hohokam burgs, probably populated by a few hundred to more than a thousand people at a time, broke up and dispersed into the smaller settlements. The scattered descendants were encountered by Cabeza de Vaca and the other three lost conquistadors.

Such climate-related movements now seem to have defined much of Mexico during the late precontact era—the Medieval Climate Anomaly (800–1300 CE) in the Northern Hemisphere, known archaeologically as the Epiclassic (600–900 CE) and early Postclassic (900–1300 CE) periods in Central Mexico and the Yucatan. In the arid lands of North Mexico, the overall trend was increasing dryness, with a notable megadrought covering the years 897–922 CE.[7] An already arid landscape of deserts and mountains was drying out even more.

There is growing archaeological and paleoclimatic evidence to suggest that this increasing aridity, if not that specific megadrought, led to the abandonment of a series of earlier Epiclassic monumental centers 700-plus miles south of the Hohokam in the lower reaches of Mexico's Altiplano, which runs all the way up to the US-Mexico border. These include the so-called Chalchihuites culture centers of Alta Vista and La Quemada, in Zacatecas, Mexico. Originally, these desert centers had emerged just north of—and because of—Classic-period Teotihuacan. After the fall of Teotihuacan, both Alta Vista and La Quemada grew even larger, developing their own distinctive practical and architectural aesthetic in the process. Seemingly, for the people in the frontier zones north of the imperial city, Teotihuacan's collapse had not been a bad thing. The builders of Alta Vista and La Quemada favored massive rectangular buildings, small rectangular pyramids, and colonnaded, monumental façades, halls, and courtyards. In addition, La Quemada possessed two I-shaped ballcourts,

Figure 6.2. Ruins of La Quemada, with colonnaded hall in background and I-shaped ballcourt to the left. Wikimedia: JavierDO, 2013. Creative Commons Attribution-Share Alike 3.0 Unported License.

one of which was very large (Figure 6.2). Another ballcourt may have existed at Alta Vista.[8] But, similar to the Hohokam, neither place possessed anything like a circular platform or a subterranean kiva. Then again, unlike the Hohokam, the residents of Alta Vista and La Quemada did worship the goggle-eyed water god known to the Aztec as Tlaloc.[9]

Major occupations at both La Quemada and Alta Vista date to about 600–900 CE.[10] Even at their peak, neither were heavily populated cities. Rather, La Quemada and Alta Vista were administrative and ritual centers into which farmers would travel for ceremonies—not unlike Chaco Canyon and many Maya cities of the day. The colonnaded porticos and halls of both sites clearly anticipate the later, Postclassic-period architecture of another prominent Mesoamerican city to the southeast known as Tula. Indeed, many archaeologists suspect that these Chalchihuites sites were the ancestral homes of people who gave rise to the residents of Tula, known as Toltecs. One might even speculate that northern desert dwellers—so-called Chichimecs—may have been among those who moved south in the late 800s to help build the Toltec city of Tula. Certainly, the archaeologists studying La Quemada believe that its abandonment around the year 900 involved the relocation of its people southward, if not southeastward.

Aztec legend supports this idea. The Aztec believed that both their ancestors and those of the Toltecs came from the north, from Chichimeca. In fact, archaeologists studying La Quemada and Alta Vista report the commonplace practice of ancestor veneration and human sacrifice, reminiscent of the later Aztecs. Specifically, parts of people were publicly displayed on the monumental walls at La Quemada until they fell off, accumulating in the rubble at the base of the structure. This practice included the hanging of human legs and arms from ropes down stone façades in the central precinct.[11] It also seems to have involved the political-ritual integration of desert farmers living in some two hundred village settlements around the monumental complex. On special occasions, formal processions of farmers would enter La Quemada, pay homage to the great ancestors and elites, bring in necessary supplies and foodstuffs, look at the rotting human limbs hung on ropes, and then return home.

It was a delicate balance easily undone by slight localized shifts in rainfall, or perhaps in the rainfall of neighboring regions. Conceivably, farmers of the Epiclassic Altiplano simply could not sustain the effort and food supplies needed in such a precarious environment. One has to wonder if a drought might have led to farmers questioning the whole idea behind such a place. In any event, the entire interior west-central Mexican zone was abandoned around the year 900.[12]

It was in that year, plus or minus a decade or two, that a close connection between the Hohokam, their Chalchihuites neighbors far to the south, and the coastal peoples of West and North Mexico was also severed. Archaeologists such as Randall McGuire use the name Sedentary period to distinguish the post-900 era from the earlier Colonial period (700–900 CE). In that later period, after 900, the Hohokam began to turn their attention away from Central and West Mexico and more toward the Pueblos and Mogollon villages of the American Southwest to the north and east. This is not to say that the Hohokam were ever assimilated fully into a Pueblo or Mogollon world. Outside of a brief historical moment up around the Grand Canyon, they never were.

In point of fact, unlike these other southwestern peoples, the Hohokam were speakers of Uto-Aztecan dialects. The Hopi, an isolated Puebloan group north of the Hohokam, spoke another Uto-Aztecan language, unlike the rest of their Puebloan counterparts to the east. There were likely blood ties between all. Certainly, Uto-Aztecan dialects are common to the south, down through pre-Hispanic Sonora, Sinaloa, Nayarit, and Jalisco. More than likely, the Chalchihuites-culture peoples spoke some version of Uto-Aztecan. So did the Toltecs. Indeed, as the name suggests, Uto-Aztecan languages include Nahuatl, the vernacular of the Aztecs.

Archaeologists are reasonably certain that the Hohokam also had a mythic narrative similar to that used by the Aztecs in the 1500s to explain the founding of their imperial city of Tenochtitlan. That is, Tenochtitlan (i.e., Mexico City) was said by the Aztecs to have been settled on an island in the middle of Lake Texcoco precisely where an eagle sat in a cactus eating a snake held in its talons. Today, that snake-eating eagle on the cactus is emblazoned on Mexico's national flag. Interestingly, this very same leitmotif was depicted by the ancient Hohokam of Arizona. There, carved bone hairpins, marine-shell jewelry, and painted pots depict scenes where large birds swallow snakes atop a vertical perch. Wear such an illustrative pin in your hair or use such a pot in front of your community and you proclaim, knowingly or not, your beliefs and your identity.

Scaling up this mythic narrative to the landscape, we might see in the archaeological remains of the great Hohokam settlement of Snaketown, near modern-day Phoenix, a parallel to Aztec mythology. Snaketown is one of the largest early Hohokam towns in Arizona, having achieved that status at the beginning of the

Colonial period (ca. 700 CE). It was built in the shadow of a mountain called Gila Butte, today right next to Interstate 10 heading south out of Phoenix. Historically, the Aztec spoke of a mountain similar to Gila Butte. Atop it, the Aztec said, their ancestors built a temple to the god Huitzilopochtli. At its base, they built a ballcourt.[13] For the later Aztecs, Quetzalcoatl was said to have played a ballgame against the dark lords of the underworld in order to retrieve and reincarnate the ashes and bones of his predecessors. The popularity of the ballgame among the Hohokam might be linked to this same mythic story.[14]

Sure enough, one of the largest ballcourts in northern Mexico or the Southwest is also found among the ruins of Snaketown. The big ballcourt measures 200 feet in length and 100 feet in width and dates to the period 700–1100 CE. Like the more than two hundred other ballcourts known across the Hohokam region, this one is a sunken feature with an elongated oval shape and open ends. Teams presumably played a local version of the Mesoamerican ballgame down in these courts, passing a small rubber ball between teams, one at either end, until a goal was scored through the open end or the team dropped the ball. Onlookers gathered around the elevated rim of the big court, some 10 feet above the sunken field, to watch the game. When not in use for the game, Snaketown residents would have also used the court as a dance ground and a site of community functions and rallies—not unlike gymnasiums and football fields in modern American public schools.

During the Epiclassic era, or 700–1100 CE in the Hohokam area (aka the Colonial and, later, Sedentary periods), the 250-acre settlement of Snaketown was home to a thousand people living in hundreds of pithouses arranged around dozens of courtyards that in turn surrounded a big plaza and two ballcourts. Pithouses were a common type of Native domicile found from the Sonoran Desert north into the Arctic and east to the Atlantic seaboard. At Snaketown, their floors were dug three or four feet below grade, and a modest wooden frame was built up from those floors covering an area of just 200 or 300 square feet, about the size of a modest modern living room. Roofs were covered with earth, affording them a cool interior even when it was stifling hot outside. Inside there was just enough room for a nuclear family to sleep and store a few household articles. Houses near the town plaza were larger than normal, suggesting that the residents were of a higher status. Their homes were built to impress, to store the additional foodstuffs and supplies the families needed, and to provide extra elbow room for entertaining and putting up visitors.

The duties of all leading Hohokam families included the care for and veneration of the dead, who were cremated, with ashes buried in urns or sprinkled around the homes. Special carved-stone palettes were made for grinding incense for use in these funerary rites, which may not have been the most pleasant to smell otherwise. Small fired-clay figurines of ancestral characters—deceased grandparents, distant aunts or uncles—and even children are found around houses and in garbage mounds, sometimes in contexts that suggest remembrance and offerings to the spirit world.

Such practices of living with the ancestral dead, and especially the use of modeled clay anthropomorphic figurines, are Mesoamerican in origin. They are in no way related to the Pueblos to the north, those from whom Cabeza de Vaca said turquoise originated. For such reasons, archaeologist Randall McGuire voices what is now most assuredly the best big-historical reconstruction of the Hohokam, at least from his southern point of view looking north. Whether genetically related to Mesoamericans or not, he thinks, they were very definitely historically related and deeply affected by Mesoamerica. From the Mesoamerican Preclassic up through the Classic period, the Hohokam way of life looks similar to that of the peoples of coastal West Mexico and interior north-central Mexico. They even acquired or copied the things of West Mexico on a routine basis, including its Red-on-Buff pottery, its copper bells, its cloisonné-backed pyrite mirrors, its colorful macaws, its snake-eating eagle imagery, and its ballcourts.

Quite possibly, the real vitality of the Hohokam is attributable to the ballgame. As among the Maya and other Mesoamericans, the ballgame (outside of Teotihuacan at least) likely played out mythic narratives involving supernatural culture heroes such as Quetzalcoatl, similar to those known among Central Mexicans and the Maya, even as it inspired community cohesion at the level of entire regions and localities. Sporting events do this. In fact, sports arenas also do this, even if used for non-sporting events.

Such celebrations of community make sense where those communities aren't defined from the top down, which is to say from Teotihuacan down. With the collapse of that great city and the dispersal of its narratives in the sixth century, the old traditional game—perhaps always played by kids informally—reemerged as the official sport of the array of independent Epiclassic communities that developed all around Mesoamerica. That reemergence was cult-like, spreading with a fervor common to religious movements, which is probably precisely what was happening. Local visionaries imagined new ways of living in the era after Teotihuacan, and the ballgame embodied their new vision, competitive spirit, and individuality. For those who spoke some variant of Uto-Aztecan, the game's rules and new meanings would have easily translated from one realm to another, up the spine of Mexico's Sierra Madre Occidental, across the Altiplano's sea of Chichimec peoples, and into the heart of Hohokam culture. At this early date, that's where it stopped—not all Mesoamerican influence, just the ballgame. Debate yet swirls around the question of whether or not the Pueblos of the American Southwest could have become Pueblos without the Hohokam and, by extension, without the events centered back in Mesoamerica.

McGuire's colleague Stephen Lekson assumes the point of view of the Anasazi world of the north looking south and west at the developments happening out of the Phoenix Basin. Lekson, an expert in Mogollon and Pueblo archaeology and a popular figure with his own cult following, suggests that the early Epiclassic (Colonial) growth of the Hohokam shocked and awed the backwater

Basketmaker-period and early Pueblo-period farmers to the east and north. Up through the 700s, these proto-Anasazi still lived in small pithouse villages.

By comparison, the Hohokam irrigation farmers were already cosmopolitan. To their backcountry counterparts, they seemed practically Mesoamerican, with a cultural vitality and infrastructural stability that made places such as Snaketown and Grewe into historical powerhouses. These places were likely known to and envied by the earliest Puebloan and Mogollon farmers to the north and east up through the 700s. The Hohokam people had things that their backwater neighbors did not, things with power from far-off lands, things made from coral, shell, copper, and colorful feathers.

They likely also possessed a military potential to be respected, if not feared, and evidence of warfare abounds.[15] A Hohokam town of a thousand people could have easily mobilized a hundred warriors to go on a raid against people to the north. Perhaps some Puebloan community might have possessed something that the Hohokam believed was rightfully theirs. Perhaps some Mogollon community had wronged a nearby Hohokam town. That wrong might need to be made right.

The distance from Snaketown, Arizona, to Zuni, New Mexico, in the north, or the Mimbres Valley to the east, is just a little over 200 miles as the crow flies. Even accounting for obstacles and the extra time to cross the Mogollon Rim, a war party on the move could have covered it within the span of a couple of weeks. The scattered pithouse villages of these proto-Puebloan or early Mogollon peoples would have been lucky to field a couple of dozen fighters in response, if they even managed to see the attack coming. People beyond the Hohokam horizon would have been sitting ducks.

And that might have been enough, historically speaking, to set up what happened at the Place Beyond the Horizon. What occurred was in many ways totally unlike anything in the Hohokam world. In some ways, it would be transcendent, changing the history of the American Southwest forever, if not also the Southern Plains and the edge of the Eastern Woodlands. In other ways, it was one of two great social experiments that were distinct from, yet completely dependent on, Mesoamerica and climate change.

Places to Visit

Casa Grande National Monument, Arizona

Owing to its four-story-high adobe ruins, its proximity to central Phoenix (just 40 miles to the north), and the increasing vandalism at the site, Casa Grande (or the Grewe site) was the first archaeological preserve in the nation, set aside by President Benjamin Harrison in 1892. It was later added to the roster of national monuments in 1918. Beginning around 700 CE, a pithouse town existed on the site. In the 1300s, a great house was built here, one of a number of impressive Hohokam adobe structures that constituted several adobe-walled compounds at the site. The town was abandoned in the mid-1400s. The modern ramada over the top of the great house was added in 1932 by the Civilian Conservation Corps during the administration of Franklin D. Roosevelt. Today, Casa Grande sits within the corporate limits of Coolidge, Arizona, off Interstate 10. Twenty miles south of Phoenix, exit Interstate 10 onto Highway 187 for the final 20 scenic miles to the park. Take Highway 187 east to Highway 87 south to the park entrance.

The Heard Museum, Phoenix, Arizona

If you are in Phoenix thinking about driving to Casa Grande, stop first at the Heard Museum, at 2301 North Central Avenue. The Heard contextualizes the Native past with the present, making the historical links that help all of us understand the ways in which the archaeology of the Southwest and North Mexico matters to both descendants and non-descendants. Its museum shop sells items made by contemporary Native artists and stocks a good number of relevant archaeology books.

Alta Vista, Zacatecas, Mexico

One of the more difficult sites to visit listed in this book, Alta Vista is located on the eastern foothill side of the Sierra Madre Occidental away from major urban areas and large international airports. It can be reached by connecting through Mexico City to Durango International Airport, in Victoria de Durango, Zacatecas. Taking a car on a long 90-mile drive south on Mexico Highway 45, cut onto smaller roads south to the little town of Chalchihuites and then due west to the archaeological ruins and the on-site museum. Conversely, one can take a three-hour bus ride from Zacatecas city to the site. The visitor might be surprised to see adobe and wooden-post construction, reminiscent of Hohokam sites. The primary ruins to observe are stone foundations and Mesoamerican-style courtyards surrounded by platforms that originally featured structures with colonnaded porticos.

La Quemada, Zacatecas, Mexico

Instead of getting off of Mexico Highway 45, one could continue all the way to the city of Zacatecas, three and a half hours south of Victoria de Durango, picking up Highway 54 for another forty minutes to La Quemada. Conversely, one could fly into San Luis Potosí and drive Highway 49 west to Highway 45 in Zacatecas, where one might spend the night. A tour of the on-site museum is followed by a walk up the hilltop, first to the ruins of a colonnaded hall and then to a great I-shaped ballcourt, the unusual Votive Pyramid, a great masonry-faced acropolis, and more.

7

A Place Beyond the Horizon

In 1535, Cabeza de Vaca, Estevanico, Castillo, and Dorantes were passing through what was left of the Mogollon and Hohokam cultures and were told stories of impressive Pueblo big houses up the Rio Grande. They decided not to venture there, although Estevanico, of course, later returned in 1539 in advance of Fray Marcos and, ultimately, Coronado. Estevanico, Coronado, and Coronado's men hence were the first Old World citizens to glimpse the Pueblo world.

By 1539, that world was already changed from what it had been during the Medieval Warm Period. It was more politically fractured and violent, with more people living in fewer, larger adobe pueblos. A great social experiment of the 800s–1100s, known by some today as the "Chaco Phenomenon" and centered on Chaco Canyon, had been left behind by its descendants.

We do not know the exact names of the people involved, nor the precise chain of events, but by the mid-800s CE what the Hopi called Yupqoyvi, or the Place Beyond the Horizon, was under construction in a stunningly empty, desolate, high-altitude canyon northwest of modern-day Albuquerque, New Mexico. Two to three centuries later, this place would become one of the great monumental complexes of the ancient world. Consisting of a dozen multistory great houses and dozens of smaller family units, Chaco Canyon is the largest complex of masonry buildings ever constructed in precolonial America north of Teotihuacan and Tula. Inside the rectilinear and curvilinear walls of each great house are multiple banks of parallel rectilinear rooms stacked up to five stories high. The rooms surround and look down upon open plazas and the flat circular roofs of subterranean public or ceremonial circular rooms known as kivas. The Spanish, thinking them hearths of the devil, called them *estufas*, or stoves. At Chaco Canyon, two or three dozen of the kivas are so large and elaborate that they are today called great kivas (Figure 7.1).[1]

Given the geopolitical realities of the Hohokam after 700 CE, it may be little wonder that, later in the eighth century CE, people living in pithouse settlements scattered all about the mesas north of the Mogollon Rim had begun to build "blocks" or contiguous rows of aboveground storage rooms as part of a transition from what archaeologists have termed the late Basketmaker III period into the Pueblo I period. This was the semi-arid Four Corners region, where New Mexico, Arizona, Colorado, and Utah meet. And here, before the year 800, the storage rooms were initially just a row of small rectangular cells placed at the backside of the yards around the pithouses. Kids played here. Women and men did their daily chores in and around the rooms. Visiting aunts or uncles stayed in some of them. Liaisons likely happened in others. The occasional angry teenager might have spent the night sulking in one.

At this time and later, the grinding of maize was one of a woman's primary activities. It was an extremely laborious job, and it was done inside a room. In some seasons, women might spend the entire day, along with their sisters or other kin, kneeling and pushing heavy stone manos across even larger stone metates to pulverize lye-processed maize kernels into a fine, powdery meal. Doing so allowed the Basketmaker and later Puebloan women to produce high-quality masa dough with which to make corn bread, among other things.

Of course, the women paid for it with their bodies. Physical anthropologists who studied their skeletons observed extremely worn-down joints from the backbreaking, repetitive work. Worse, mistreatment and physical abuse seem to have been a part of ordinary life for some

Figure 7.1. Great kivas. Top: excavated example in Pueblo Bonito; bottom, Casa Rinconada, Chaco Canyon, New Mexico. T. Pauketat, 2012, 2003.

Puebloan women, possibly captives or other low-status members of the community. In certain times and places, some captive foreigners were treated little better than slaves. Their crania show repeated evidence of having been struck in the head with a blunt instrument.[2]

Such gendered labor and abuse developed over the course of the eighth century, depending on where a person lived and who they were.

At about the same time, the rows of aboveground rooms were converted from storage rooms for foodstuffs, work rooms for grinding corn, or temporary housing for visitors into the living and sleeping rooms of almost all Puebloan families. Possibly this was because flexible domestic architecture was in demand by families on the move during this dynamic time leading up to the 800s CE. Of course, such reshuffling was seldom easy, and sometimes led to both intragroup violence—as with that directed at women—and intergroup violence, which is to say warfare.

Unlike the lands to the south in Mexico, there is no evidence that northwestern New Mexico was drying out over the long term. Instead, tree ring data from the more northerly regions suggest that the Medieval Climate Anomaly in this region was typified by a series of "anomalously wet periods that temporarily increased the carrying capacity of this semi-arid environment."[3] One of these wet periods began in the late 700s and spilled into the early 800s. It was followed in the mid-800s by a mega-drought, but the weather soon cycled back into another wet period. This is how it went in the high desert of the Colorado Plateau. According to the guru of southwestern climate change, Larry Benson, a retired geochemist with the United States Geological Survey, the pattern was conducive to the productive rain-fed farming practices typical of the Pueblos, though the oscillation around a mean might have encouraged farmers to look to the gods for help from time to time. Along with the cultural pressures emanating from the Hohokam to the south, the climatic variability probably also encouraged people to look to each other for security in bad years.

Under these conditions, a few locations and a few families living there were propitiously sited to emerge as central points of articulation in the fluctuating social and demographic webs of the Colorado Plateau. One might even imagine that such points and people were anchored to special places that emanated singular, supernatural qualities. One can feel such qualities today in Chaco Canyon. The skies are clear, blue, and warm in the daytime and brilliantly star-studded, black, and cold at night. The land smells of juniper, piñon, and sage. The masonry layers of the silent great houses mimic the natural rock layers of the canyon walls. In the past, as today, travelers presumably would have returned as much to encounter the spiritual powers of the place itself as to socialize with the locals. Ancestral Puebloan peoples would mark such places with shrines—simple arrangements of rocks and offerings. They would spend the night nearby, with more elaborate shrines outfitted with formal pilgrim housing.

Even today Chaco Canyon beckons to pilgrims. The majestic Fajada Butte still sits like a gateway monolith at the mouth of the canyon, which opens up to the northwest, toward the great houses, and to the southeast, toward agricultural fields and the ruins of a large ancestral Basketmaker III village. The canyon is a half-mile wide and walled in by opposing 100-foot-high cliffs of stratified sandstone. Near Fajada Butte, the light brown sandstone is interbedded with layers of black lignite. All along the northeastern canyon wall, massive sections of the rock face have separated from the cliff itself. With one exception, these have not yet fallen. They overlook the great houses, which probably were built intentionally near the balanced rocks, perceived to have been held up by some mysterious force of nature. Such places and rock features possess a power that the Chacoans respected.

The acoustic qualities of the canyon, especially its central "downtown" area, are notable.[4] So, too, are its visual qualities. One can view much of the canyon from one of the oldest great houses at the canyon's north end, Peñasco Blanco. A series of rock shrines, often just simple circles of stones, line the mesa tops nearby. Indeed, from those tops one can see for hundreds of miles in some directions. More to the point, the many people who were tied to Chaco could also see into the canyon by standing atop one of the other prominent landforms that surround the canyon.

Twelve monumental masonry buildings—great houses—and a series of other monumental facilities, walled-off road segments, and cut-stone staircases line the canyon floor and climb the rocky escarpments to the mesa summits. In the center of the canyon is a dense cluster of rock art, intersecting roads, and great house constructions: Pueblo Bonito, Chetro Ketl, Pueblo del Arroyo, and Pueblo Alto. Each is a veritable theater wherein performances by a few in the plazas or atop the room blocks could have been broadcast to the many looking down from higher ground (Figure 7.2). Originally five stories high in its rear, Pueblo Bonito itself was the supreme amphitheater; in its final form, it had a D shape when viewed from above. The earliest honored burials were in the early 800s, with two men and their matrilineal relatives carefully interred in a lower back room of this oldest and greatest great house.[5] They were probably the founders—the designers—of this extraordinary place. Their burial room and Bonito's other back rooms were discovered full of offerings: vases, pitchers, metates, and wooden wands used in ritual sword-swallowing performances, among

Figure 7.2. Chacoan great house, Chetro Ketl, as viewed from Chaco Canyon rim, showing circular tower kiva and great kiva. T. Pauketat, 2008.

many other things.[6] Included were a few elaborately chipped, double-edged Edwards Plateau flint knives.[7]

Threatening Rock, the large rock that stood along the canyon wall behind Pueblo Bonito, fell in 1941, crushing the back wall. Visitors walk over the rubble today. South of that collapsed standing rock, a later Chaco-era extension of Pueblo Bonito, known as the Hillside unit, is still visible. It includes a masonry base for what must have been an impressive monumental staircase and ladder that climbed 100 feet from the floor of the canyon to the top of the cliff beside Threatening Rock. Between the Hillside unit and the next great house to the southeast, called Chetro Ketl, was an anthropogenically enhanced rock wall with extraordinary auditory qualities. From various points on the canyon floor, from atop Great House roofs, or from the mesa rim above, orators, singers, drummers, and trumpeters blowing conch shells would have commanded audiences in the thousands. From multiple points in multiple directions, the monumental constructions layered auditory and visual effects one upon another.[8]

The visual experience of Chaco Canyon extends into the heavens. The canyon, as it turns out, is naturally aligned to a maximum south moonrise and, in the opposite direction, a maximum north moonset.[9] These are the extreme points on the horizon sometimes called "lunar standstills" or "lunistices" where the full moon will rise and set in succeeding months once every 18.6 years, or about once every human generation. The phenomenon was possibly marked around the world at places such as Stonehenge in England, the Hopewell earthworks in Ohio, and Ur in Mesopotamia, but it is especially well documented in the middle latitudes of North America, where ancient people discovered the pattern by repeated observations of heavenly movements from single points on the landscape.[10] Chaco is one of these notable places, and its greatest great house, Pueblo Bonito, established in the 800s, sits in the middle of the canyon's primary lunar axis.

This observation was originally made by Anna Sofaer and her Solstice Project team in the 1980s, after she had discovered the famous Sun Dagger petroglyph atop Fajada Butte. There, the play of light and shadow through three slabs of sandstone strikes two spirals, pecked into the rock by some unknown Chacoan priest centuries ago, to mark the annual cycle of the Sun and the generation-long cycle of the Moon. Great houses in the canyon, and at various Chacoan "outlier" sites across the Four Corners region, have walls and rooms aligned to these same solar and lunar events. One pictograph painted on the underside of a ledge below Peñasco Blanco is widely thought to depict the supernova of 1054 CE. The Chacoans were avid skywatchers.

One distant Chacoan outlier, Chimney Rock in southwestern Colorado, was built and repeatedly remodeled and expanded during a lunar standstill year, when the rising and setting full Moon reached its extreme northern and southern positions on the horizon.[11] The Chimney Rock Great House sits atop a thousand-foot high mesa that features two prominent rock spires (i.e., chimneys) between which the full moon can be seen to rise once every 18.6 years. More locals moved onto the mesa as well, building homes in their own local style, which used cobbles in stark contrast to the block masonry of the nearby Chacoan great house. Half a century later, when these locals became disillusioned with Chacoan religion and the demands of its priests, they emigrated to a new location far to the east, shedding as many vestiges of their former Chacoan affiliation as they could.[12]

Perhaps Chacoan politics by that time had become too intense, too hierarchical, or too susceptible to control by fundamentalists. Those in charge in the canyon itself, for example at Pueblo Bonito, could have used force to maintain that order against those outside, had they wanted. And perhaps they did, maybe against perceived threats from, say, the Hohokam. While there is no evidence of great wars, indications of conflict are found around the perimeter of the Chacoan region, possibly a result of the absence of Chacoan governance out there. Steve Lekson uses the term "Pax Chaco" to describe the apparent peace maintained inside the Chaco region, and he considers that it may have been similar to the Pax Romana in the ancient Mediterranean. And like Rome, Chaco may have enjoyed a kind of peace at home by suppressing any political resistance or competition that arose in the periphery.

None of that detracts from the idea that the heart of Chaco was still built around the spiritual powers of the canyon or other locations, such as Chimney Rock. Chaco's various celestially aligned monuments bespeak a cultural and political phenomenon based on cosmic experience. The Sun and Moon would have been perceived to move around the canyon, and outlier great houses were sometimes linked to each other by formal roadways. Along these, people and spirits may have processed on the occasion of major ceremonials, with the people carrying materials, supplies, timbers, and maize into the canyon. As a result, Chaco Canyon must have felt to those who participated in the processions as if it was both at the center of the universe and in the "middle of time."[13]

More than coercion, such ritual experiences were the best ways to motivate thousands of people to work hundreds of thousands of person-hours to construct and maintain Chaco's monuments. Even the constructions of Egypt's Old Kingdom pyramids, which incorporated slave labor, were reliant on the manufacture of belief in local communities that would thereafter feel a part of something larger, cosmic, and lasting. Sentiments are produced through participation and coordinated physical and emotional movements. With time, however, various people usually begin to realize that such all-encompassing social, political, and religious constructs are grand illusions.

Those who did and do come to their senses, so to speak, might resist. Of course, defiance of a politico-religious order rooted in the experience of a landscape is difficult. How does one oppose the very movements of the Sun and Moon? In Chaco Canyon, at Chimney Rock, and at a host of other Chacoan outliers, the Sun and Moon, not human leaders, were what coordinated the movements of farmers. People watched these all-important celestial bodies moving across the sky and, based on past experience, predicted where the orbs would appear over the course of a year or a generation. The people timed their own daily prayers, agricultural activities, family events, political rituals, or travels and pilgrimages accordingly. It's a phenomenon well known to archaeologists, and it hasn't changed through time. All ancestors of all peoples did it at one time or another. It's the basis of civilization. And we all still do rely on celestial movements to some degree, if only in their regulation of daytime and nighttime. We simply tend not to think much today about the fact that all major cultural holidays—from Christmas to Passover, or Ramadan to Easter—are based on a celestial calendar.

At Chaco, such cosmic cycles seem to have brought waves of pilgrims into the canyon, the best evidence for this pattern being well-dated "pulses" of great house construction. At many of the great houses, every decade (9.3 years) or two (18.6 years) a new wall would be added, a room block expanded, old doorways blocked up, or kivas sealed up and built over. Processions of people would enter the canyon carrying timbers cut from distant mountains, pots made by distant potters, and food to feed the many people who would labor to build the marvelous multistory monuments that grew bigger with each pulse. They would have heard the stories of their own parents, grandparents, aunts, and uncles, and they would, in turn, tell their own children of their wonderful works.

Any one pilgrimage and construction pulse was a veritable religious movement, with a visionary or priestly architect possibly being the one who presented the people with a reinvigorated or reinterpreted cosmic design that, once executed, left everyone who took part with a new sense of purpose and direction. The visions and cosmic designs themselves would presumably motivate people best if the structures built from them contained in their very walls multiple powerful references that might inspire awe or wonder—even if few of the people understood the full meaning or obscure references involved. And in such ways, Mesoamerican influences, Mesoamerican things, perhaps even a few Mesoamericans—maybe West Mexicans or Huastecans—themselves would have entered the Place Beyond the Horizon. They were pulled in, walked in, or were carried in by the powers of this place.

During one particular pulse, around 1040, the Chacoan realm was expanded and great kivas were designed and upgraded into the monumental rooms that we see today. These oversized and overbuilt kivas had local roots, evolving from traditional pithouses into spaces with religious and communal overtones as early as 600 CE.[14] By the ninth century, formal kivas appear, though it remains unclear when these became associated with the Mesomericanoid wind and rain god in the form of conch shell trumpet rituals.[15] The earliest great kivas in the canyon's two Basketmaker III pithouse villages, however, lacked a fundamental characteristic of Ehecatl-Quetzalcoatl shrines in Mesoamerica at the time—verticality.

This may have been remedied by later great kivas and "tower kivas"—those with exaggerated vertical walls. Kiva verticality came along during the pulse of monumental construction in 1040, the beginning of the so-called Bonito phase. At that time, several of the best and biggest great kivas were constructed with exterior walls that projected 6 to 10 feet above the ground, giving them massive, elevated, flat roofs that could have doubled as stages in ritual performances.

The most singular such vertical great kiva, Casa Rinconada, occupies the very center of Chaco Canyon, opposite Pueblo Bonito (Figure 7.3). In this setting, it is elevated atop a prominent colluvial slope along the south canyon wall, one of two or three anthropogenically sculpted slopes on that side of the canyon. Assuming that Casa Rinconada was roofed (and some have suggested otherwise), any orator or singer could have been heard distinctly from its rooftop stage by those listening from the tops of other great houses or from the Chaco Canyon rim.[16]

Tower kivas were even taller, two or three stories. Some of these were not stand-alone towers but aboveground constructions built inside rectangular rooms, perhaps to stabilize their walls. One such tower encased inside the northwestern corner of a late-dating great house in the canyon, Kin Kletso, was built quite intentionally atop a large unmodified boulder of sandstone that had fallen from the canyon wall

Figure 7.3. Great kiva at Aztec, Colorado. Top, as seen from plaza; bottom, reconstructed interior. T. Pauketat, 2017.

100 feet above centuries earlier. The boulder comprises beautiful large mollusk-shell fossils. Constructing the entire great house wall and kiva atop it, Chacoan masons carefully fitted their blocks into every irregularity of the natural boulder in a clear attempt to preserve the fossils on the face of the rock and, presumably, link the building above with the ancient watery realm preserved in the fossilized rock below

(Figure 7.4).[17] Here again is the common North American connection between circular form and primeval waters.

Another such linkage might have been made just a few years earlier at yet another of the canyon's great houses, Pueblo del Arroyo. In this case, around the year 1109, the earliest Puebloan circular tri-walled public building was constructed overlooking a bend in Chaco Wash. With a footprint about the same diameter as a Chacoan great kiva,

Figure 7.4. Kin Kletso's exterior wall built atop fossiliferous sandstone boulder, Chaco Canyon. Sandstone masonry blocks are 6 to 12 inches in length. Courtesy of David Boyle, 2021.

this special building was a late addition that dates to an early twelfth-century construction pulse in the canyon (Figure 7.5). At that time, Chacoan labor and laborers were moving out of the canyon to build a new Chaco to the north, at a location today called Aztec (misnamed by nineteenth-century Euro-Americans).

There are a couple dozen more bi-, tri-, and even quadri-walled buildings scattered across the late Chaco to post-Chaco (Pueblo III) landscape to the north, including a couple at Aztec. There is also one to the south, atop Cerro de Moctezuma, overlooking the ruins of Paquime (see Chapter 1). It and the northern examples usually consist of a central circular room surrounded by two concentric rows of small rooms, all of which, panopticon-style, open onto the interior room. The interior room, evidence now suggests, was typically taller, taking the form of a tower with one or two outer, lower walls successively stepping down from the inner summit, forming a kind of terraced

Figure 7.5. Remains of a circular tri-wall masonry building, Aztec ruins. Wikimedia: SkybirdForever, 2012. Creative Commons Attribution-Share Alike 3.0 Unported License.

circular construction that would have looked like some Postclassic Mesoamerican circular pyramids (Figure 7.6).

Steve Lekson has made a study of such buildings. On the interior, they appear to him to have been more secretive and restricted—perhaps the chambers or temples of priests and administrators.[18] Viewed from the outside, they are strongly reminiscent of the more elaborate elevated Maya water shrines, including the Caracol observatory at Chichen Itza and some of the circular pyramids of the Toltecs and Huastecs.[19]

In many ways, Chaco Canyon and its numerous outliers—spread all over the Four Corners region of New Mexico, Arizona, Utah, and Colorado—were unlike the centralized cities of Mesoamerica, such as Tula, Tamtoc, or Teotihuacan. Chaco Canyon's twelve great houses hint at an extraordinarily low-density urban core, even less thickly populated than the low-density cities of the Maya, such as Tikal, since the thousands or even tens of thousands of people in those jungle cities yet clustered around the monumental cores. Chaco's population was truly scattered, many living in villages in the Chuska

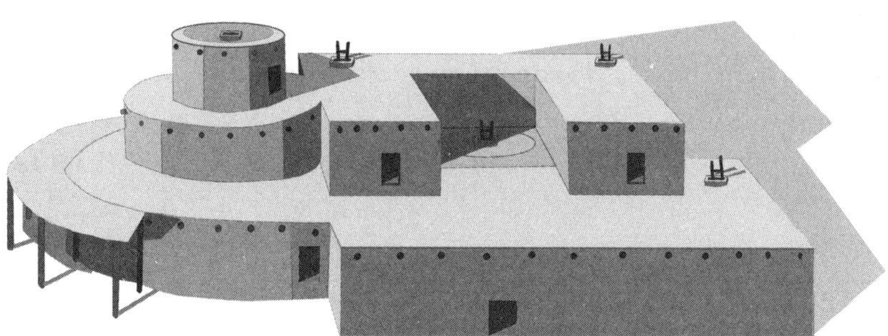

Figure 7.6. Reconstruction of tri-wall at Mitchell Springs great house. From David M. Dove, "Greathouse Formation: Agricultural Intensification, Balanced Duality, and Communal Enterprise at Mitchell Springs," *Southwestern Lore* 87, no. 1 (2021): 5–49, fig. 6. Courtesy of David M. Dove.

Mountains 50 miles to the west, and Chaco's outlier great houses probably were largely autonomous, depending the religious fervor of local citizens as much as on political support or management from the canyon itself.

★★★

Back in the canyon, more pulses followed. Around the same time as the Pueblo del Arroyo tri-wall construction, Mesoamerican-style colonnades were added to the public façade of Chetro Ketl, one of the largest and most central of Chaco Canyon's great houses. The façade has a rectilinear Chacoan feel, but nothing like it had ever been built before, at least not this far north of Alta Vista. And that Chalchihuites site, 900 miles to the south, is the likely inspiration. Of course, by the 1120s, Alta Vista was already abandoned, so we aren't talking about a Mesoamerican-based colonial enterprise, trading mission, or outreach program moving from south to north. Rather, this would have been a Puebloan-centered effort to incorporate the places or things of mythical pasts or powerful far-off gods into the masonry constructions back home on the Colorado Plateau.[20]

In yet another pulse, most likely during the 1120s, a large ponderosa pine log, estimated at 60 feet tall down to its roots, was carried in from the Chuska Mountains and set vertically in the open plaza of Pueblo Bonito.[21] We can presume that it was used in great central rituals, perhaps as a gnomon or solar observation post, or perhaps as a great world tree that was climbed in Chaco's very own pole-climbing ceremonies. Soon thereafter, nearing the mid-1100s, Kin Kletsin and several other McElmo-style great houses were built.[22] McElmo was a typical northern style associated with the Aztec site and Mesa Verde, where Chaco's expatriates were moving. The style involved the use of larger sandstone blocks to construct smaller buildings that, in turn, commemorated northern historical ties to Chaco Canyon proper, which by then was being emptied of its human population. McElmo architectural constructions presented impressive exteriors but were compact with nearly non-functional interiors. At Mesa Verde, one can even see a miniaturized version of Pueblo Bonito in the form of a D-shaped "Sun temple."

Mesoamerican things were very definitely carried into Chaco Canyon: West Mexican copper bells, tropical macaws, and powdered chocolate. Of the various imports, chocolate, made from the cacao bean, is proof positive of commerce of some kind, direct or indirect, with Mesoamerica, at least during the sixty or so years of the Bonito phase (1040–1100 CE).[23] The cacao plant's range at the time extended from Huasteca south on the Gulf Coast, and less intensively from Nayarit and Jalisco south on the Pacific side. Cylindrical jars were used to mix the imported chocolate powder with water to produce a bitter ritual drink themselves, and these jars seem to have been modeled after special Huastec, West Mexican, or Maya cylindrical vases that are a foot or more tall. Most of jars used in the ritual consumption of chocolate were found buried in a dark, secret back room of Pueblo Bonito, stacked there around the year 1100 CE as part of an official termination rite—possibly as part of yet another pulse.[24]

Perhaps whoever brought the caffeine-rich drink mix into northwestern New Mexico also came with a cage or two of colorful macaws. That person or persons may have been Mesoamerican. Alternatively, they might have been Chacoan, maybe a priest returning from a religious journey or a traveler who hailed from the Hohokam or Mogollon region. If the latter, they might have been middlemen, like Cabeza de Vaca centuries later. We might call what they did "trade," but the term is deceptive, implying an economic rather than cultural or religious motivation. Indeed, "trade" is an inadequate explanation of Chaco. It misses the point and diminishes the actual historical effects of the movements of people and powerful things. Better to simply think of this as a kind of overland circulation that helps to explain the apparent historical connections between north and south.

Everywhere one looks, there were active, if intermittent, physical and communicative connections across the southwestern landscape into North Mexico and, from there, West Mexico and the rest of Mesoamerica. People traveled to and from one place to another.

Waves of pilgrims visited Chaco. Chaco's politicians and priests made their own pilgrimages, of sorts, south to the Gulf of California or into the storied lands of Zacatecas and, from there, Mesoamerica proper. They probably returned with special objects, new friendships, and visions that would then be translated into terms understandable to their followers back home.

That translation process entailed very real cultural filters that prevented certain information from passing into the north. Even something as seemingly obvious, experiential, and communal as a ballgame did not translate into the Puebloan heartland at the height of Chaco. Then again, the ballgame did appear to the west of the Place Beyond the Horizon just after the eruption of Sunset Crater, in north-central Arizona, between 1068 and 1080 CE. There, at Wupatki, a copy of a Chacoan great house was built next to a Hohokam-style ballcourt (Figure 7.7). The ballcourt sits next to a volcanic vent that forces out or sucks in air, depending on the season.

Residential structures at Wupatki's outlying sites include Hohokam-style houses.[25] Some of Wupatki's inhabitants were, clearly, immigrant

Figure 7.7. Wupatki Great House, northern Arizona. T. Pauketat, 2013.

Hohokam. Others were expatriate Chacoans. Today, the Hopi are the closest Puebloan group to the Sunset Crater region, and they trace a connection back to the Place Beyond the Horizon. What's more, they speak a Uto-Aztecan language, like their ballgame-playing counterparts among the Epiclassic or Colonial- and Sedentary-period Hohokam, due south of them in Arizona.

As it happened, the ballgame had ceased to be a Hohokam sport by the time ballcourts appeared in the late Pueblo era at places such as Wupatki, near the Grand Canyon. The Hohokam were now building their own great houses out of adobe and at the same time conducting important ritual gatherings atop rectangular Mesoamerican-style platform mounds. Chaco was long gone by then, having been converted into a ghostly vacant site of religious worship after the severe drought of the 1130s–1150s. Descendants speak of having emigrated out of the canyon as part of a larger plan, presumably by the mid-twelfth century. They were abandoning the canyon, they say, because the political power of the priests and leaders of this great social experiment had gotten out of control.[26]

***

Ultimately, the rise and demise of the Place Beyond the Horizon holds several key lessons for our understanding of the big-historical relationships between people, place, spirituality, pilgrimage, and climate change. Chaco Canyon and other key locations around the Four Corners region were endowed with spiritual powers perceived by people. Fajada Butte and the naturally lunar-aligned canyon were exceptional long before people built the first great house. And unlike other parts of North Mexico, California, and the American West, northwestern New Mexico in the early years of the medieval warming provided people with ample sustenance and safety from outside threats.

All of this thanks to the gods. And so Chaco's leaders honored those gods, traveling long distances to the south to find and understand them, entertaining strangers who traveled to them from those

Mesoamerican lands, and building what they learned through such contacts into their wonderful buildings. Among the most important were circular structures that assumed new Mesoamerican meanings thanks to the Wind-That-Brings-Rain.

Unfortunately for the Chacoans, people whose lives depend on the spirits of the wind and rain suffer when such spirits cease to favor the people. In the end, the Chacoans could not sustain Chaco Canyon. The builders of the last McElmo-style masonry structures moved north. Others went south, and still others headed west. They did not forget their heritage. Instead, people with Chacoan family legacies remained powerful for generations after the mid-1100s. Some of them were even subject to attack by those fearful of the expatriate Chacoans' latent supernatural power. At a place called Sand Canyon in southwestern Colorado around the year 1260, one such man—an elderly polydactyl craftsman—and his small pueblo were targeted by raiders. He was shot while standing atop his two-story village, and the killers dropped his body into a dark interior room, tossed stones onto it, and then burned the entire pueblo to the ground.[27]

The powers of other senior Chacoan descendants were handled in more respectful ways upon their deaths. At Ridge Ruin, 200 miles west of Chaco and just south of Wupatki, a deceased Chacoan priest was buried with all of his religious paraphernalia and magical materials. Archaeologists initially dubbed him "the Magician," since he was interred with wooden wand-like swallowing sticks, special mixing bowls, and other priestly items not unlike those found with the back-room Pueblo Bonito men. Having died around 1170 CE, the Magician appears to have been a migrant from the east, from Chaco. He had moved west into the so-called Sinagua cultural area—a land "without water"—near Wupatki and the Grand Canyon. His death appears to have been the impetus for the people of Ridge Ruin to leave their settlement in the 1170s.[28] Presumably, the burial of his person and supernaturally powerful possessions was the only way to safely contain the cosmic forces that he embodied.[29] The trick for the living in dealing with such power, it seems, was to channel it or stay out of its way. Those who did the former particularly well might become visionaries or prophets in their own right. Those who didn't do the latter might end up dead.

The later 1100s were a time of great ethnic and religious change, as the social webs that had once clearly defined the Hohokam, Mogollon, Ancestral Pueblo, and Navajo were blurring.[30] New visionaries appeared from time to time, and those with particularly compelling messages—increasingly conveyed in things, not at places—appeared again and again in the later 1200s along the Mogollon Rim, where archaeologists identify a new kind of polychrome pottery with designs called Salado. Salado is known for its Mesoamerican imagery, usually associated with a sunny, colorful vision of an afterlife filled with birds, flowers, and butterflies—a veritable heaven on earth known as the Flower World. Salado art and its associated religious practices were birthed in the towns and villages that followed Chaco's demise, preceding by a matter of decades an even more widespread Katsina religion that appeared in the fourteenth century and spread northward through or out of the multistory, urban Mogollon pueblo Paquime. The Katsina gods brought the people water from the mountains, above which rain clouds form, and include allusions to storm and rain deities strongly reminiscent of Mesoamerican gods.

Unlike some other pulses of religious fervor, the Katsina religion stuck, at least among the descendants of the Pueblo and Mogollon cultures. It survives in some ways even today. Gods whose images were pecked into Puebloan rock art or painted on pots in the 1300s still visit Puebloan descendants today during special community rituals. Less tethered to place, the Katsina gods appear to Puebloan communities if and when beckoned by people. The deities' survival, it now seems, owes in part to the demise of Chaco Canyon, which, not unlike Teotihuacan centuries earlier, had held a kind of mental hegemony over the people. When that was broken, the people and the gods were freed.[31] Katsinas spread a new Mesoamerican-inspired, pan-southwestern religion, even though largely cut off from direct overland ties to Mesoamerica. In terms of content, the Katsina religion was the culmination of the wave of Mesoamerican inspirations associated with the Epiclassic and early Postclassic periods. By the fourteenth century, these explicitly included the imagery of Mesoamerican gods: the feathered serpent Quetzalcoatl and the water god Tlaloc.[32]

Of course, by then, the Hohokam great houses and large towns that had inspired Chaco Canyon were themselves being abandoned in favor of scattered small settlements. More than the Pueblos, and despite the Katsina religion, the Hohokam had always been more Mesoamerican in some sense. Yet they never bought into the big Epiclassic religious movements or cults of Ehecatl-Quetzalcoatl and Tlaloc (or their cognates). They never built circular kivas, steam baths, or shrines. That was for the Maya, Teuchitlanos, Toltecans, Huastecans, Puebloans, Mogollons, and, as we are about to see, the people at the end of another "corn road" running northeast into Texas.

Places to Visit

Chaco Culture National Historical Park, New Mexico

Do not attempt to drive into Chaco Culture National Historical Park in the rain. You won't make it. And do not even consider pulling a camper trailer or, worse, driving a Winnebago into this sacred landscape. This greatest of archaeological preserves in the United States, treasured by its Native descendants, is threatened from all sides. It does not need thoughtless tourists. Take a tent, but go online ahead of time and reserve a camping space at Gallo campground. You will need two days just to get started seeing the great houses and hiking the mesa lands of this park, established in 1907 by President Theodore Roosevelt. Nearing the entrance on the rough, washboard road, you spy the top of Fajada Butte, and then descend slowly into the canyon. Just past the campground, Fajada Butte appears around a bend. The road winds past the greatest of the great houses: Hungo Pavi, Chetro Ketl, Pueblo Bonito, Pueblo del Arroyo. You can hike to others by parking your car and filling out a backcountry permit at the parking lot. Hikes are peaceful, invigorating, and sometimes strenuous. Leave the artifacts lying where you see them. When you return to the campground that night, voices surround you in increasingly hushed tones. Campfires crackle, aromas fill the air, and the blue sky fades to Milky Way black.

Aztec Ruins National Monument, New Mexico

The misnamed Aztec site is located in New Mexico some 50 miles due north of Chaco Canyon. Take US Route 550 past the turnoff to Chaco and continue north toward Durango, Colorado. Aztec was founded in the late 1080s and constructed over succeeding decades to mimic the configuration of three of Chaco's great houses (Pueblo Bonito, Chetro Ketl, and Pueblo Alto). You will see only one of the three pieces of the larger complex overlooking the Animas River within the city limits of Aztec, Colorado. Unmistakably Chacoan in its masonry construction, the Aztec site was expanded using McElmo block construction after Chaco's 1140 CE depopulation. The reconstructed great kiva conveys the awesome, performative qualities of these public spaces. The room block to the north reveals the characteristic T-shaped doorways on former exterior walls. These seemed to have constituted special portals through which one passed when moving from the outside world into the living spaces of Chacoan descendants.

Chimney Rock National Monument, Colorado

From Aztec, Colorado, continue north 30 miles toward Durango, and then east another 40 miles on Highway 160 to Chimney Rock. There, high atop a narrow razorback mesa, local people and Chacoans built an isolated great house in 1076 CE to commemorate the long cycle of the Moon. Consider staying in a bed-and-breakfast in Pagosa Springs, Colorado. Drive to the relatively new national monument, created by

President Barack Obama in 2012, and walk up to the top. As you do, you pass Pueblo I–II pithouses and room blocks built using smoothed boulders. These were not Chacoan homes but those of local people who lived here through the Chacoan period. They no doubt did most of the work on the Great House under the supervision of Chacoan architects. The great house sits a thousand feet in the air. From its summit, Chacoan priests could have watched the full moon rise to the northeast—here at the very edge of the Chacoan World—one out of every 18.6 years.

Wupatki and Sunset Crater National Monuments, Arizona

Drive up to the Wupatki great house and visitors center. An easy, wheelchair-accessible stroll down to this impressive masonry structure and the ballcourt beyond reveals a uniquely hybrid archaeological complex, reminiscent of both Chacoan and Hohokam monumental buildings. Adjacent to the ballcourt is an amazing volcanic vent that alternately blows out air or sucks it in, depending on the season. For the adventurous, hike (or drive) to Sunset Crater, a great cinder cone that remains from a volcanic eruption in 1085 CE. That eruption was the reason for the construction of Wupatki during the 1100s. Fewer than two hundred people ever lived in the great house, but a thousand or more farmers, living in hundreds of settlements nearby, helped to build and maintain it until its abandonment around 1275 CE.

8

The Other Corn Road

The surviving members of the Narváez expedition, out along the Rio Grande in southwest Texas, might have acquired a better sense of the Katsina religion, with its Mesoamerican-style gods, had they chose to follow a "cow road" north instead of a "corn road" west.[1] This is because the cow road would have led them to great herds of bison on the Plains, but it probably also would have led them to prosperous pueblos practicing the Katsina religion that procured bison meat from the Plains tribes.

For starving travelers, the thought of a good hunk of fatty meat might have been a powerful inducement. The men deliberated. There was a lot of open country to traverse. The corn road was said to be an arduous month-long trip with little food or shelter to reach villages of maize agriculturalists—no bison meat. Yet they chose it anyway as the surer route back to Mexico City.

Long before this fork in the road, Cabeza de Vaca and his comrades had decided against turning south, since the Sierra Madre Oriental would channel the travelers back toward the Gulf Coast, where they'd be in peril of being recaptured by coastal foragers. At this point in their journey, the travelers also wouldn't have considered turning back into the Woodlands of east Texas, though doing so would have been a reasonable escape strategy back in the autumn of 1528, just after their barges had crashed on the Galveston coastline.

At that time, walking north from modern-day Galveston, it would have taken the castaways about two weeks to reach the populous nation of the Hasinai Caddo. The Hasinai, in fact, were located on another corn road headed north and east out of Mexico. It would later become known as El Camino Real de los Tejas, connecting Mexico City to the Texas and Louisiana territories. And had Cabeza de Vaca and the others gone in that northerly direction in those initial weeks and months, they might have later cut westward through the High Plains of west Texas, traveling along the Red or Canadian Rivers to reach the Rio Grande pueblos.

Over the centuries of the Medieval Climate Anomaly (800–1300 CE), there had been intermittent communications between the Pueblos and the Caddos. In fact, as with the Southwest generally, the medieval period saw more rain in north and west Texas, the open scrubland between the Pueblos and the Caddos. Such conditions would have facilitated one-off trips and long-distance connections between the two, and might have been responsible for both the arrival of maize into eastern North America and, as we shall see, the transfer of lunar astronomical knowledge to or from the Puebloan Southwest.

Then again, the remains of expatriate Chacoans are unknown east of the Rio Grande, as are the Hohokam ballgame and the Puebloan Katsina religion. The Texas scrub seems to have filtered out much routine human movement between the Southwest and the Southern Plains. That filtering effect persisted, to some degree, into the 1500s, when the Hasinai occupied the western front of Mississippian civilization, due east of the Southern Plains. The Hasinai were sedentary town-dwellers in northeast Texas who spoke a distinctive Caddo language. At this late date, they ventured out into the Plains only episodically, to procure bison and other goods from more distantly related Caddoan-speaking Plains Village neighbors, such as the Wichita and Pawnee of north-central Texas, Oklahoma, and Kansas.[2] From east-central Texas into the Red River and Arkansas River valleys of northern Texas, eastern Oklahoma, and western Louisiana and Arkansas, the town-dwelling Caddo were a kind of borderland culture, farming maize, beans, and squash, evincing cultural trappings of La Florida's

Mississippians and hinting at Puebloan and Mesoamerican inspirations behind some of their practices.

Before the climatic shifted away from the warmer, wetter medieval weather in the late 1200s, Caddo towns had been relatively large, made up of hundreds of people and centered on one or more earthen platform mounds. Those mounds elevated the most important Caddo temples, shrine buildings, and elite homes. Some were rectangular. Many were circular.

Yet few archaeologists consider the origins of Caddo mounds, among other things, in Mesoamerica.[3] They've been trained not to. The argument goes, to paraphrase one such archaeologist, that Mesoamerican cultural influences can't be proven, so we should ignore them. Somehow, even mentioning connections between the Caddo and the people south of today's US-Mexican border seems perilous to many archaeologists, lacking as they often do the material evidence of regular, sustained Mesoamerican trade relations. It's true: we have yet to find copper bells, Mesoamerican chocolate, or macaws in eastern North America, so it's safe to conclude that there was, in fact, no regular commerce between the civilizations of Mesoamerica and the people of eastern North America.

To complicate the picture, so much of what we know about the Caddo was learned before the advent of radiocarbon dating in the 1950s, and we have yet to connect all the dots. Thankfully, with high-precision dating possible and with advanced statistical methods for narrowing in on the actual calendar year being dated, things are becoming clearer. The most recent calibrations of radiocarbon dates now reveal that the first Caddo towns were founded during the Formative Caddo period (900–1050 CE) at about the same time as the Epiclassic spread of Ehecatl-Quetzalcoatl imagery and Toltecan and Huastecan practices in Mesoamerica.

One of the earliest Formative Caddo towns sits at the southernmost edge of the Caddo world. The George C. Davis site—aka Caddo Mounds State Historic Site—is located 160 miles north of Galveston on the Neches River. Its layout is simple: two rectangular mounds and one circular mound situated on a ridge around which families built dozens of scattered, circular, pole-and-thatch domiciles. Unlike the masonry homes of the Pueblos or the stone foundations of the Toltecs, Caddo homes only survived for a single human generation before rotting away. Archaeologists can detect the postholes and living floors that remain using geophysical techniques that measure subtle disturbances below the surface. Careful scientific excavations reveal them clearly, and if they were put to the torch centuries ago, the charred remains of the poles and thatch used in their construction can still be found.

The foundational deposits of the one flat-topped circular mound at the Davis site date to this Formative Caddo period.[4] Believed by some to be an accretional burial mound, based on a less than critical study of such monuments, this circular tumulus, Mound C, was in reality a platform, periodically raised with the addition of more earthen construction fill. And this Caddo mound was a contemporary of the circular platforms at the Las Flores site at the mouth of the Pánuco River, 650 miles to the south.

Unlike the Las Flores mounds, however, the George C. Davis site circular mound was apparently not surmounted by pole-and-thatch architecture. Instead, excavators noticed a series of shaft graves that extended down from each successive flat summit.[5] Elsewhere in the Caddo world, shaft graves were dug into the floors of both circular and rectangular mound-top structures, the walls of which consisted of posts set in individually dug postholes or wall trenches.[6] In the early periods, many graves consisted of groups of people laid out in rows, side by side, as if all of those interred in single pits had died simultaneously. At Davis, the pits contained men and women of reproductive age, with the occasional child, arranged in ways suggesting a group death. Possibly this means human sacrifice, conceivably involving the relatives or retainers of deceased community elites.

Such mass graves are among the things that distinguish Formative Caddo (900–1050 CE) and Early Caddo (1050–1200 CE) people from their neighbors. Outside of Central Mexico and, as we shall see, Cahokia, human interments lined up in rows are rare to unknown. Another typical Caddo attribute that continues up through the historic era, also rare outside of Mesoamerica, was the opulence of burial. In many North American cultures, the dead were interred with only modest accoutrements—a pot or a favorite stone tool, a pendant around the neck. Caddo people, however, buried their dead with many offerings—multiple pots, smoking pipes, chipped-stone arrowheads, and ornaments that would have adorned the deceased or festooned the ritual costumes they were wearing. Some such adornments and offerings were imports, including delicately carved stone earspools covered with sheet copper. But most were made locally by Caddo artisans in distinctive Caddo styles.

Of the locally made items, the most elaborate and easily identifiable Caddo products were finely incised and engraved pottery bottles, cylindrical vases, and bowls. Archaeologists named some of the most beautiful Holley Fine Engraved, Spiro Engraved, and Crockett Curvilinear, the last after a nearby town that was in turn named after the Texas hero Davy Crockett, who roamed the Neches River region in the 1830s. By anyone's standards, these pots were "handsomely decorated with engraved designs, carefully and gracefully drawn in many complex forms, and the designs intensified by filling the lines with red or white paint."[7]

The origins of these designs suggest inspirations—"irritatingly nonspecific but nonetheless genuine cultural resemblances"—drawn both from neighboring groups to the east and from Mesoamericans far to the south.[8] The designs include interconnected bands of volutes or spirals, the spaces in between sometimes filled with opposing nested arcs, each successive arc getting smaller until they reach a vanishing point (Figure 8.1). The effect of the combined spiral and nested arc design elements is sometimes called a "scroll," and has been likened to a marine conch shell cut in half. Some variants of the scroll motif are evocative of serpents or, as likely, serpentine vines (see Figure 8.1). Virtually the same motif, unknown in the Caddo region before 900 CE, is widespread across Epiclassic and early Postclassic

Figure 8.1. Caddo pottery with wind, water, or breath/speech scrolls. Left: bottle (9.2 inches tall); right, bowl (12.2 inches wide). Adapted from Clarence B. Moore, "Some Aboriginal Sites on Red River," *Journal of the Academy of Natural Sciences of Philadelphia* 14 (1912): 481–644, plate XL and fig. 49.

Mesoamerica at the same time, where it has been connected to the Wind-That-Brings-Rain god Ehecatl-Quetzalcoatl.

Some classic Caddo motifs were transferred to the large conch shell dippers, obtained from the Gulf Coast, from which the Caddo used to drink special potions. Unlike the pots, however, these dippers were also engraved with the images of god-like characters, most often humanoid men or their disembodied heads, but frequently featuring snakes, birds of prey, and spiders. The images, think some analysts, tell of events in the netherworld, not this world, though communing with such spirits can happen via trances induced by such things as psychotropic drugs.

There is a mesmerizing 1960s psychedelic or op-art quality about the curvilinear and spiral Caddo decorations on marine shells and pottery, especially since the complex designs are often repeated over and over, encircling the pottery containers and making the user feel as if she or he is in motion. The sensory impacts of the scrolls and other such motifs on the small bottles, vases, bowls, and dippers, whether ceramic or shell, might have exacerbated the effects of drug use in public ceremonies involving individuals pouring and drinking some potion in front of a gathered throng of onlookers.

Contemporary evidence from the Cahokia site, 400 miles to the north of the Caddo heartland, suggests that similar fineware drinking containers—some almost certainly made by immigrant Caddo potters—were used for brewing and drinking a caffeinated tea made from the yaupon holly bush (*Ilex vomitoria*) beginning in the late 900s. Importantly, that bush is not native to the Cahokia region, which sits at latitude 38 degrees north, but it does grow locally in southwestern Arkansas, which is at latitude 33 ± 2 degrees north in Caddo country.[9] Cabeza de Vaca witnessed it being consumed, and described how it was boiled down to produce a frothy beverage by people living in the lower Rio Grande valley.[10]

Yaupon holly tea, also known as the Black Drink, is not the only potion likely to have been imbibed by participants in religious ceremonies.[11] While there is as yet no firm evidence of liquid Mesoamerican chocolate, there is evidence of the consumption of other psychotropic potions made from both jimsonweed (*Datura* sp.) and morning glory (*Ipomoea* sp.).[12] Even some of the small mixing bowls or drinking cups found in Caddo country, as well as in other Mississippian and Puebloan locales, have spiky exteriors made to look like *Datura* seed pods.

Such potions were used widely by shamans and priests in Mesoamerica, too. The morning glory mixture was at least as potent as the jimsonweed drink because it contained a chemical, lysergic acid amide (LSA), that has similar effects on human beings as the modern synthetic drug lysergic acid diethylamide (LSD). No less a man than filmmaker and drug alchemist John Waters noted, in an NPR interview, that morning glory was the one drug that he'd never do again.[13] Not only was it exceedingly psychotropic, he noted, but morning glory possessed some nasty side effects. Not that these stopped Aztec priests, who drank *tlililtzin*, a morning glory beverage, to get in touch with their gods. Other Mesoamerican shamans or healers used similar morning glory concoctions for medicinal purposes.[14]

Arguably, the serpentine form of the plant's vine and the mind-bending effects of a potion made from the plant might help to explain the intricate curvilinear designs on pots. They might also account for the shape of the arrowheads so commonly interred with the Caddo dead. How that is so rests on recognizing a common Indigenous metaphor for healing. Across the continent, the act of shooting an arrow into a person, including people presumed to be witches (and witch-like enemies), is an act of healing. Accordingly, it may be less than coincidental that some Formative and Early Caddo period chipped-stone projectile points, most less than an inch long, were made to look like the leaves of morning glory and jimsonweed plants. These include examples that possessed odd barbs along their sharp edges, similar to jimsonweed leaves. They also include a type of chipped-stone projectile point with long needle-shaped tips, bulbous midsections, pronounced barbs, and prominent basal attachments, virtually identical to morning glory leaves (Figure 8.2). Not incidentally, the natural range of psychotropic morning glory (*Ipomoea tricolor*) extends

Figure 8.2. Morning glory leaf and a Caddo-style projectile point. Left, T. Pauketat; right, courtesy of the Illinois Department of Transportation.

from Mesoamerica into the Great Bend region of Texas and Arkansas, but little farther north.

The George C. Davis site sits in the middle of that range, near the modern-day town of Alto, Texas, in the highlands between river valleys. In that location, the Davis site also sits on what became, in the 1600s, El Camino Real de los Tejas—the royal Spanish road between Mexico City and the Spanish administrative capital of the Texas territory (Los Adaes, today in modern-day Louisiana). The royal road, also called the San Antonio Trail, ran just east of the rugged Edwards Plateau of interior Texas where it gives way to the more easily traversed Coastal Plain. Here, a moderately dissected hilly landscape was covered in prairie grass and could be crossed with relative ease. This was the other corn road.

Such colonial-era roads often formalized pre-contact-era Native traces, and El Camino Real was almost certainly no exception. The location of this early Caddo civic-ceremonial center, at the southern edge of Caddo country and on high ground, likely means that an overland trace had existed through this part of Texas at least since 900 CE. Cabeza de Vaca, in escaping the coastal foragers in a southward and then westward direction, missed it. Or perhaps he ignored it.

Archaeologists in the 1940s referred to the route as the Gilmore Corridor, named by a prominent ethnobotanist who was interested in the possibility that maize agriculture diffused through the corridor's grasslands.[15] The development of Formative Caddo culture, that is, may have been a consequence of what was, for all intents and purposes, a conduit to Mesoamerica. The corridor, and the colonial-era trace that ran through it, connected Texas with Huasteca, the Altiplano desert of the Chichimecs, and finally Central Mexico. As noted earlier, no smoking-gun evidence has been found, and perhaps none will be. Archaeologist J. Charles Kelley, who did most of the work on the site of Alta Vista, in Zacatecas, believed that his Texas-archaeologist colleagues were shortsighted and focused on the wrong lines of evidence.

"Perhaps if the archeologists were less preoccupied with their search for the camp sites or other material evidence of the putative 'migrants' through or around the Texas 'cultural sink,'" Kelley complained, "and more alive to the significance of the observed behavior of groups such as the Jumano and the Coahuiltecans, the question of Mexican-Southeastern contacts would appear much less a problem." But the problem remains, and so Kelley's lament in 1955 is relevant today: "The entire question of cultural relationships of this order, the process whereby they develop, and the agents thereof is as yet inadequately explored."[16]

Old monolithic theories of culture, where traits were understood to have been gradually adopted or rejected through time, misled archaeologists.[17] So did a later hyperfocus on localities that insisted that each and every population across the continent adapted first and foremost to their local environment, and that adaptation is what explains the history of cross-border America. It's a very Anglo-centric viewpoint that forgets about the existence of sophisticated cultures just south of the border. It's the kind of exceptionalism that makes Ross Hassig bristle.

Not finding a continuous distribution of maize agricultural societies diffused across the Gilmore Corridor, most archaeologists today think little about how the rise of the Caddo might have been connected either to Mesoamerica or to climate change. Yet all, ironically, would acknowledge that a Mesoamerican food crop, maize, inspired the historical changes in population density, agricultural intensity, and ceremonial practice during a period of significant climatic warming and climate-induced hydrological change. The fact is that the Mesoamerican cultigen arrived in Caddo country around the year 900, when parts of Mexico, California, Texas, and the Mississippi valley were undergoing markedly reduced or, alternatively, increased precipitation. Such climatic fluctuations likely induced people to respond with practical agricultural measures as they sought to maintain a stable food supply. Importing maize was one such response. More than likely, it entered eastern North America by way of the Puebloan Southwest, perhaps via western Rio Grande intermediaries (archaeologically known as the Toyah).[18] Some seed corn could also have been imported directly from Mesoamerica—namely, Huasteca—but if so, its genetic signature has been swamped by that of the Puebloan strains.

Out in the Four Corners region of the American Southwest and North Mexico, maize had been grown for centuries by this time. The earliest known corn in Arizona and New Mexico dates to about 2000 BCE, carried northward by proto-Uto-Aztecan-speakers to whom maize metaphors made sense. Certainly, its adoption into the gardens of pithouse horticulturalists in that region helped pre-Hohokam and pre-Puebloan (i.e., Basketmaker) settlements grow large. Of course, even earlier maize varieties are known from Mesoamerica itself, where the crop was first domesticated from a wild native grass known as *teocentli*. The earliest domesticated maize recorded is more than six thousand years old and was found in archaeological deposits in dry caves located in the Mexican state of Guerrero.

Notoriously sensitive to altitude and latitude, the maize plant had to adapt to life in the northern latitudes' shorter growing seasons, a process that would have begun out in the Puebloan Southwest. Farmers experimented with different strains to see which grew best. Many archaeologists and plant geneticists believe that this slow, gradual testing and hybridization process took centuries. Indeed, the Northern Flint corn from the Eastern Woodlands—most especially the later Northeast and Great Lakes regions—appears to have been derived from a pre-adapted southwestern variety.[19] Even a paleo-ethnobotanical study of the Davis site corn concluded that it was an eastern North American variety that had developed from an imported Southwestern strain.[20]

A few archaeologists have argued that maize phytoliths—microscopic bits of silica that are found in some grasses such as maize—appear in two-thousand-year-old soot on the outside of broken pots all the way up into New York State. Their argument is that farmers experimented with this crop for centuries, perhaps in the final centuries BCE up to 900 CE.[21] But there are no actual charred pieces of the maize plant itself—macrobotanical evidence that would prove corn to be truly ancient—in the Eastern Woodlands until the eighth and ninth centuries CE.[22] Thus, some researchers have returned to an older school of thought that places the arrival of maize in both Caddo country and the American Midwest at or just before the year 900. They presume that an experimentation phase would have begun at that point in the Eastern Woodlands, lasting until about 1200 CE—much later than maize in the Southwest and thousands of years later than its widespread adoption in Mesoamerica.

In other words, the earliest corn in the Mississippi valley was adopted at just about the time that Chaco Canyon was coalescing out in northwestern New Mexico, and soon thereafter appears at the other end of the Santa Fe Trail and south a bit—on the Arkansas River in the middle of what is called the Plum Bayou culture. The Arkansas River can be followed upstream into the Plains and then into the Puebloan Southwest. From the Arkansas River, maize must have been very quickly carried into the Mississippi valley, arriving around modern-day St. Louis, Missouri, around 900 CE. From that jumping-off point, later varieties were carried to Wisconsin's Woodland Indians in the 1000s and to New York's early Haudenosaunee or Iroquois farmers in the early 1100s. Newer, better strains emerged as corn adapted to its new eastern home, and these were later passed back into the Caddo region.

An overland route for the first arrival of maize in the Eastern Woodlands directly through the Gilmore Corridor or along the Gulf Coast now seems less likely, at least for most strains of the crop. But the most important question isn't the specific origins of eastern maize but the late time frame for its arrival. That is, setting aside questions of genetics and lengthy experimentation phases, why would Woodland people have waited so long to adopt maize if there was a northern variety already out in the Southwest? There were two cultural reasons.

First, maize wasn't adopted before the year 900 in eastern North America because there were preexisting culinary and agricultural traditions there. It isn't as if people hadn't farmed domesticated crops for centuries in the Eastern Woodlands. They had. Beginning as early as the so-called Late Archaic period (ca. 2000–300 BCE) and picking up steam through the so-called Woodland era (300 BCE–900 CE), squash, local grasses—varieties of pigweed (*Chenopodium* sp.), knotweed (*Polygonum* sp.), and maygrass (*Phalaris* sp.)—and oily-seeded plants such as sunflower (*Helianthus* sp.) were all domesticated and farmed across the middle latitudes and southlands of North America.[23] Living in sedentary villages or towns and tilling the earth was not a foreign concept.

It is not inconceivable that Woodland people, from time to time, came into contact with the mysterious foreign crop called maize. To quote Steve Lekson, "everyone knew everything," right? But most people, under the conditions in which they lived before 900 CE, didn't actually need or even desire corn, and their traditional culinary practices would have ensured inertia. Tradition, after all, is what leads to desire, even today: if your family doesn't eat sage stuffing on Thanksgiving Day, then it is unlikely that your descendants will in the future. This is because the way we grow, harvest, cook, and serve food is the physical manifestation of our family identities, which define our wants and tastes. In short, you are what you eat, and a kind of cultural or identity-based resistance to corn likely existed in parts of the ancient Americas.

Beyond that, there is the little matter of climate change. Given that the maize plant was domesticated from a wild grass in southern Mesoamerica more than six thousand years ago, it needed a lengthy frost-free growing season and rainfall or irrigation at the right time in its life cycle to prosper. Such warm, stable hydroclimatic conditions existed in North Mexico and the American Southwest by 2000 BCE, and by then the plant had been hybridized so that it could tolerate the climate of southwestern deserts and the Colorado Plateau.

However, elsewhere in eastern North America, hybrid varieties and suitable climatic conditions were not prevalent until the ninth century and the Medieval Climate Anomaly. When introduced at the start of the medieval period (the Mesoamerican Epiclassic or early Postclassic and the Formative Caddo periods), it yet needed time for the plant's genetics to adjust—all with the help of Native farmers, of course, selecting those plants that had performed best the preceding growing season. Over the course of the earliest centuries of the medieval era, the plant adapted to its new home, as human beings and corn plants experimented with each other in the northern and eastern climes. Today, the maize plant has been subject to so much human and natural selection that the American Midwest produces way more corn than would have been possible in the old fields of either Mesoamerica or the Southwest. And, of course, it has spread around the world, with maize being a staple field crop in places ranging from Europe and Africa to China.

Back in medieval America, maize farming could be readily expanded because, unlike the situation across much of Mesoamerica (from the Maya heartland in the Yucatan Peninsula to the arid Chichimec interior of the north-central Altiplano), the American Midwest and Mid-South had grown warmer and wetter. In fact, portions of the Mississippi valley had become lush between the ninth and twelfth centuries. This was a good place and time to be a corn plant, and it was an even better place and time to be a corn farmer. Immigrant farmers poured into the Mississippi valley heartland during these centuries.

Larry Benson, geochemist and Chaco Canyon climate change expert, has argued this point for years, especially for the middle portion of the Mississippi valley. Benson has compared archaeological reconstructions of the past to hydroclimatic models that cover the Medieval Climate Anomaly. Working with dendroclimatologist Edward Cook, of the Lamont-Doherty Earth Observatory at Columbia University in New York, their Palmer Drought Severity Indices are based on ancient tree ring information collected from around the continent and generalized to infer the amount of precipitation-fed water in lakes and rivers, from the American Southwest into the Eastern Woodlands. Certain portions of the Midwest, they conclude, were ideal for rain-fed agriculture from the 900s into the early 1100s.[24]

***

The correlation between climate change, corn, and cultural expansion is readily evident between Texas and Oklahoma, where the Red River enters northwestern Louisiana near Texarkana, Texas. This is the so-called Great Bend region, where the drainage turns rather abruptly south after flowing eastward for hundreds of miles. From the Great Bend west, you could have paddled upriver in a wet year almost to modern-day Amarillo, Texas. From Amarillo, you would need to walk overland to the Canadian River, to the north, which would then lead you straight into the Puebloan Southwest. Downriver from the Great Bend, however, you would pass through the expansive floodplain of the Red River, complete with overlapping meander scars, into the deep woods of modern-day Louisiana.

The de Soto expedition passed through here, after its leader's death, in search of a southwesterly overland route home. Not satisfied with the possibilities, and perhaps advised by locals against cutting through the prickly pear homelands of dangerous foragers to the south, de Soto's men doubled back and, instead, floated down the Red River to the Mississippi. From there they fought their way downriver and entered the Gulf of Mexico around present-day New Orleans. Then, sailing southwesterly along the Texas and Tamaulipas coasts, they did what Pánfilo de Narváez had failed to do. They reached the Pánuco River and followed it upstream back to Mexico City.

No doubt the Caddo people of the Great Bend region were glad to see de Soto's men go. Later, French explorers encountered the thriving Kadohadacho tribe of the Caddo Confederacy in 1691 in this same region, the descendants of those encountered by the de Soto expedition. The Kadohadacho are northern neighbors of the Hasinai, who reside along the Neches River, and maintain their own traditions. The Kadohadacho believe that they originated in a cave (which is to say, a tomb) inside a specific mound in the Great Bend region. As recorded by early twentieth-century anthropologists, that mound appears to have been located at a cultural site today called Crenshaw.[25]

Crenshaw is the largest Formative-period civic-ceremonial center in the Caddo heartland, with six large platform mounds, two rectangular and four circular (Figure 8.3). Similar to the situation at the Davis site, we don't know for sure if the circular mounds at Crenshaw, such as Mound E, were the substructures for pole-and-thatch temples, shrines, and homes. This is because of the way these poor tumuli were butchered in earlier twentieth-century excavations

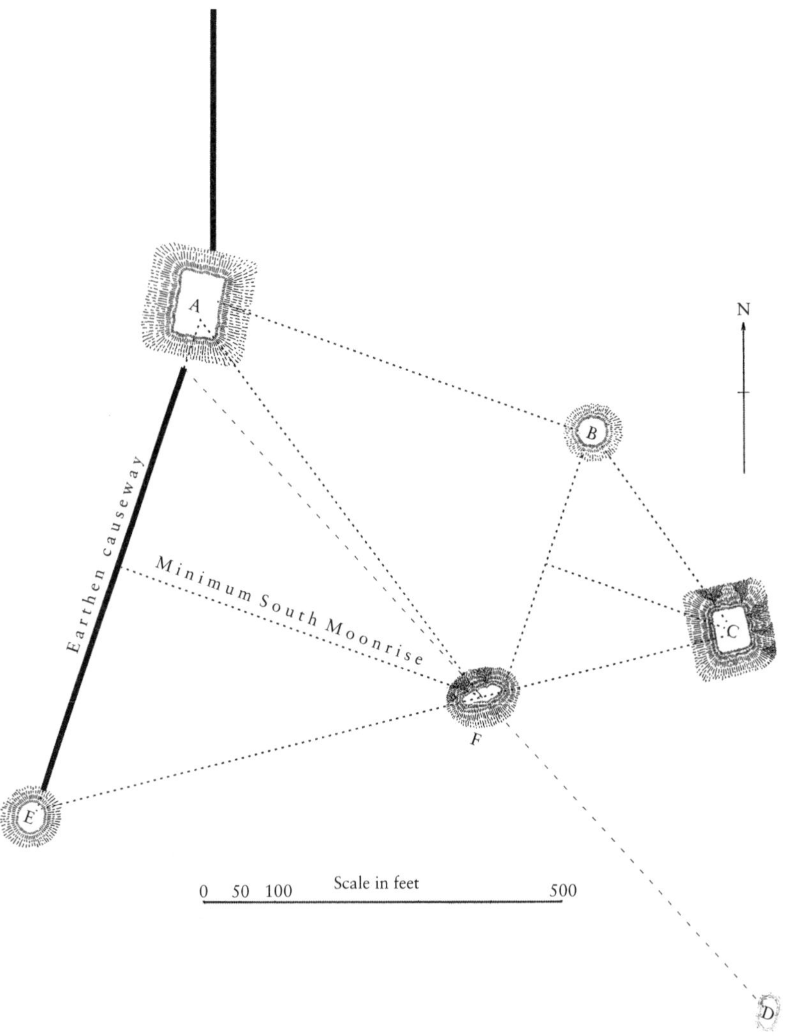

Figure 8.3. Crenshaw site plan map, showing astronomical features and lines of sight. Adapted from Clarence B. Moore, "Some Aboriginal Sites on Red River," *Journal of the Academy of Natural Sciences of Philadelphia* 14 (1912): 481–644, fig. 122.

by Euro-American treasure hunters seeking to possess the objects that the Caddo placed with their dead. These diggers simply assumed that the mounds were primarily intended for burials, as were earlier Woodland mounds, because the diggers sought pots and things buried with the dead. These same diggers, and a couple of generations of archaeologists, also wrongly assumed that the various Caddo mounds were built in rather haphazard locations.

Looking down at Crenshaw today from a few hundred feet in the air, the opposite is verifiable: one can see the design and order established by the builders around the year 900.[26] There are two 600-foot-plus lines in the form of earthen causeways. A linear off-cardinal earthen causeway connects the circular Mound E with the rectangular Mound A. Another causeway extends north from Mound A to the edge of the old channel of the Mississippi River, effectively splitting the solar year in half were one to watch the rising and setting positions of the Sun throughout the year. At the north end of this north-south causeway, at the water's edge, Crenshaw's dead were buried. Perhaps offerings to water spirits were thrown into the river.

The rectangular Mound E to A causeway is oriented at 20 degrees of azimuth relative to true north. In that direction, the lower causeway would have traced the path of the Milky Way at a specific time of the year, when it could be seen up in the night sky on important occasions. At the latitude of Crenshaw, and given the low horizon angle that obtained at this location, the off-cardinal causeway also precisely marked the orthogonal of a minimum south moonrise, as fixed by the placement of the large Mound F. This was the position where the full moon would rise halfway through its 18.6-year cycle, or 9.3 years after the maximum moonrise and moonset, as previously noted for Chaco Canyon. Interestingly, the triangle formed by Mounds A, E, and F via the causeway is roughly 600 feet on a side, double that of another triangle between Mounds B, C, and F. Neither triangle is perfectly equilateral, and the historical disturbances to the mounds impede our ability to measure precisely, but the site's combined solar, lunar, and stellar orientations and linked circular-rectangular mound patterns attest to its status as a cosmic center.

A similar site layout is evident at the George C. Davis site, where the circular platform, Mound C, sits to the southwest of the rectangular platform, Mound B (similar to Mounds A and E at Crenshaw). At Davis, Mound C is also due north of the rectangular platform (called Mound A), which was a substructure platform that elevated important buildings. Thus, similar to Crenshaw, cardinal directions and a minimum south moonrise are implicated in the design, perhaps evocative of the path followed by the Moon through the Milky Way on its nightly journey through the sky.

Such lunar-based geometry (comparable to that of Chaco Canyon) and the references to the Milky Way in the founding centers of Caddo culture, Davis and Crenshaw, are consistent with the cosmic orientations of the Caddo generally. For the Caddo, as with so many Indigenous peoples in North America, the Milky Way was the Path of Souls, the spirit trail along which the souls of the dead would travel once they departed the body.[27] The Moon was a part of this Milky Way trail, because it moved across the sky and cut through the Milky Way from east to west during the nights leading up to and after a full moon.

Not incidentally, the Caddo traditionally revered the Moon as a god, the powers of which might be summoned by the town's high priest. Indeed, the high priest of each major town was called Tsah Neeshi (Lord Moon). The elder priest of the entire Caddo Confederacy was Gran Tsah Neeshi (Lord Full Moon).[28] Given its placement in the lunar-aligned double-triangle configuration of Crenshaw, Mound F might even have been the Caddo's earthly manifestation of the otherwise intangible, perhaps topped by a Moon temple used by an original Tsah Neeshi.

Unfortunately for us, especially modern-day Caddo descendants, the Red River up to the Great Bend was navigable by steamer in the nineteenth century, and a well-known Ivy League gentleman-graverobber by the name of Clarence B. Moore turned his family inheritance and his steamboat up that river in 1911.[29] Moore arrived at the Crenshaw site on March 19, 1912, with a team of twenty men—a captain, pilots, an engineer, a steamer crew, and eight or more diggers—and proceeded to do there what he had done for twenty years at other major Mississippian town sites across the American South. Over the course of just two days, these diggers dug into all six of the major mounds, especially Mounds B, C, and D. The pots they took from the individual and mass burials they uncovered there encouraged everyone—looters, well-intentioned enthusiasts, and later scientific archaeologists—to excavate even more of the mounds from the 1930s through 1960s. As a result, today, only two mounds, those connected by the causeway, remain in anything approaching their original condition.

Of the other four principal mounds, Mound C was most important. Its lower levels were found by Moore and later archaeologists to predate the Caddo period. Those lower levels date as early as 700 CE, during the preceding Woodland era's Fourche Maline period. Pre-Caddo Fourche Maline culture is known for its small impermanent residential sites and dome-shaped, accretional burial mounds. Before the year 900, Crenshaw was a small but special place where Fourche Maline people gathered to conduct ceremonies for the dead. Between the years 700 and 900, Mound C grew large as community members died and were added to the mound, with more and more earth heaped over the location with every interment. This changed markedly, and possibly abruptly, in 900 CE. At the time, Mound C was converted into a platform mound (conceivably to elevate a circular temple), and the double-triangle configuration of the site was established. After that founding moment, the mass burial of bodies (as many as sixty men, women, and children at a time) commenced, each major interment followed by an enlargement of the mound into which the burials were made.[30] The scale and periodicity of these mass graves remain mysterious. Were these sacrifices made on the occasion of the death of a prominent community leader? Were they offerings timed to the 18.6-year cycle of the Moon? So far, we aren't sure. Intentional human sacrifice seems likely, but it often leaves behind few traces on the skeletal remains themselves.

In any event, after 900 CE tomb burial for Caddo community elites was common across the Neches and Red River regions up into the northern outliers of Caddo Country in the Arkansas River basin. At least one tomb at the George C. Davis site, and another far north at the famous Caddo site of Spiro, show evidence of having been supported by massive upright timbers, as if the vaults were built of wood, filled with bodies, and then covered over with earth. These events likely were special and intended to honor the elite dead. The sacrifice of family members or retainers may have been part of the ceremony, followed by the placement of bundles of arrows, groupings of pots, and other possessions or community objects into the grave. The descendants of a place such as Crenshaw would even remember that there was one Caddo tomb—or cave—from which their entire bloodline, if not their Caddo heritage generally, might be traced. It was from there that they all emerged at the beginning of this world.

No doubt, other contemporary peoples in other places across the Mid-South and lower Mississippi valley—Caddo and non-Caddo—had other ideas about where they and their kind originated. Some people might even have entertained multiple origin stories, mixing Caddo and non-Caddo accounts via multiethnic or polyglot social contexts, where their community heritage was distinguishable from their language or ethnicity. However, in terms of creation stories, the Caddo are the most similar to Puebloan, Hohokam, and Mesoamerican peoples in believing themselves to have emerged from the earth below. By contrast, most all other people in eastern North America considered their mythical place of emergence to be in the sky. These non-Caddo easterners would have believed the first human beings to have descended from heaven in primordial times. That said, there is every reason to suspect that later maize farmers blended foreign mythic Southwestern or Mesoamerican accounts of creator goddesses, corn mothers, and hero twins in an underworld with their own ancient stories once they adopted maize.

***

If one walks for about a week, or 122 miles, northeast from Crenshaw into central Arkansas, sticking to the flat Coastal Plain along the eastern edge of the rugged Ouachita Mountains, one comes to the edge of the Caddo homeland. Here, outside of modern-day Little Rock, Arkansas, sits a large formative-era Late Woodland mound complex amid the cypress-studded swamps and backwater lakes of the Arkansas River. It is the misnamed Toltec site, thought by early Euro-Americans to have been built by the ancestors of the Aztecs.

Arkansas's Toltec site has eighteen of the largest rectangular flat-topped pyramids ever constructed by midcontinental Americans of the era, between the years 700 and 1050 CE. All of the mounds, it appears, were ceremonial stages that elevated theatrical rituals, not substructural mounds elevating temples and elite homes. In this way, Toltec is similar to Formative-period Crenshaw and George C. Davis. However, in contrast to these Caddo sites to the south, there were no circular platforms among Toltec's mounds. Neither were there elaborate mass burials of Caddo elites, leading most archaeologists to suspect that the residents of Toltec were not ethnic Caddos. Then again, Toltec's mounds were built in conjunction with movements of the Moon, much like those at Crenshaw. In fact, all of Toltec's rectangular pyramids face a once-in-a-generation maximum south moonrise even as they also back up against a wide bayou.[31] This lunar-based, water-connected monumental design must have been put into place when Toltec was founded, around 700 CE. If so, then Toltec's lunar design would predate Chaco Canyon and Crenshaw. We just don't know for sure.

What we do know for certain is that the Toltec complex was abandoned sometime around 1050 CE. In fact, the entire central Arkansas River region around Little Rock was depopulated during this same mid-eleventh-century moment. This leaves uncertain the question of where they migrated. Did they all leave at the same time and travel in one direction? Or was there a rift that splintered the people of Toltec, some going north and some going west, just as the Formative Caddo world was coming into its own as a cultural region?

Some answers can be found by continuing our journey to the northeast for another 230 miles, straddling cypress swamps to the east and the mountainous Ozark escarpment to the west. Do this, and you pass through what is now the Bootheel region of Missouri before coming to the Mississippi River at a place called Thebes Gap. In the middle of the Bootheel, you would have encountered a natural causeway bending up from the southeast to meet you, making easy your walk to Thebes Gap. This was a freak of ice age geology—a 250- to 550-foot-high, 1- to 12-mile-wide band of windblown silt (loess) today known as Crowley's Ridge. During the Miocene and into the Pleistocene, the ridge separated the truly ancient courses of the Mississippi River to the west from the Ohio River to the east. Millions of years ago, these great watery serpents joined each other around present-day Memphis, Tennessee, before flowing to the Gulf of Mexico.

Today, the ridge is covered with the remains of nine-thousand-year-old, early Holocene-epoch Native forager base camps and cemeteries. More than likely, Crowley's Ridge was both a pathway and a boundary marker for these people and the herds of extinct bison that they hunted. It remained something similar down through history, all the way to the arrival of Hernando de Soto, who noted that the ridge was wooded but bordered a grassy plain, with scattered bison in the lowlands to the west. If one follows Crowley's Ridge to the north, one ends up at Thebes Gap.

A well-known stopping point for both Native and early Euro-American explorers, Thebes Gap was a narrow constriction of the river marked by great boulders. These boulders once blocked river traffic up and down the Mississippi. Mark Twain described them in his book *Life on the Mississippi*: they were "a chain of sunken rocks admirably arranged to capture and kill steamboats on bad nights."[32] At low water, one might even cross the river on foot at this location, hopping from boulder to boulder from the Missouri side into Illinois country. Certainly, before the Army Corps of Engineers began dynamiting them in the 1840s, anybody boating on the river had to stop, get out of their watercraft, offload their supplies, and portage everything around the line of rocks before continuing upriver. Many camped here and rested up overnight. Meriwether Lewis and William Clark did this in 1804.

Hammered into one of the boulders at this location, one can still see the outlines of a nine- or ten-century-old Mississippian-period rock art map.[33] The map appears to diagram the Thebes Gap crossing, the course of the Mississippi River, and the locations of Indigenous towns and ethnic groups north and south of here in the 1200s (Figure 8.4).

Were you to canoe upstream from Thebes Gap centuries before that time—in the year 700 CE, for instance—you would have traveled from the cypress swamplands south of the crossing into the more temperate deciduous landscape of the central Mississippi valley. In the flat bottomland beyond the river was a wild tangle of forests and backwater lakes teeming with all manner of amphibians, reptiles, birds, and mammals. Great flocks of migratory waterfowl happily paddled the open ponds behind beaver dams in the spring and autumn. Farther upstream, the floodplain narrows, hemmed in by limestone bluffs up to 200 feet tall. When you reach the vicinity of modern-day St. Louis, Missouri, the bluffs diminish in height and the valley floor widens on the Illinois side, thanks to geological serendipity—a weakness in the bedrock that permitted the ancient Mississippi to meander across a much wider area.

In this section of the valley, great things were to happen after 900. However, in the centuries before that time—before the arrival of corn—you would have been singularly unimpressed with the scattered horticulturalist-hunters who eked out a living along this stretch of the Mississippi River. The Woodland people here lived quiet, peaceful lives in small winter villages of a dozen or so pithouses. In the summertime, they'd break into small family units to harvest seeds, tend seasonal gardens, hunt, fish, and, come autumn, collect nuts.[34]

After 900 CE, when these farm families adopted maize, they were pulled inexorably into relationships with a few, increasingly large year-round villages. What's more, because of maize, they also began to

Figure 8.4. Thebes Gap rock art map. Left, the slab in position on the riverbank; right, a portion of the river motif. T. Pauketat, 2005.

quarry modest amounts of limestone and to clear and burn the forests, all to obtain the raw materials (lime and ash) to process (nixtamalize) corn. Within a generation or two, their villages grew large and the social and physical landscapes of their collective experience underwent significant change. Another century more, and communities of hundreds of people were living in several burgeoning settlements opposite modern-day St. Louis. Two or three contiguous sprawling villages occupied the banks of Cahokia Creek in what would become the city of Cahokia.

Most ordinary farmers in these pre-urban decades would have suspected that the rain and corn spirits favored their bustling village communities in this northern land. Distant people—southerners from the Bootheel of Missouri, from the Toltec site, from Crenshaw—would have eventually caught wind of this vibrant new land of bounty and spiritual balance thanks in large part to the warmer and wetter midcontinental expression of the medieval climate. The unique stretch of wide floodplain, they would have surmised, was special. Descendants of later French settlers would colonize this same stretch of bottomland in the 1690s because it was devoid of human inhabitants (after 1776, they called it the American Bottom).[35] This particular expanse of the Mississippi floodplain and the Indigenous city of Cahokia in its middle had been abandoned by its builders some four centuries earlier.

The climate was turning cooler and drier at the onset of a little ice age in the 1300s. Cahokia would not be sustained. But that it arose in the first place was a direct result of historical ties to the Caddo along roads that permitted travel between the Pueblo lands to the west and Mesoamerica to the south. The maize plant itself had moved into eastern North America from these distant lands via the Caddo. Caddo ceremonialism and origin stories reflect multiple linkages with Mesoamerica. And Caddo flat-topped circular pyramids on lunar orientations belie both Mexican and Puebloan entanglements. This pan-continental history was underwritten by the climatic shifts of the Medieval Climate Anomaly. The Postclassic droughts and population reshufflings in Mesoamerica were complemented by cultural expansions in the Southwest and Mississippi valley. All would be overseen by a pantheon of spiritual forces at the center of which was a powerful, invigorated, thundering god—the Wind-That-Brings-Rain.

Places to Visit

Caddo Mounds State Historic Site (aka George C. Davis site), Texas

A modest complex of three platform mounds, the Caddo Mounds or Davis site remains a center of cultural activity for Hasinai Caddo descendants. Reach Alto, Texas, from Dallas, Houston, or Shreveport. Once in Alto, take the old Camino Real, now State Highway 21, southwest of Alto for 6 miles. Tour the grounds and visitors center. Works Progress Administration excavations into and adjacent to the large Mound A in 1939–1941 produced the remains of circular public and private buildings, including an elaborate, repeatedly rebuilt lodge, initially just 14 feet in diameter, with a formal covered entrance and three rectangular alcove extensions, about 25 feet wide. Dubbed the "maze" by perplexed archaeologists, the alcoves were likely altar rooms that held powerful medicine bundles. The circular Mound C was a flat-topped platform that had been enlarged several times, each enlargement associated with one or more mass burial. The Davis site was a driving force behind the southern Caddo history of the Neches River valley, also called the Alto region until the 1200s.

Toltec Mounds Archaeological State Park and Old State House Museum, Arkansas

A trip to Little Rock, Arkansas, is incomplete without a stop at the Old State House Museum, where superb exhibits of precontact history are on display. From Interstate 30 (toward downtown Little Rock), take the Markham/2nd Street exit and go toward 2nd Street until you reach Center Street, then turn right. Go, if only just for the singular Cahokian work of art known as the Seated Warrior or Big Boy pipe, found at Spiro, Oklahoma, but made at Cahokia around the year 1100 CE.

Afterward, drive to the Toltec Mounds Archaeological State Park. From Little Rock, take US Route 165 south 16 miles to the park. From the 700s to the 1000s, Toltec was the big kahuna of the American mid-South. Great things probably happened at Toltec, an impressive complex of eighteen platform mounds and surrounding earthen embankment, situated where the Arkansas River bottomlands emerged into the Mississippi alluvial plain from the Ouachita and Ozark Mountains. Quite possibly, it was a multiethnic town of proto-Siouan- and Caddo-speaking peoples supported by Plum Bayou–culture farmers living all around it. It is also quite likely that events to the north at Cahokia, if not to the west at Spiro, led to the depopulation of this site and the entire central Arkansas River valley region in the mid-1000s.

9

Paddling North

Only water existed at the dawn of time. From water came land; from land and water all forms of life were created, including [hu]mankind. Because all life comes from the same source, we are all interconnected, and I am as much a part of the clouds as they are of me.

—Vernon Masayesva, past Hopi tribal chairman, 2002, to Winona LaDuke[1]

No Spanish conquistador had ever come close to the American Bottom, although it was—in the form of the precontact urban phenomenon of Greater Cahokia—the birthplace for the Mississippian civilization later encountered by the men of the Pánfilo de Narváez and Hernando de Soto expeditions in 1528 and 1539–1543, respectively. De Soto's men met some likely descendants of this great city near present-day Memphis, Tennessee, but by then Cahokia was but a distant memory, having been depopulated with the close of the Medieval Climate Anomaly in the early 1300s. Possibly, the legendary city of Quivira—described by the Pawnee guide to Francisco Vásquez de Coronado as being out on the Great Plains near the Missouri River—might have been that memory.[2]

Then again, Quivira may have been a word used for any number of Mississippian towns, similar to Tollan or Place-of-Reeds among Mesoamericans. But even if that's true, Cahokia was still the archetype, the urban complex that defined what Mississippian civilization would be. That archetype had everything to do with water, situated as Cahokia was in the middle of a large marshy stretch of fertile Mississippi River floodplain known as the American Bottom.

This bottomland was so crisscrossed in places by old channels of the Mississippi River, with soils so black with humus and subject to periodic inundation, that one famous visitor—Charles Dickens in 1842—couldn't understand how anyone could live here. Today's archaeologists think a little differently. In fact, Susan Alt, of Indiana University, thinks she knows what was special about the American Bottom that led to the Indigenous city of Cahokia.[3] The cultural developments that took place there, beginning around 900 CE, weren't simply a function of climate change, she thinks, although the Medieval Climate Anomaly no doubt enabled maize farmers to realize the agricultural potential of this unique region. The social changes that followed 900 CE weren't merely a result of bumper maize crops, although the abundant yields of the newly introduced, high-fructose grain crop were surely a function of great agricultural surpluses. Finally, the big-historical shifts about to take place in the middle of the eleventh century weren't merely the consequences of the propitious size, shape, and latitude of the so-called American Bottom, splayed out in the middle of the vast Mississippi River watershed near the mouth of the Missouri and Illinois Rivers.

Returning from her visit to Actun Tunichil Muknal (the Cave of the Stone Sepulcher) in central Belize, Alt has begun to think differently about water and its role in the ancient world of Cahokia. Water, she thinks, is more than a resource to be located and controlled as part of a rationally constructed agricultural system. It is more than a liquid that we drink to sustain life. And it is more than an essential ingredient in the life cycle of the maize plant.

Of course, water is and has always been the great mediator of biological life. Obviously, it is essential to the maize plant, a high-yield and highly water-sensitive crop. And, of course, water can be and was controlled in an economic and political sense. But for many Indigenous people, ancient and modern, water assumes a spiritual quality, a life-force. Even today, among "Siouan-speaking descendants or neighbors of descendants, water is one of the four major powers—water, wind, earth, and fire. . . . The world began as water and the first creatures were water creatures."[4] One has to look little further than the pantribal, multination Mní Wičóni movement that accompanied the start of construction on the Dakota Access Pipeline in 2016–2017.[5] Water, especially to Indian people on the Plains, is life. Many of these same people have at least some Cahokian blood running through their veins today.

Moreover, there are many kinds and forms of water and water powers, as Susan Alt elaborates. For the "ancient Cahokians," she says, "thunder, lightning, and water from the sky would have been perceived very differently than groundwater, especially that which seeped out of a hillside." To almost all Cahokian descendants, and neighbors of descendants, "thunder, lightning, and rain belonged to the Thunderers, masculine sky-rain spirits who in some legends confronted underground beings in epic battles. Groundwater, on the other hand, would have more likely been associated with underground beings, spirits, and feminine forces" (Figure 9.1). The differences parallel those of Mesoamerica, where the Aztecs distinguished the masculine Wind-That-Brings-Rain god and the water god Tlaloc from the groundwater goddess Chalchiuhtilcue.

Geochemist and climate change researcher Larry Benson and his dendroclimatologist colleague Ed Cook, well known for their work evaluating centuries-long sequences of tree rings across the western and midwestern United States, estimate the amount of water in the past hydrological system of the Greater Cahokia region by comparing tree rings from across the United States. The pattern around Greater Cahokia is clear: ample water for rain-fed maize agriculture was present from the start of the medieval period to the early 1100s, when a series of severe but not necessarily devastating droughts would have impacted the region's farmers. Many of those making a living farming for Cahokia in the uplands to the east of the city appear to have abandoned their fields by 1150. Conditions grew worse and less predictable in the decades afterward, and human population dropped

Figure 9.1. Falling Spring waterfall emerges from bluffs into the American Bottom, 7 miles south of Cahokia's St. Louis Precinct. T. Pauketat, 2017.

precipitously such that Cahokians radically downsized their urban experiment by 1200. In that year, religious rituals dedicated to rain, or to the Thunderers, appear to have been terminated. Circular buildings atop circular mounds ceased being built and used. Water was everything at Cahokia.

Proof positive of the high religious significance of water has been discovered at an all-important shrine complex, sitting on an isolated hilltop at the edge of an open prairie that began 15 miles east of Cahokia. This is the so-called Looking Glass Prairie, an expanse of native tall grasses atop a rolling plain named in the eighteenth century after the wavy appearance of old mirrors. Charles Dickens visited this prairie near the end of his American tour in 1842. By then, the region's hydroclimatic conditions were returning to the same wet and warm levels known in the Medieval Climate Anomaly, largely thanks to the end of the Little Ice Age and the beginning of the Industrial Revolution. Dickens would get a taste of what the region had been like in Cahokia's heyday.

Holed up in the middle of the gritty commercial hub of St. Louis, Missouri, in April Dickens traveled down the Ohio and up through Thebes Gap to St. Louis to see an American prairie before he returned to London. His hosts, traveling with Dickens in three horse-drawn carriages and a two-wheeled gig, had planned to catch a ferry across the Mississippi, travel east to the modest burgs of Belleville and Lebanon, Illinois, and then return via an old Indian trace-turned-wagon-road, which would take them through the middle of the ancient city of Cahokia. At sunset on that first day of the trip, they would sup on the summit of a hill under the orangish blue sky of the Looking Glass Prairie.

As it turned out, the evening before the jaunt into the prairie was extraordinarily hot and humid. And that night it rained. Not a little; a lot. St. Louis, says Dickens,

> had been—not to say hot, for the term is weak and lukewarm in its power of conveying an idea of the temperature. The town had been on fire; in a blaze. But at night it had come on to rain in torrents, and all night long it had rained without cessation.[6]

The next morning, after crossing the Mississippi, the group's carriages slowed while navigating standing water and axle-deep mud. The party followed a dirt two-track lane that skirted lakes and marshes and kept to the higher bottomland ground, such as it was. Dickens recounted:

> The air resounded in all directions with the loud chirping of the frogs, who . . . had the whole scene to themselves. . . . [T]hough the soil is very rich in this place few people can exist in such a deadly atmosphere. On

> either side of the track, if it deserve the name, was the thick "bush"; and everywhere was stagnant, slimy, rotten, filthy water.[7]

Once in the forested uplands fringing the bottom, the caravan picked up speed, stopping briefly in the relatively new German American settlement of Belleville and then continuing to the northeast, following the crests of a series of loess-covered glacial hills toward Lebanon, where the forest would give way to a savannah studded with invasive cedars and then to open tall-grass prairie. Nearing their destination, immigrant English, Welsh, and German farmers had begun to break the thick prairie sod using new plows, made of steel and pulled by oxen. Exposed to the sunlight, earthworms wriggled in the overturned deep-black chernozem where once they had lived among the roots of big bluestem, butterflyweed, and Indian grass. Beyond Lebanon to the north and east, the expansive Looking Glass Prairie conquered the eye. The setting was austere, "a perfect solitude, without a living thing," said one Euro-American pioneer traversing the Looking Glass.[8] The Dickens party likely rode out into this sea of tall grass east of the town and stopped atop another prominent glacial hill. It was nearing the vernal equinox, and Dickens looked back, due west, at sunset.

> Looking towards the setting sun, there lay, stretched out before my view, a vast expanse of level ground; unbroken, save by one thin line of trees, which scarcely amounted to a scratch upon the great blank; until it met the glowing sky, wherein it seemed to dip: mingling with its rich colours, and mellowing in its distant blue. There it lay, a tranquil sea or lake without water, if such a simile be admissible, with the day going down upon it: a few birds wheeling here and there: and solitude and silence reigning paramount around.[9]

Given the panorama afforded the great Charles Dickens, he might have seen the green-grass-covered eminence on a hill just two or three miles to the north. Perhaps he inquired: What is that? If he had, then Dickens would have been told that the protrusion was Emerald Mound, the largest of a dozen mounds clustered together on the summit of yet another glacial ridge in this sea of prairie grass.

Figure 9.2. Artist's line drawing of a portion of the Emerald Acropolis in 1881, with the Great Mound visible behind a Victorian-era farmhouse, and a flat-topped circular platform visible in foreground. Public domain.

Emerald Mound and its eleven sister mounds were well known to westward-moving Euro-American pioneers. Pioneers, in fact, watered their horses and replenished their supplies at an effluence just north of the largest of the Emerald mounds before continuing on to the American Bottom. Unbeknownst to Dickens and his thirsty forebearers, the spring that slaked travelers' thirst was not entirely natural, but had been enlarged and managed for centuries by Cahokians, whose shrines had been built across this anthropogenically enhanced hilltop eight centuries earlier (Figure 9.2).

Those shrines are what Susan Alt, her colleagues, and students are here to investigate. They have found hundreds of religious buildings, including dozens of small rectangular prayer buildings denoted by their special yellow-plastered floors and hearths. And they have found dozens of circular steam baths, laid out atop the artificially enhanced ridge surface and, presumably, surmounting each of the complex's

Figure 9.3. Virtual reconstruction of a Cahokian module of ceremonial buildings at the Emerald Acropolis. Image by Alex David Jerez Roman for the Emerald Acropolis Project. Courtesy of Susan Alt and T. Pauketat, 2016.

eleven circular platform mounds (Figure 9.3). The Cahokians built these mounds and structures in rows or at angles that align with the off-cardinal angles of both the ridge and the Emerald site's twelfth great mound, an 18-foot-high rectangular platform with a secondary rectangular terrace off the northwest side. Here it has rested for centuries, faceted and covered in green grass in the spring, like an emerald gemstone. At their unique angles, the off-cardinal axis of the mounds, ridge, and other buildings points directly to a maximum north moonrise. Reminiscent of the Caddo sites in the Red River's Great Bend, or great houses in Chaco Canyon far to the west, the Emerald Mound complex oriented people's bodies and practices to the Moon.[10]

Why? Watch the Moon throughout the year or pick up a farmer's almanac and you will see that certain weather systems—namely, warm fronts that bring steady rains—are often preceded by an atmospheric condition most often associated with a full moon. Known as a 22-degree halo, this condition produces a circle of light around the Moon.[11] Farmers worldwide use the ring around the Moon to predict rain. For Plains neighbors and descendants of Cahokia—Caddo-, Caddoan-, and

Siouan-speakers alike—the Moon is a "rain bringer" and, by logical extension, a circle is a sign for rain and water. Still today, Omaha women are named after the Moon.[12] At the old city of Cahokia, girls and young women were sacrificed to pay homage to the spirits associated with this mysteriously attractive celestial orb.[13] For the Caddo back in Texas, Oklahoma, and Louisiana, raindrops were the "tears of the Moon."[14]

The American Bottom and surrounding uplands are awash in unusual watery places. Emerald is just one. To the north, south, and especially west of the ancient city of Cahokia (which sits in the bottomland) are karst uplands. Here, extending for miles behind limestone cliffs that rim the floodplain, is a rugged wooded landscape of natural sinkholes—openings in the earth that lead down into caverns and underground streams formed before the ice age, the result of surface precipitation percolating down through the sedimentary bedrock, gradually dissolving the softer layers of limestone as it went. In the larger caves are flowstones, stalagmites, and stalactites. Historically, the region's karst attracted later German immigrants, who stored beer in St. Louis's many caverns, giving rise to the Anheuser-Busch empire.[15] During and after the Civil War, bands of Missouri renegades and outlaws, including Jesse James, hid out in the Ozarks' caverns farther west and south of the city.

In the middle of all of this was the widest expanse of Mississippi River floodplain north of Thebes Gap, where an overland trace running up from central Arkansas along Crowley's Ridge may have debouched. Great oxbow lakes yet crosscut the wide American Bottom, attracting flocks of waterfowl migrating to their winter and summer destinations in the far south and north, respectively. The wide floodplain, with its fertile sandy terraces and ridges as well as its seasonally wet swales and marshy lowlands, also allowed maize agriculture to establish a strong foothold among the Late Woodland village farmers of the early tenth century CE. And with that, a process of social change and immigration began that would produce the nearest thing to a Mesoamerican city north of the Pánuco. Within seven or eight human generations, the city of Cahokia would dominate the Mississippi valley.

The city itself was not like a modern industrial or commercial hub. Instead, it was similar to a low-density Maya city, its temples elevated above the morning mists that shrouded the houses and fields all around its edges. In the inner sancta of the city, water features, causeways, and prominent elevated temples were hubs of religious activity that, in turn, defined the unusual urban economy and polity. In fact, the city itself was not highly nucleated but was made up of three semi-distinct urban precincts strung out along two ancient oxbows—old beds of the river abandoned two thousand or more years prior—and the active channel of the Mississippi River. To the northeast, in the middle of the floodplain, was the largest precinct, today mostly subsumed within Cahokia Mounds State Historic Site. Originally, the Cahokia precinct covered 6 square miles, centered on the largest pyramid, Monks Mound, and the largest public plaza north of Teotihuacan (Figure 9.4). At least 120 pyramids, hundreds of prominent freestanding poles, equal numbers of thatched-roof temples, and thousands of smaller houses arranged in a dozen or more neighborhoods constituted this precinct.

The Cahokia precinct trails off to the southwest for a couple of miles along the aptly named Indian Lake until we reach the second precinct, a 2-square-mile aggregation of fifty earthen pyramids, plazas, poles, temples, and hundreds more houses at East St. Louis. Less than a mile across the river from it was the third precinct, built atop the low bluffs in what

Figure 9.4. Panoramic view of Cahokia's principal pyramid, Monks Mound. Wikimedia: public domain, Tim Vickers, 2009.

is now downtown St. Louis. Here were twenty-six more mounds and at least one major plaza. Here also were two or more access points into the underworld. One was a sinkhole just off the site's main plaza. The other was a cavern entrance below the largest mound, a great ridgetop-shaped burial mound. Before the Civil War, young boys playing hooky from school could be found hiding out in the cavern.

As far as we know, the entire three-part urban complex of Cahokia was designed and built around the year 1050 CE, with each part likely selected for its special features, such as the caverns below St. Louis. Extensive archaeological excavations at the East St. Louis and Cahokia precincts have shown that tremendous alterations to the landscape took place at this same mid-eleventh-century moment, when urban changes were being imposed through large-scale public works projects and associated social engineering. At that time, earthen fills were dug up from nearby sources to elevate low-lying areas, atop which the people implanted a series of great upright poles—mostly the trunks of huge cypress trees 1 to 3 feet in diameter and perhaps 50 to 100 feet tall—and built pyramids and housing, the latter via an expedient type of house foundation style (wall trenches) that likely involved prefabricated walls built and installed by work crews. These new wall trench foundations are strikingly similar to the wall channels discovered at Las Flores, in Tampico, Mexico.

At that same time, Cahokians initiated pilgrimages to the far-off lands of the upper Illinois and Mississippi River valleys to establish religious shrines. Some ambitious pilgrims went north to special natural locations 900 miles away near present-day Stoddard and Trempealeau, Wisconsin.[16] At Trempealeau, a series of Cahokian shrines was built to overlook the Mississippi River and the opposing bluffs of Minnesota. To construct the most elaborate, at or just before the year 1050, Cahokian builders lowered one side of a bluff-top ridge spur and raised the other, in the process creating a bilaterally symmetrical rectangular mound-and-causeway complex aligned to a minimum north moonrise. From the remains of rebuilt Cahokia-style prefabricated houses on the site, archaeologists can deduce that at least three such long-distance pilgrimages were made, possibly in conjunction with the long lunar cycle. Guesstimates of the numbers of travelers involved in any one trip between Trempealeau and Cahokia range from a couple of dozen up to one hundred.

From the near absence of local pottery and tool debris on site, archaeologists can also tell that the Cahokians were not there primarily to engage the local human population. Rather, they were likely in the far north to commune with the primeval spirits of ancestors, rocks, water, and the Moon. Equally likely, these were high-ranking, would-be leaders and priests, along with some contingent of farmers and workers. The best guess, based on the distribution of Cahokian shrines and wayfaring stations, is that they traveled up the Illinois River—a calm, wide dugout ride north to present-day Peoria, Illinois—and from there cut across country to the Rock River.[17] Upon reaching the Rock River, they floated in their canoes downstream until rejoining the Mississippi and then paddled north into the rugged lands of what is today known as the Driftless Area.

Drift, for a geologist, is the unconsolidated gravels deposited by ice age glaciers tens of thousands of years ago. Wisconsin's Driftless Area, therefore, was a region spared by ice age glaciers that scraped across the ancient continent, all thanks to a geological fluke a million years ago.[18] For Cahokians to make such a journey into its midst, they would have needed to leave in the spring, after the river ice melted. Later that year, if they didn't wish to experience the harsh cold of the north, the Cahokians would have returned before the river refroze in December. In returning south, the elite travelers may have followed the migratory flocks of ducks, geese, and cranes, moving with the changing colors of the deciduous trees from north to south. If they had planned well, they would arrive in time for Cahokia's great harvest festivals in October or November. At that time, the region's farmers, pilgrims, and other visitors, primarily from the south, would have poured in for the Thanksgiving-style festivals.

Cahokia was alive with activity and, no doubt as a result, immigrants by the thousands flooded into the city during the decades after 1050.

The majority were probably rural folks from the hills and valleys all around who moved into new digs within the city and accounted for a five- to ten-fold increase in the city's population. Cahokia's human population swelled to around fifteen to twenty thousand during the second half of the eleventh century.[19] A similar population increase happened beyond the urban core as well, with new farmsteads and hamlets popping up across the floodplain and into the uplands in the late 1000s on both the Missouri and Illinois sides of the Mississippi River. A decent guesstimate of the human population of the more-than-1,000-square-mile Greater Cahokia region by around the year 1100 CE trends upward to fifty thousand.[20]

This is not to say that we should restrict our considerations of the urban phenomenon of Greater Cahokia to living human beings, because Cahokians clearly did not. Although the frogs were an annoyance to Dickens, for instance, Cahokians celebrated water creatures—especially frogs—through their artwork and monuments. Some water creatures were probably viewed as persons who possessed souls. Few Native North Americans rigidly demarcated the human realm from the animal realm. At Cahokia, stone carvings of bullfrogs are common, usually in the form of oversized tobacco smoking-pipe bowls. Some are shown holding rattles, perhaps used in rainmaking rituals.

Also at Cahokia, ducks, frogs, beaver, fish, serpents, and other mythical water creatures are modeled on pottery bowls. Spiders, whose webs gather the morning dew, are depicted on gorgets made from marine shell imported from the Gulf of Mexico. These were elaborate centerpieces of necklaces worn by special people on special occasions. The beads of such necklaces, also made from imported marine shell, were produced by the thousands at Cahokia. They were the primary medium by which Cahokians identified themselves vis-à-vis the cosmos.[21] A few prized Cahokian possessions found along the Atlantic or Gulf Coasts of Florida and Alabama confirm that the Cahokian web was widespread, and it facilitated the movement of shell northward.[22] One such possession is a Cahokian redstone smoking pipe bowl, found on Dauphine Island off Mobile Bay in the Gulf of

Mexico. Cahokians had carved it to look like a crayfish. The survivors of the ill-fated Narváez expedition had floated past the island with little thought of or care for the history resting just to the north.

Ducks, frogs, beaver, fish, serpents, and crayfish: these were water creatures woven into the tapestry of Greater Cahokia, and rooted in the riverine and lacustrine lowlands of the American Bottom. The sights and sounds of the watery marsh and black swamp are thick in the American Bottom, as Dickens observed, adding to a sense that Cahokia was a city both of water and of the powers and creatures thereof as much as it was a place for people. Dickens could not imagine that such an environment might have been capable of supporting an Indigenous city. But Dickens didn't think like Cahokians.

The environmental conditions that some might find oppressive had positive emotional impacts on the Indian peoples of the Midwest, given their unique histories, given their water-sensitive corn crops, and given the unpredictably uber-positive agricultural conditions under which they found themselves in the 900s–1100s CE. With the ontological sensibilities that they surely possessed—predispositions to see the combination of black humic soil, standing water, high humidity, and water creatures in a positive light—we may presume that Native midwesterners experienced the dark, misty, wet places of the American Bottom in spiritual terms. In point of fact, descendants and other heirs of the ancient city of Cahokia view water and darkness as portals that enable one's spirit to move between the worlds of the living and the dead—doorways that might allow them to commune with ancestors and gods for the benefit of the living. For Cahokians, the evidence was all around, and it takes no great cultural insights to appreciate that rainwater is absorbed into the same ground from which plant life springs and in which loved ones are laid to rest, and that the water that seeps out of the earth, whether from caverns or springs, hence comes from the earth and the realm of the dead.

Earth itself takes on special meanings in such a world, as it did for Mississippians and Plains villagers alike well before the arrival of Columbus, Cabeza de Vaca, Coronado, and de Soto. At Cahokia, one of the least appreciated features of the central city are its elevated earthen walkways. They are the Cahokia precinct's backbone, connecting the northern neighborhoods with the periodically inundated black humic lowlands of the precinct's southern end, a zone of croaking, chirping frogs, especially when the Moon is full.

The largest Cahokian causeway traversed the central complex for two-thirds of a mile, from the great pyramids and plaza of the living in the north to a southern ridgetop burial mound in the south.[23] The burial mound, in turn, was surrounded by a dozen or so barely visible circular mounds that outline a large rectangle, and this rectangle was probably laid out at the city's foundation.[24] The diagonals of that rectangle point to a maximum north moonrise and the winter solstice sunrise, respectively.[25] A line that bisects the rectangle through its short axis establishes the 5-degree offset baseline from which the entire precinct was laid out.

The second least appreciated earthen features at Cahokia proper are the borrow pit lagoons (Figure 9.5). From select locations rimming

Figure 9.5. Short causeway at Cahokia leading from circular mound (out of view to the right) to rectangular platform (center) surrounded by the water of a borrow-pit lagoon. T. Pauketat, 2019.

the southern end of the main precinct, Cahokians dug or "borrowed" earthen fills with which to level the Cahokian landscape and to build the mounds, leaving behind sizable depressions that can cover many acres. These filled with water almost immediately, and hence would have been both a ready source of drinking and cooking water for people and a habitat for Cahokia's aquatic, non-human inhabitants. In one such lagoon bottom, investigated in the early 1970s, archaeologist Robert Hall found the skeleton of a prepubescent juvenile. The child's body had settled into the soft sediments of this former water-filled depression. She or he—archaeologists often cannot know for sure at this age—was likely an offering placed in the water, just off to the side of two circular platform mounds.

The sacrifice of young people, mostly female, was a relatively common practice at and around Greater Cahokia after 1050 until sometime around 1200 CE. In one Cahokian carving, a primordial earth goddess seems to be offering up a young child for sacrifice (Figure 9.6).[26] Sacrificial events saw the killing of from one to fifty-three individuals at a time, with the suggestion from one of Cahokia's ridgetop mounds, Mound 72, that this happened every few years beginning in the late eleventh century and lasting into the twelfth. That such was the case must have been completely foreign and shocking to local families the first time that they saw or heard about it. These locals would have still possessed simpler Woodland-era sensibilities. Human sacrifices may have been difficult to understand, much less witness. And the Cahokian sacrifices were likely public, theatrical, and connected to rituals surrounding Cahokia's many upright cypress poles.

It is worth noting that in Mesoamerica, cypress trees were the "world trees" that supported the cosmos—as retold in creation myths involving good and bad creator or redeemer gods such as Quetzalcoatl and Tezcatlipoca. Cypress wood was also associated with rulership because it was rot-resistant and lasts for generations.[27] Perhaps the wooden poles at Cahokia had similar connotations. Archaeologist Robert Hall connected them generally, plus a historically known "arrow sacrifice" among Caddoan-speaking peoples in the Great Plains, to rebirth

Figure 9.6. Carved stone smoking pipe bowl showing a Cahokian feminine goddess and a human offering. Courtesy of Thomas Emerson, 2021.

ceremonialism and the Mesoamerican god Xipe Totec, a supernatural brother to the Wind-That-Brings-Rain god Ehecatl-Quetzalcoatl.[28] Whether or not that is true, they were most definitely common, and emplaced all around Cahokia, with dozens to hundreds standing at any one time (Figure 9.7). Their post pit foundations are found by archaeologists everywhere around the urban complex, constituting a defining feature of Greater Cahokia.

Two such post pits were discovered under the ridgetop-shaped Mound 72. In one burial trench under Mound 72, piles of crystals, a tube of copper, a bag of gaming stones, and bundles of arrows tipped with expertly made stone and carved-antler arrowheads were heaped atop a row of bodies. The effect, if not intent, was remarkably similar

Figure 9.7. Lower portions of a large cypress pole discovered by archaeologists in 1960. Courtesy of the Illinois Department of Transportation.

to that of the early Caddo mortuary program known from the Red River south to the Neches. In fact, an entire quiverful of arrows in this one Cahokian burial were actual Caddo arrows, made not in the American Bottom but in Caddo country. One smashed pot was a Caddo pot, not a Cahokian vessel. Cahokia's sacrificial rites, that is, are Caddoan in character and, perhaps, Mesoamerican in spirit.

The contexts and alignments of other trenches full of offered bodies in Mound 72 and other ridgetop mortuaries at Cahokia are instructive. Some sacrificial pit burials were almost certainly laid out to intentionally reference the 5-degree Cahokia precinct grid. Others were aligned to a particular maximum moonrise or moonset. Still others, beneath Mound 72 or elsewhere in the Cahokian precincts, were buried in the open pits from which sizable upright poles had just recently been removed.

There are six known archaeological instances of post pit or post-hole burials involving sacrificed children or young women. In each case, one or more bodies were placed in the holes where the poles had stood just moments earlier. In at least one instance, the sacrifice was connected to a rain ceremony. In one poignant case, a child approximately nine years old was placed into the open roof-support post pit of a dismantled temple. The post hole itself was then filled with water, perhaps during a thunderstorm, as inferred by the laminated sediments in this layer of the pit. In fact, the entire dismantled temple was washed over with silt from a rainstorm, perhaps as some sort of offering to a Wind-That-Brings-Rain god or a local version of a rebirth and fertility god similar to Xipe Totec. Then the child was covered with more earth by whoever was on hand.[29]

There are other such posthole or post pit burials; one is beneath Mound 72, where the bodies of nineteen young women were laid into an enlarged former posthole.[30] Another such instance in Cahokia's main plaza at the foot of Monks Mound was found to be the final resting place of an infant who had been laid into a post pit just after its great pole had been removed. The bodies of two young adult women were buried in a similar manner at East St. Louis, one in a fetal position and the other, with wrists and ankles bound, facedown at the bottom of an open hole that minutes earlier had held a 3-foot-wide upright pole.[31]

When originally standing, these large poles would have been highly visible markers, allowing priests to make visual alignments between the earth on which they stood and celestial events above their heads, such as the rising and setting of full moons. The poles themselves might have been viewed as living beings, much like those of the Sun Dance on the Plains or the Venerable Man pole of the Omaha today.[32] But the size of Cahokia's poles, and the frequency with which they seem to have been emplaced and then removed, over and over again, suggests something more. That "something more" likely involved a Mesoamerican-style pole-climbing ritual. After all, the Cahokian poles measured from 1 to 3 feet in diameter and may have projected skyward as much as do *voladore* poles in Mexico today—100 or more feet. At that height, some of the great posts on top of platform mounds were subject to being struck by lightning, much as archaeologists experienced when they experimented with a telephone pole atop the summit of Monks Mound. Twice that summer it was struck and shattered by lightning.[33]

In any event, there are iconographic hints that the Cahokian poles, if not their Caddo counterparts, were the centerpieces of Mesoamerican-style pole-flying ceremonies. These hints start with depictions in the Indigenous picture books of Mesoamerica, known as codices, that survived the Spanish conquest and subsequent Catholic purge of Native records in the 1500s and 1600s. In several of them, the pole is shown with a four-sided framework at the top from which the flyers would hang from ropes. The flyers are shown in raptor masks and costumery, and a rope is shown twisted around the pole from top to bottom.[34] To the right of the pole in the image, an arrow sacrifice was taking place—in honor, we presume, of the Wind-That-Brings-Rain's brother, Xipe Totec.

Turning to Cahokian and Caddo artwork, we see similar depictions of Thunder Gods or their disembodied, raptor-mask-wearing heads arranged around a striped pole. In the case of one fragmentary Cahokian sandstone tablet, the disembodied heads of men wearing raptor masks are arranged around pole-and-rope motifs on one side, and the heads of ivory-billed or pileated woodpeckers—birds that chisel into poles—are similarly depicted on the reverse side (Figure 9.8). The pole's diagonal stripes, more than likely, are a simplified wind motif, much like that seen on Cahokian pots. They might also be rope motifs, connecting the raptor men of the Mississippi valley with some version of a Mesoamerican-derived pole-flying ritual.[35] Either way, it seems unlikely that Cahokian poles were merely passive marker posts that simply stood like an obelisk in one place for multiple seasons or years. Rather, these were active ritual monuments around which Cahokians performed, either on the ground or as flyers hanging from ropes.[36] That's probably why they were so massive, so tall, and so frequently put in and pulled out. The Cahokian pole ceremony was transplanted from Mesoamerica, and later morphed into some early version of the Plains Sun Dance (Figure 9.9).

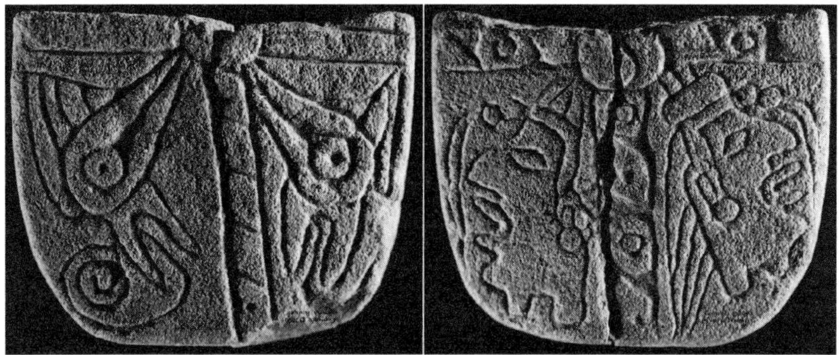

Figure 9.8. The Ramey tablet (4 inches tall). Left, ivory-billed woodpecker heads and pole/rope motif; right, Cahokian bird-men heads and stripe-and-dot pole motif. Courtesy of Pete Bostrom, 2021.

Figure 9.9. Cahokia's Woodhenge, reconstructed, with central post in foreground and Monks Mound in background. Wikimedia: QuartierLatin1968, 2011. Creative Commons Attribution-Share Alike 3.0 Unported License.

Post pits are known from the top of Monks Mound as well, as was a now-destroyed circular platform mound that overlooked the main Cahokia plaza from the southeastern corner of the great central pyramid's summit. In that position, the small circular mound on the great mound was the highest point in all the city, elevated about 110 feet about the people below. This mounded peak was created, we now know, to be in alignment with the causeway that stretched out to the south. Given its position, occupying both the city's baseline and its highest point, this modest circular mound and the building atop it was the *axis mundi* of the entire precinct, the point at which heaven and earth were connected and the place at which the powers of the cosmos were focused on earth (Figure 9.10).

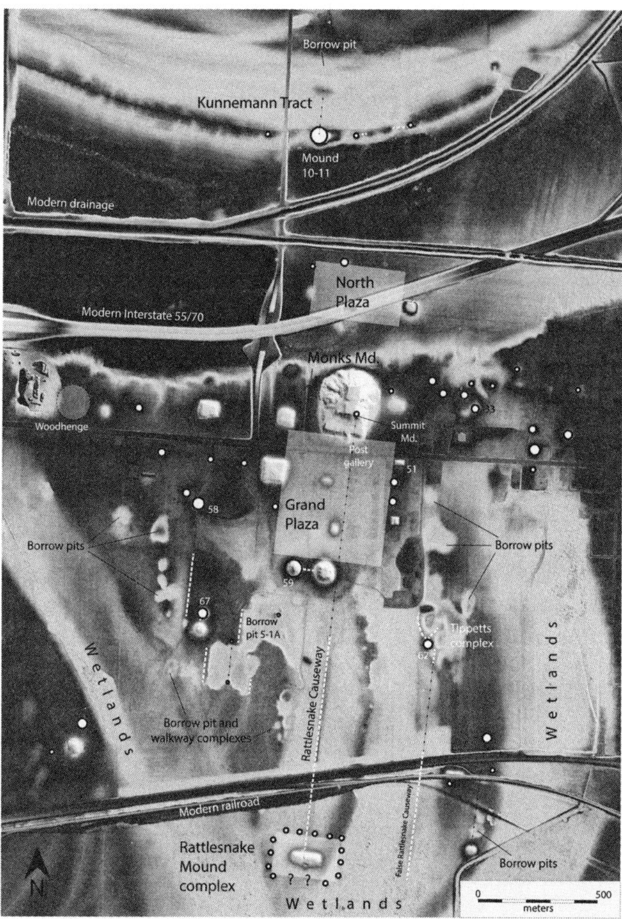

Figure 9.10. Bird's-eye view of the central Cahokia Precinct, showing locations of primary causeways, circular platform mounds, and borrow-pit lagoons. LiDAR base map courtesy of the Illinois State Archaeological Survey.

In 2021, a crew from the Illinois State Archaeological Survey discovered the wall trench foundation and internal hearth of a circular steam bath on this exact spot. It was one iteration of what the team now thinks was the foundation for a series of circular steam baths or water shrines built and rebuilt here, on Cahokia's *axis mundi*, as the rectangular pyramid was enlarged through time. Nearby and also atop the great mound were the post pit foundations for vertical poles, perhaps used in Cahokia's *voladore* ceremonies—for eagle or falcon dancers to climb, dance, and then rotate to the ground on ropes.

Even given our uncertainties about the Cahokia pole-flying ritual, the number, size, and prominence of *voladore*-style poles at Cahokia is unique compared to the few known instances of these features at other Mississippian towns or civic-ceremonial centers in eastern North America. Reasonable estimates of the number of oversized poles standing at any one time around the city of Cahokia easily reach into the hundreds. Also exceptional are the number of circular pyramids and circular water shrines. There are an estimated fifty circular mounds, most truncated cones or platforms, within the Cahokia precinct alone, along with an unknown number at East St. Louis, a row of four in St. Louis overlooking the Mississippi River, and eleven at the Emerald site overlooking natural seeps.[37] These circular pyramids are often paired with rectangular ones, the two resulting paired mounds linked by earthen causeways similar to those known at Crenshaw in Caddo country.

The Cahokian causeways, realized Robert Hall, are reminiscent of the Lakota's ceremonial pathways of earth sprinkled between the circular *inipi* sweat lodges and the sacred fire outside, most often to the east. Inside the Cahokia steam bath, or the Lakota sweat lodge, men sat in the dark. They listened to the priest, just outside, muttering prayers and building up a fire that would heat the stones which were to be carried into the circular building's interior. The men bowed their heads, looking up when the priest flipped open the heavy blanket door and entered. He carefully moved the hot stones from a wooden bowl into the recently redug hole in the middle of the earthen floor, then exited. Outside, there was more muffled chanting and prayers before the flap opened again and the priest entered with a pot of water. After speaking a few words, he splashed the water onto the rocks, then left once more. The rocks sizzled and steamed, the men now sitting alone, inhaling the vapor, feeling the sweat bead on their backs, chests, arms and legs. At the edge of consciousness, at least one man could have had a vision of a Thunder Being or Beings—the Wind-That-Brings-Rain god or gods of Mesoamerica, the powerful spirit who brought Black Elk's vision centuries later.

Outside the sweat lodges were upright posts that beckoned the Thunderers and related spirits of the above and below worlds. One must remain pure before these spirits. Any physical movements must be made carefully. Hence the sprinkled earth outside the Lakota lodges. Hence the monumental causeways at Cahokia. These unpolluted walkways, it seems, enabled spiritual movements and spiritually sanctioned human movements between the temples or shrines on the summits of the circular and rectangular pyramids. It is even a good bet that the ancestors of the Lakota, somewhere in the upper Midwest, would have met Cahokians in the eleventh and twelfth centuries—perhaps at a place such as Trempealeau. From the Cahokians, the ancestors would have obtained or adapted the *inipi*. The initial transfer would have happened via a medicine bundle, from a Cahokian bundle-keeper or priest to a foreign apprentice who was visiting a Cahokian shrine (if not the city itself) to learn the bundle's secrets. Many more bundle transfers would follow.

There is archaeological evidence at Cahokia that circular ceremonial steam baths did indeed occupy the summits of some if not most of the circular platform mounds. And such features—water temples—look a little like the Caddo mounds at the George C. Davis and Crenshaw sites. In Caddo country, these were in part an adaptation of earlier Woodland (Fourche Maline) burial mounds and in part the adoption of a circular flat-topped pyramid similar to the circular mounds of Huasteca. They appeared in both regions by 900

CE, roughly the same time at which great kivas were being built in Chaco Canyon.

At Cahokia, the earliest flat-topped circular platforms dated no earlier than the founding moments of the city, around the year 1050 (Figure 9.11). Circular steam baths and rotundas were introduced at the same time, the earliest ones found in the heart of the Cahokia precinct and atop the Emerald acropolis 15 miles to the east. These ranged from small personal-sized buildings, similar to Plains sweat lodges, to great public buildings. At the north end of one Cahokian neighborhood,

Figure 9.11. Cahokia's circular architecture: the 40-foot-tall "Roundtop" Mound 59 adjacent to large borrow-pit lagoon. T. Pauketat, 2017.

for instance, overlooking a wet marsh, small steam baths cluster on the bank near contemporary rectangular houses. A few hundred yards to the east, on that same bank, sits a great rotunda 75 feet in diameter, too big to have been capable of containing steam, and in some ways reminiscent of later Plains Indian Sun Dance structures.

All such buildings indicate that something unusual had happened at Cahokia that was not to be repeated elsewhere in the same way or at the same scale. These buildings were associated with new ceremonies imported into the new city around 1050. There are no known circular platforms and no circular lodges or rotundas anywhere in the American Bottom or the adjacent uplands up to that year. In fact, there are none from neighboring regions either, at least not until that mid-eleventh century—not until the Medieval Warm Period.

That climatic anomaly brought great historical change to the continent. But it, just like the Indigenous city of Cahokia, would end—the two developments causally intertwined and closely paralleling each other. The key to understanding this parallelism is the circular building, which appeared and disappeared with the expansion and contraction of Cahokia's political, economic, and cultural power. Where did it come from? The closest known circular pyramids and circular lodges in use before Cahokia's startling urban emergence were in the Caddo country of southwestern Arkansas. Others, even more similar to Cahokian circular temples, were already in place down along the Pánuco River, among the Huastecs.

Places to Visit

Gateway Arch National Park, Missouri

A visit to the ancient city of Cahokia begins in St. Louis at the visitors center of Gateway Arch National Park. Fly into St. Louis and take a car downtown via Interstate 70 to the arch. Cahokia's St. Louis precinct, with its twenty-six mounds and subterranean passages, sat just a few hundred feet to the north of where you stand in the visitors center. Here you will begin to learn answers to the question "What happened because of Cahokia?" Ride up to the top of the arch and look down at the mighty Mississippi River. Get a sense for the landscape all around, but then walk slowly through the visitors center. See how the collapse of the Mississippian city opened up a landscape and allowed the French to establish one of their three premier North American colonies, later lost to the British and Americans. Next see how the gateway city became a mercantile center during the Civil War, and then an industrial city, all the while ignoring the rich Native archaeological heritage all around.

Horseshoe Lake State Park, Illinois

To begin your tour of the archaeological site of Cahokia, start with some environmental context by driving across the Mississippi River on Interstate 55/70 just a few miles to Illinois Route 111. Turn north and drive a few more miles to the entrance of Horseshoe Lake State Park. Entering the park, you will immediately see a great oxbow lake in front of you. The other side of this lake is actually an island, with the oxbow and the park continuing to the industrial landscape on the horizon. Even today, Horseshoe Lake and its teeming animal and plant life give you a good idea of the richness and variety of the landscape a thousand years ago. Archaeological surveys of the park revealed that Late Woodland farmers in the locality moved to Cahokia when that city was under construction (ca. 1050 CE). This was followed by a more highly organized agricultural landscape during the Mississippian era (1050–1350 CE), studded by a few important Cahokian sites, including a small town and mound complex on the northwest corner of the lake along which a park road passes today.

Cahokia Mounds State Historic Site, Illinois

There are a number of ways to enter Cahokia, sitting as it does in the midst of a residential and commercial zone also known as State Park

Place. From Horseshoe Lake State Park, drive south on Highway 111 until you reach Collinsville Road (US Route 40) and turn left. Here used to sit the second-largest earthen mound at Cahokia, a great ridge-top burial mound. Driving east on 40, you follow the route taken by Dickens in reverse. In a couple of miles, a reconstruction of the site's Woodhenge marks the beginning of the central complex of earthen pyramids, and Monks Mound looms in the distance. Past it, turn right into the Interpretive Center. After touring it, exit the building on the west side and walk into the site's Grand Plaza. Ignore the mowed green grass, which would not have covered the grounds centuries ago. It takes ten to fifteen minutes to traverse the plaza to the front steps of Monks Mound, which you climb to reach the 100-foot-high summit. From the top, you can see Horseshoe Lake to the north, St. Louis to the west, and the bluff horizon to the east and south.

Stand on the southeast corner of the summit and notice that it appears as an isolated semicircle. This was the city's *axis mundi*, the former location of a circular mound topped with a circular steam bath. From here, look nearly due south into the trees that cover that part of the park; that was the site of a 60-foot-wide causeway that led through a wet marshland to another large ridgetop mound, known as Rattlesnake Mound, almost a mile away. In most directions, and with the aid of the park's augmented reality, you can imagine neighborhoods of small pole-and-thatch homes, surrounding the occasional larger temple or special public building. The largest such building on the site was at the north end of the summit of Monks Mound.

Before leaving the park, be sure to walk beyond the south end of the Plaza to Mound 72, with its interpretive signage. From there, peer into the woods to your east and look for the foot-high causeway. To the west is one of the largest borrow pits, and you can see more by following the trail around it and looping back to the museum.

10

Smoking Daggers

> They said at that time there wandered about the country a man whom they called "Bad Thing," who . . . would come in and take hold of anyone he chose. With a sharp knife made of flint, as broad as a hand and two palms in length, he would then make a cut in that person's flank, thrust his hand through the gash, and take out the person's entrails. . . . [A]sked . . . where he came from and where he had his home, he pointed to a rent in the earth and said his house was down below.
>
> —Álvar Núñez Cabeza de Vaca, survivor of the Narváez expedition, 1542[1]

Hundreds of miles north of Huasteca, south of Cahokia, east of the Pueblos, and west of the Mississippi, the Caddo and their Caddoan-speaking neighbors, the Pawnee and the Wichita, were in the middle of everything. Coronado had come near them, following a captive Pawnee guide—"the Turk"—into the Central Plains. Hernando de Soto and his expedition had fought some of them and had tried to head back to Mexico overland via the Great Bend region of the Red River. Possibly, a well-established footpath through the Gilmore Corridor, later to become El Camino Real de los Tejas, ran through the George C. Davis site, connecting it with Huasteca and Central Mexico as early as 900 CE. The first maize plants in the Eastern Woodlands might have passed through here or, as likely, come in from the American Southwest.

Given their position in the middle of it all, it may be less than surprising that Caddo people are almost certainly responsible, at least to some extent, for the beginnings of the city of Cahokia. Cahokia's descendants probably include members of the Dhegihan-speaking Kaw, Osage, Omaha, Ponca, and especially the Quapaw. Other descendants likely include Chiwerean-speaking Missouria, Otoe, and Ioway, Algonkian-speaking Peoria, Potawatomi, and Miami, and various delegations of Caddoan-speaking Pawnee and Caddo-speaking peoples from the Red and Arkansas Rivers.[2] It also remains possible that other southern Mississippian peoples, the descendants of whom were encountered by Hernando de Soto and other would-be Spanish conquistadors, have Cahokian blood coursing through their veins.

The lines of evidence supporting the contention that Caddo people, or at least elite contingents of Caddos, resided at Cahokia include big-historical patterns. The site of Toltec—possibly inhabited by proto-Caddo peoples—broke up in 1050, some likely taking their pyramid-building habits and lunar knowledge northward to the land of plenty that was the American Bottom. But more direct evidentiary reasons include the presence of actual Caddo artifacts and practices at early Cahokia. In point of fact, Cahokians built circular platforms and special circular steam baths, the former similar to Formative Caddo (and Huastec) mounds and the latter hinting of Formative Caddo houses (and Huastecan mound-top buildings).

In addition, Cahokians sacrificed people and placed their bodies in rows within shaft tombs, much like Caddos. Cahokians laid bundles of arrows tipped with actual Caddo arrowheads in at least one such Cahokian shaft tomb. Cahokians made elaborately incised and engraved decorated pottery drinking cups and bowls that look a lot like those known among the Red River Caddo. Cahokians prepared and drank a caffeinated Black Drink and used a variety of psychotropic potions, the ingredients for which were imported from Arkansas, Texas, and Louisiana. Even Cahokia's wind-water leitmotif, the so-called Ramey scroll, has Caddo pottery precedents, in turn traceable to

Epiclassic and Postclassic Mesoamerica. On top of this, the evidence of Cahokia-Caddo relationships is mutual: Cahokian objects are buried with the Caddo dead in Oklahoma, Arkansas, and Louisiana.

As it turns out, besides circular water temples, there are objects and bodily practices that appear de novo at Cahokia just after 1050 that speak to the question of direct Mesoamerican contacts. These things include a series of unprecedented small maskettes made in the city from either imported marine shell or copper. These maskettes are little shield-shape faces, with circular goggle-shaped eyes, small slit mouths, and excessively long and bent noses. The maskettes were made to be worn on the ears and are depicted in artwork made at Cahokia and at the Caddo site of Spiro, in Oklahoma. In fact, a foot-high Cahokian stone sculpture found at Spiro shows a masculine character, seated in a possible trance state and wearing just such a pair of earpieces, a bead necklace, a cape, and nothing else. Other Cahokia carvings and maskettes have been found distributed from Wisconsin and Minnesota in the north to coastal Florida in the south, indicative of the reach of Cahokia's influence.

The maskettes are famously referenced in twentieth-century legends of Native Ho-Chunk and Ioway people in modern-day Wisconsin and Iowa. Robert Hall believed that the maskettes were the embodiments of twin water spirits, well known to be connected to the Thunderers on the Plains.[3] Ultimately, Hall and others also suspected, as should we, that the idea of wearing "long-nosed-god" maskettes as ear ornaments was a Mesoamerican derivative.[4] They could be Cahokian-made renditions of a rain god—Tlaloc or Chahk—but are more likely derived from the good and bad creator deities who bring rain: the Thunderers, aka Quetzalcoatl and Tezcatlipoca. They first appear in the second half of the eleventh century at the same time as all of the other novel objects and practices of urban Cahokia, of which two more stand out.

The first is raptor-man imagery. Up until the mid-eleventh-century Cahokian expansion, the Woodland horticulturalists of the Mississippi valley were not in the habit of creating either human or humanoid images, whether in two or three dimensions. This changed rather abruptly around 1050 CE, when miniaturized faces of raptor-men, perhaps apparitions of humanoid spirits, were lightly sketched onto the exteriors of pots used in rituals.[5] Other three-dimensional carvings followed. Most depict anthropomorphized gods or heroic superhuman characters. The sketched disembodied heads or spiritual apparitions show the unmistakable hooked, beak-like noses and wing-like motifs of a raptor-man who flies in the air. On at least one late-dating sandstone tablet, raptor-man heads are arranged around a pole motif. The conjunction of ghostly faces, pole imagery, and bird-man symbolism may indicate the presence of pole flyer or *voladore* ceremonialism imported from Mesoamerica. The same character would seem to hint at a thunderbird-turned-human.

A second Mesoamericanoid object appeared at Cahokia at the same time as the Thunderer sketches and earpieces. Archaeologists have long puzzled over these chipped-stone daggers, 6 to 10 inches in length, narrow at the bottom, and wide at the top.[6] In size and shape, they are dead ringers for Toltec- and Aztec-style *tecpatl* from Central Mexico, such as those buried at Tlatelolco and Tenochtitlan as offerings at the base of Aztec temples to Ehecatl-Quetzalcoatl. Even the flint-knapping technology used to chip out the Cahokia artifacts is similar to Mesoamerica's dagger-chipping technology (Figure 10.1).

Flint (or obsidian in Mesoamerica) was often considered to have been created through lightning by the sky gods, including creator god cognates of Quetzalcoatl and Tezcatlipoca.[7] Indeed, Tezcatlipoca among the Aztecs was directly connected with obsidian, as was one of the Hero Twins or creator gods named Flint by the Native people of eastern North America and the Great Plains. In the art of the Toltecs, whether at Tula or Chichen Itza, the daggers are depicted on chacmools as worn in an arm strap, presumably associated with the killing and carving up of human sacrifices. The Toltec and Aztec gods Quetzalcoatl and Tezcatlipoca (and, later, Huitzilopochtli), the dual Wind-That-Brings-Rain gods, are invoked in myths of earlier episodes of creation in which the gods themselves are killed.

Figure 10.1. Chipped-stone daggers: Postclassic Mesoamerican *tecpatl* (left) and Cahokian knife (right), each 7 inches in length. Courtesy of Pete Bostrom, 2021.

In fact, we should suspect that the story of the "Bad Thing" heard by Cabeza de Vaca in south Texas or Tamaulipas in 1535 directly references the same Mesoamerican stories of a dagger-wielding Tezcatlipoca, a violent twin or counterpart to the heroic Quetzalcoatl. After all, Cabeza de Vaca was just 200–300 miles north of the Pánuco River at the time he heard the story of this monstrous underworld being who would cut out a living person's entrails with a sharp knife made of flint. Moreover, if he was right to locate the story in actual events "fifteen or sixteen years ago," then the Avavares people who told the four survivors the story might have been remembering the capture and sacrifice of some of their own by Huastecs or Aztecs to honor Tezcatlipoca just before the time of Cortés's final conquest of Tenochtitlan in 1521.

Interestingly, like the Edwards Plateau daggers known archaeologically in south Texas or the human-head earpieces made at Cahokia, the Cahokia daggers were not made in Mexico. Rather, they were mass-produced at workshop villages in the Missouri Ozarks or the rugged Shawnee Hills of southern Illinois and then toted to the great American Indian urban experiment in the American Bottom. The earliest known Cahokian chipped-stone dagger, locally called a Ramey knife, was made from chert (or flint) and left behind inside a house at Cahokia right around the year 1050. It was about 7 or 8 inches in length and was expertly chipped from a single block of southern Illinois stone. That knife seems to be a copy of the Mesoamerican *tecpatl*, and there were hundreds more examples crafted after 1050 in or near the Greater Cahokia region. Most were virtually identical in size and form to those found in Mesoamerica.[8]

Such daggers became even more common after 1200 CE and were found in considerable numbers from Cahokia southward. At the Caddo site of Spiro, wooden examples had been carved and then sheathed in copper.[9] Some later Mississippian versions of the daggers reached sword-like dimensions and were depicted as held in the hands of god-like dancers by Native artists who engraved the scenes on the exteriors of large marine conch shells.[10]

Back near Cahokia, archaeologists discovered a series of objects plowed up in a farmer's field that included two Ramey knives, a lead-ore paint-stone, and a long-stemmed ceremonial axe head or "spud" of a variety made in Tennessee but commonly found in Caddo country (Figure 10.2).[11] The farmer's plow had ripped through the burial of an individual who had notched incisors—a practice of dental mutilation common in Huasteca and elsewhere in Mesoamerica, and at Cahokia.[12] A couple of potsherds in the field suggest that the burial dates to the early 1100s. Unfortunately, not much remained of the burial itself, which was likely of a woman. At Cahokia, the practice of dental mutilation was most common in women. Only a handful of Mississippian individuals with filed teeth are known outside the Greater Cahokia region—none from Caddo country. At Cahokia, the

Figure 10.2. Long-stemmed ceremonial axe head or spud from near Cahokia. T. Pauketat, 1981.

earliest such dental notching dates to the mid- to late eleventh century, circa 1050 CE, and continues until the great civic-ceremonial complex was depopulated, around 1350 CE.[13]

More importantly, the timing of the practice—nearly simultaneous with the arrival of *tecpatl*-style daggers, long-nosed god maskettes, and circular water temples—suggests three things. First, at the time of Cahokia's urban expansion there were cultural complexes in place to the south, in both Caddo country and Mesoamerica, from which Cahokians drew inspiration. Second, given the coincident appearance of the foreign-object styles and practices, such inspiration was not a slow process of diffusion. Third, since the things in question were made or performed locally, their abrupt appearance indicates not long-distance trade but, rather, a cult-like belief in the power of the shapes or styles of particular things, possibly associated with priests or leaders.

The timing of and importance assigned to these things suggests an event-based acquisition of knowledge more likely to have been the result of one-off episodes of travel. Perhaps the travelers ended up living for a period in a foreign land, such as the Great Bend region of the Red River, the mouth of the Pánuco, or even Tamtoc or Tula, in order that they might learn the rituals associated with a medicine bundle that contained copies of the powerful objects and their secrets. Remember, bundles can be replicated, and a Cahokian returning with one might have then proceeded to replicate her or his bundle, in effect kicking off an entire religious movement rooted in a foreign practice transplanted into a new land.

With that in mind, let us return to the question of the origins of Cahokia's circular mounds—unprecedented in the American Bottom until the year 1050. At Cahokia, all instances of flat-topped circular mounds from which we have any evidence at all were topped by circular steam baths, water temples, or freestanding vertical poles. These are Mesoamerican traits. By contrast, the earliest of the Caddo circular mounds may not have been surmounted by circular pole-and-thatch architecture (although we are not certain). Only later do we know for sure that circular Caddo mounds were topped by circular buildings.[14] Thus, the circular pyramids that look most similar to and predate Cahokia's water temples, complete with circular building outlines and wall trench or wall channel foundations, are at Las Flores, the coastal Huastecan site in Tampico at the mouth of the Pánuco River.

Like Huastecan circular mounds and mound-top buildings, the Cahokian water temples and even many off-mound steam baths overlook bodies of water or springs. At Cahokia, for instance, the largest circular mound or water temple (Mound 11) towers over the marshland of an old river channel, with Monks Mound in the distance. Attached to it is a rectangular platform extension, and next to that are two other pairs of circular and rectangular mounds, each pair connected via a short earthen causeway. The second largest water temple (Mound 59) overlooks the great plaza to the north and a large lagoon to the south. It, too, is paired with a rectangular pyramid via a causeway. From its summit in the 1940s, a boy found a serpent ornament made out of hammered copper. There are other such pairs and suggestive archaeological discoveries.

The reasons for such close associations of water temples or steam baths and bodies of water no doubt begin with the need for water in steam-bath rituals. To make steam, one needs water and red-hot rocks. Afterward, supplicants might be required to jump into the nearest body of water as part of a ritualized cool-down. But the watery associations of Cahokian steam baths and water temples go well beyond the obvious needs to sweat and then chill. Like water temples or steam baths among the Maya, on the other side of the Gulf of Mexico, Cahokians also associated the shells of marine gastropods, conchs and whelks, with the sacred sweat lodges or water temples. On the floors or roofs of the circular buildings on or below Mound 33, due east of the great pyramid of Monks Mound, excavators in 1922 found hundreds of such shells, including one whole conch dipper or drinking cup.[15] There were also pieces of natural flowstone that Cahokians must have collected from a cave or spring. The associated circular buildings found at the base and lower stages of the mound date to the late 1100s—near the end of the pinnacle of Cahokia's urban phase.

Cahokia's Mound 33 monument and its marine shells and flowstone now seem to mark the end of a century-and-a-half-long history of water temple ceremonialism. Whereas steam baths are found across the civic-ceremonial landscape of urban Cahokia and its farmlands before the year 1200 CE, only three or four possible examples are known to postdate the turn of the thirteenth century. Archaeologists had struggled to understand the implications of this region-wide change, at least until recent evidence was discovered that hints strongly of major political events in the heart of Greater Cahokia at the end of the 1100s. Of the late twelfth-century events, a few might prove coincidental: the burning of several homes or shrines of prominent Cahokians, the nearly coeval burials of Cahokian families in ridgetop mounds, and the construction of a great palisade wall complete with bastions around the core of the Cahokia precinct. There might even be an instance in which elite women and children were sacrificed for political expediency.[16]

However, one event in particular speaks to the magnitude and implications of what was taking place. Sometime around the year 1170 or a little after, someone put the torch to an entire segment of the East St. Louis precinct. The fire appears to have been set inside a walled-off elite compound, and the scores of thatched-roof huts inside its walls burned, along with the dozens of pots, wooden bowls, stone tools, bags of shelled maize, and temple objects that sat inside them.[17] After the burning, someone cleaned up the site, sweeping charred debris into holes and burying at least one offering in the ashes of one of the former huts. From then on, the grounds sat empty. Rains washed over the location, and months passed. No one rebuilt the destroyed buildings, which had included both circular and rectangular temples on platform mounds. In the decades that followed, a few large rectangular mounds were built on the site, probably with standard rectangular temples on their summits. But the thousands of residents who had called East St. Louis home vacated the precinct.

Their departure as part of this large-scale, ceremonial termination by fire may also coincide with the closure of two or more ridgetop mound tombs (at Mitchell and East St. Louis) and the removal of a great cypress post at the Mitchell site. Even more status items and ornaments, most probably parts of sacred medicine bundles, were buried with the dead in the ridgetop mounds.[18] Some have suggested that this marked a regime change, but if a prestigious lineage had indeed come to an end, then it was also the case that these people had been associated with Cahokia's steam bath ceremonialism if not also its Thunderer or *voladore* poles. Both the poles and the circular steam baths are absent in Cahokia's precincts thereafter. That is, whoever died or left town around 1170 included the keepers of medicine bundles that had previously afforded Cahokians direct access to the rain or Wind-That-Brings-Rain gods. It's as if the legend of Topiltzin-Quetzalcoatl leaving Tollan in the 800s or 900s was being replayed 1,400 miles north and three or four hundred years later.

One might even assume that expatriate Cahokians would return to their families' ancestral homelands. In fact, in that vein, there are three more tantalizing archaeological and cultural links that help us bring the story of Cahokia to a close. The first is the simple observation that after 1200 CE the close Caddo-Cahokia connections appear to have been broken. At Spiro, Oklahoma, many Cahokian artifacts were buried by the Caddo in a mortuary feature in the 1300s. At the same time, Caddo artisans adopted less Cahokian-looking stylistic conventions in favor of Postclassic Mesoamerican ones.[19] Twin heroes in rattlesnake garb, wearing Huastec-style diadems and holding *tecpatl*-style daggers in one hand and lightning sticks in the other, are shown in marine shell etchings stepping out of a V-shaped rent in the back of a serpentine earth monster. Mesoamerican-like motifs depicting speech, not unlike the speech bubbles of modern cartoonists, emanate from the mouths of many of the Spiro images. Cahokia, that is, had been largely forgotten.

The second link to help us close the Cahokia story sits at the end of Crowley's Ridge, on the Mississippi River just south of Helena, Arkansas, and north of Clarksdale, Mississippi. Here, Crowley's Ridge was truncated by the ice age confluence of the Ohio and Mississippi Rivers. And here, on an old bend in the Mississippi River, sits what used to be the second-largest grouping of Indian mounds known in eastern North America. Named the Carson site by locals, there were eighty mounds here laid out along an axis that aligns with a southern position of the Moon on its long 18.6-year cycle. The mounds include a completely anomalous double-conical variety, alongside standard circular and square flat-topped pyramids. Recent salvage excavations by the Mississippi Department of Archives and History identified both a late Mississippian fortified town, built and abandoned just before De Soto passed through this area, as well as much older Cahokian houses. The Cahokians, it now seems, came here on one or more of their long-distance trips south and stayed awhile.[20] While here, they built houses, established ties to local people, explored the nearby Ouachita Mountains, and, possibly, constructed a few of the site's eighty mounds. Sometime before 1100 CE they left, possibly moving on to other points farther south.

But the die had been cast. The Cahokians had cemented their interests in the south, where a third link helps us wrap up the Cahokia story. That link has been largely overlooked by archaeologists, at least until they recently joined forces with Indigenous scholars and activists. This link is also the answer to a question: other than those of Caddo ethnicity, where did expatriate Cahokians go after the late 1100s? The answer: they returned to the south.

Since the late 1800s, Euro-American settlers crossing Crowley's Ridge had seen large circular mounds from Forrest City north to Jonesboro, Arkansas. Five of them sat on the western slopes of Crowley's Ridge, overlooking a wide expanse of lowlands to the west, at a place called Cherry Valley. Treasure-seekers or "pothunters" had plundered most of the mounds, but by 1958 they had not yet entirely penetrated these 13- to 18-foot-high tumuli. In that year, a self-trained archaeologist arrived on the scene with the financial backing of the Gilcrease Institute, in Tulsa, Oklahoma, to dissect the three remaining Cherry Valley mounds. His finds suggested "unquestionable affinity to similar artifacts at Cahokia."[21]

The initial mounds of the Cherry Valley site were low, flat-topped circular platforms, one in association with a circular lodge nearly identical in size, shape, and interior arrangement to Caddo buildings from Texas and Louisiana north into the Pawnee and Arikara country of the Central Plains. Another was topped by a simple square funerary house. Both had been built and rebuilt at least two times. A series of pit burials were dug through the building floors when they were dismantled, Caddo-like, and the platforms were subsequently mounded over and used for generations as a burial site. The pots buried with the dead, however, were not Caddo-style containers but plain and painted Mississippian bottles, jars, and bowls along with Cahokia-style Black Drink cups.[22]

Citizens of today's Quapaw Nation are descendants, and Carrie Wilson, former repatriation director and chairwoman of the Quapaw

Cultural Committee, leads efforts to return artifacts to the Quapaws. The cups, elaborate versions of the classic Cahokian originals, were made by her ancestors. Both the Quapaw people and their elaborate beakers have roots in the great Indigenous city of Cahokia, as has long been advocated by Wilson and as supported by a preponderance of archaeological evidence. The beakers' cylindrical shapes and long projecting handles are distinctive. These were intended to be used in great libation ceremonies involving the Black Drink, the beakers themselves presumably left here, at Cherry Valley, for further use by ancestral spirits in the land of the dead.[23]

As for the original builders of the Cherry Valley mounds, their living sites have never been located, and the Cherry Valley mounds seem to have been the centerpieces of a vacant hilltop shrine complex and burial ground "unusual in that interment at the ceremonial center apparently was widely available" to people of many different cultural backgrounds.[24] Several other such Cherry Valley culture mound complexes are known nearby, all on Crowley's Ridge. Given this, it now seems likely that the original Cherry Valley mound builders—ancestral Quapaw among them—may be the missing link in the history of Cahokia's thirteenth-century abandonment. For whatever reason, that is, some segment of Cahokia's population, those who were responsible for the all-important rites of the circular water temples, left their city at or just before the year 1200. Of course, some of Cahokia's movers and shakers were, in fact, Caddos, as can be seen in the presence of Caddo-style pottery, mortuary practices, and medicines in special cups in the old city. Others, we can presume, were ancestral Quapaws who may have adopted some Caddo practices or married Caddo spouses. Thus, here in east-central Arkansas around the year 1200, the existence of hybrid Caddo-Cahokia-Quapaw-style practices 275 overland miles south of the withering urban experiment of Cahokia along a natural causeway (which might have led some of their ancestors north in the first place) makes a good bit of sense.

Ultimately, the city of Cahokia had come apart at the seams, likely due to atmospheric shifts happening across North America at the time, which saw the critical medium of water cease to mediate fundamental (ontological) relationships between human and non-human. In the late twelfth century, Cahokians stopped rebuilding their official steam baths and water temples. They burned a few. They dismantled others, burying marine shells on the floors of at least one. The reasons were almost certainly hydroclimatic—reduced rainfall or periodic droughts that stemmed from climate change.

The late medieval hydroclimatic changes that now appear to have been at the heart of such pan–North American shifts were, of course, a little different everywhere. Some regions would have continued to get rain. Other regions would have experienced droughts far worse than those that happened around Cahokia. Unlike the Southwest or Altiplano Mexico, for instance, a drought at Cahokia may not have decimated maize agriculture. But it might still have adversely affected the overabundance on which Cahokian rituals depended. Thus, a Cahokian drought might have shaken people's confidence in the Thunderers—the primary storm and rain spirits—and the Thunderer priests who oversaw the circular water temples and great upright posts of Cahokia. The people lost faith and then took action.

After the burning of the East St. Louis compound, Cahokia was downsized, but it continued on as a center of governance and ceremony for a shrinking residential population until 1350. Once the last few clans left the city, it was largely forgotten by descendants and, soon thereafter, lost in the mists of time. In 1842, Charles Dickens described hydroclimatic conditions that were likely similar to those of the Medieval Climate Anomaly. For him, these conditions were oppressive. Passing through the ruins of the Cahokia and East St. Louis precincts after his day trip out to the Looking Glass Prairie, Dickens could scarcely understand how an ancient city might have arisen in this extreme environment.

> After breakfast, we started to return by a different way from that which we had taken yesterday. . . . Looming in the distance, as we rode along, was another of the ancient Indian burial-places, called The Monks' Mound.[25]

Mistaking the great flat-topped pyramid for a burial mound, Dickens commented on the early nineteenth-century Anglo-American occupants of the mound. A "body of fanatics of the order of La Trappe, who founded a desolate convent there, many years ago," were, he concluded, "swept off by the pernicious climate." As Dickens's carriage made its way through the very heart of ancient Cahokia, the man inside was singularly unimpressed with the region and its new European immigrants. His jaunt to the Looking Glass Prairie was concluded with a few summary remarks:

> The track of to-day had the same features as the track of yesterday. There was the swamp, the bush, the perpetual chorus of frogs, the rank unseemly growth, the unwholesome steaming earth. Here and there, and frequently too, we encountered a solitary broken-down wagon, . . . the team of oxen crouching down mournfully in the mud, and breathing forth such clouds of vapour from their mouths and nostrils, that all the damp mist and fog around seemed to have come direct from them.[26]

The damp mist, vapor, steaming earth, stagnant water, chirping frogs, and rain in torrents: here is what was special about Cahokia. The weather of the Medieval Climate Anomaly proved that the Thunderers had favored the people and the land. The Cahokians likely traveled far and wide—to the craggy Driftless Area landscape in the far north and through cypress-swamp bottomlands south into Arkansas, Texas, and Oklahoma. At least a few Cahokians likely made pilgrimages into northeastern Mesoamerica. The evidence that they did so sits here, in the form of long-nosed god maskettes, *tecpatl* daggers, and flat-topped circular mounds—the temples and objects of the rain, storm, and water spirits. The first few to build Cahokia's water temples might even have known the name of the foreign gods: Ehecatl-Quetzalcoatl, Ehecatl-Tezcatlipoca, and other members of the Epiclassic and Postclassic Mesoamerican pantheon.

That the gods favored the new city was readily evident to the people. Maize grew well here, and the water temples ensured balance, at least until the climatic fluctuations began in the twelfth century. It may seem counterintuitive that, in this lush land, water might have been the reason for both the rise and fall of the city, but that argument becomes more intuitive once we begin to feel water in all of its dimensions and with all of its historical and hydroclimatological implications. With the termination of the region's water temples, the Cahokians might have been attempting to rebalance a hydroclimatic and social world that was out of balance. As archaeologists see it today, that balance was achieved only by the departure of the Cahokians from their city. The depopulation and emigrations out of Cahokia that began in the mid-1100s were completed in the mid-1300s, five hundred years before Dickens rode in his carriage through the moldering, muddy ruins of the swampy city.

Places to Visit

Quapaw Nation Tribal Center Museum and Downstream Casino Resort, Oklahoma

Drive on Interstate 44, west of Joplin, Missouri, to Miami, Oklahoma. One of the first things to see as soon as you enter Oklahoma is the Quapaw Nation's Downstream Casino Resort. Nearby, in town, is the Tribal Center Museum. Both are open to the public, who are invited to learn firsthand about Quapaw history and tradition, both precontact and recent. The art and architecture of the impressive Downstream Casino Resort draws on the rich heritage of the Quapaw, and this is a great place to spend some time and play some games. In both the museum and casino, there are Mississippian-era pots, artifacts, and images of the Quapaw people past and present. Also nearby are the cultural centers and casinos of the Peoria, Miami, and Shawnee, all with equally rich histories that stretch back into the pre-contact-era Illinois, Mississippi, and Ohio River valleys.

Spiro Mounds State Historic Site, Oklahoma

Two and a half hours' drive south of Miami, Oklahoma, is the well-known Spiro site. Reach it by connecting to Interstate 40 and driving east from Oklahoma City or west from Little Rock, Arkansas. The site sits to the south of the interstate and the Arkansas River, surrounded by distant hills. A modest interpretive center is the first stop on a walking tour out onto the site. The main complex of eight platform mounds arranged in a rectangular pattern around an open plaza sits on a hill overlooking the lower floodplain of the Arkansas River. Between 1933 and 1935, looters tunneled into the sacred inner tomb of the Craig Mound, an unusual composite of four circular mounds in a row. Inside, these graverobbers removed a vast hoard that was dubbed "A King Tut's Tomb on the Arkansas" by a local newspaper. The men of the mining expedition sold some artifacts on the spot, dispersing a treasure trove that Caddo people and archaeologists have spent years recovering. In recent years, University of Oklahoma archaeologists have discovered the remains of dozens of temporary houses in rows all around the Craig Mound, apparently all dating to the same great mound-building or mortuary festival held on the spot in the 1300s.

Crowley's Ridge State Park and National Scenic Byway, Arkansas

Much farther to the east in Arkansas, one crosses Crowley's Ridge. This landform is unique, dates to the Miocene era, and stretches from Thebes Gap in the north to Helena, Arkansas, in the south. It resulted when the ancient Mississippi River paralleled the ancient Ohio River before joining south of gravelly deposits in between, later to be capped with windblown silt a hundred feet thick—Crowley's Ridge. The great, forested, elevated feature, near Paragould, Arkansas, is named for its first Anglo-American settler, Benjamin Crowley. He is buried in a cemetery that's now part of Crowley's Ridge State Park, a favorite place for camping and hiking and home to public

Civilian Conservation Corps architecture dating from the 1930s. You can begin a drive here to follow a series of interconnected highways known as the Crowley's Ridge Parkway and National Scenic Byway. Heading south on Highway 1, you will pass through Forrest City and then Harrisburg, Arkansas, before reaching the small town of Cherry Valley on the western flanks of Crowley's Ridge. The mounds sat on the ridge to the east. Continuing south, you reach the end of Crowley's Ridge at Helena, Arkansas, on the Mississippi River. There, visit the Forrest L. Wood Crowley's Ridge Nature Center and the Delta Cultural Center. Here, if you cross the river, you travel a short distance south to the Carson Mound group.

Carson Mounds, Mississippi

Hidden away in the Mississippi Delta, north of the crossroads where the blues were born, are the remains of the great mile-long and half-mile-wide Carson site. Two of its biconical mounds are yet visible in an active corporate farming landscape, as are two or three of its largest platforms, partially preserved because of twentieth-century homes built on their summits. Stay overnight at the Shack-Up Inn on Highway 46 just south of town. In the morning, drive the Oakhurst-Stovall Road north 6 miles. Just past the birthplace of Muddy Waters, turn left onto McWilliams Road and proceed through its intersection with Route 1. Beyond lies the heart of the Carson site, marked as one of the sites along the Mississippi Mound Trail.

II

First Medicine

Water is our first medicine.

—Bobbi Jean Three Legs, Standing Rock activist, 2017[1]

Before the Spanish conquest and the entangling of Old and New World histories, the Indigenous people of North America had developed their own distinctive ways of living in or relating to the world. Importantly, these ways developed *because of the world*—including its climatic conditions—as much as they developed because of people. The people of precolonial North America, from the Yucatan up through Mexico and into the Southwest and Mississippi Valley, lived as if the winds and waters that came with rains and storms were animate, spiritual beings or gods.

We can see such ways of relating to the world through Native peoples' stories and imagery, especially those that involve great Thunder Beings or creator gods that resided in the sky. Teuchitlan-culture people and later Huastecans climbed poles to engage Ehecatl or Ehecatl-Quetzalcoatl. The Maya venerated Kukulkan in their rural Terminal Classic shrines and great Postclassic cities. Cahokians and later Plains and Mississippian peoples worshiped the Thunderers in circular sacred buildings. These gods brought rain to people who relied on the water-sensitive maize plant, people who understood that water is the first principle or "medicine" of all life.[2]

Many readers will think of the term "medicine" in a purely pharmacological sense, as the natural or synthetic substances used to treat maladies or injuries. And to be sure, the pills, serums, injections, and ointments prescribed by physicians today might be conceived to be quite unlike the foods and nutrients that we consume daily. Foods and nutrients, after all, allow organisms to regulate metabolism or dissolve compounds that pass through the body. The water that we drink, one might conclude, is a nutrient, maybe even a food. But is it medicine?

In ancient America, if we define medicine as that which heals, and if we understand healing to be more than just a physiological process, then water was indeed medicine.[3] In point of fact, medicine for many Indigenous Americans was and is directed at more than just human bodies. In the past, healing was psychological, social, and even atmospheric as well as physiological, involving the rebalancing or repositioning of the spirit, mind, and body, on the one hand, and earth, sky, and water vis-à-vis human communities, on the other. Healing might have entailed a driving away of evil spirits that caused aches, disease, and mental illness, or a replenishment of that which made the birds sing and the game animals return the next season. It might have happened by way of a vision, the waving of a hand, or the shaking of a rattle adorned with owl feathers. Special substances or basic sorts of things—tobacco, the Black Drink, and ocean shells—were valued not just because they served some purpose in a ceremony. They were valued *and* served some ritual purpose *because they possessed healing effects.*

A shaman's trance might open a gateway to the spirit world through which healing power might be transferred to a patient. So might a visionary's dream telling of things to come—powerful medicine. In fact, shooting an arrow into an evil spirit, sacrificing a witch in dark cave, or offering a child or young woman to the spirit of a *voladore* pole might have been big medicine as well. In Huasteca today, community medicine resides in a ceremony where the flyers climb these poles, spin upside down from ropes, and drop to the ground to the cheers of the crowd. It's also great theater.

To be sure, this kind of healing is not based in abstract religious beliefs about invisible, imaginary worlds. Rather, this sort of healing, even generalized holistic healing, is palpable, multidimensional, and multisensorial. That which heals may come from tangible forces that transcend human know-how, but one can see, smell, hear, and touch those medicinal forces. They belch smoke and lava from volcanos. They hold up the great rocks along southwestern canyon walls. They are aligned to the Moon and Milky Way along the Red River. They thunder out of a cumulonimbus cloud that pours down rain, and they seep out from the sides of isolated hilltops in the Midwest's prairies. They are inside the bowl of a smoking pipe, a sacred bundle, an engraved drinking cup, or a shrine house. Healing powers as perceived by Indigenous Americans were tightly interlocked with these very real things, substances, and phenomena.

For Black Elk, the Lakota visionary and holy man, these powers were visions that he could see, smell, and hear:

> When a vision comes from the thunder beings of the West, it comes with terror like a thunder storm; but when the storm of vision has passed, the world is greener and happier; for wherever the truth of vision comes upon the world, it is like a rain.[4]

Rain cleared the air and made the grass grow and birds sing. A rainbow may have followed. Along with thunder, lightning, and rain, rainbows were real, powerful, and medicinal. They exuded effects—visual, audible, and olfactory qualities—that people felt, and that left impressions in their minds.

Similarly, Black Elk could feel and see the effects of a sweat in his circular *inipi* lodge on supplicants, who would emerge happy, purified, and enlivened (Figure 11.1). Those who entered were made whole, and felt better when they exited; never mind the positive physiological effects of unclogged pores, reduced joint pain, and decongested sinus cavities. Like a Huastecan *voladore* rite, the Lakota priest could also witness the power of the Sun Dance, which would bring the medicine of the above world down through a sacred tree and its

Figure 11.1. Cheyenne sweat bath, 1910. Edward S. Curtis Collection, Library of Congress. Public domain.

attached ropes into the bodies of men and, from there, returning balance and renewal to the community. Drums would thunder rhythms and spur on dance. The men looked skyward.

Of all such powers, water possessed a spiritual vitality or inherent energy that was as powerful and pervasive as any. Consider H_2O's properties. Water, strictly speaking, isn't a thing. Rather, it is an ever-changing substance. Sometimes it is a near-invisible vapor that escapes as breath from your mouth. It flows and moves, assuming the form of that which contains it. Water readily changes states—solid, liquid, and gas—in ways that absolutely mediate biological and social life and death. In climes north and south of the tropics, water freezes, and the snow and ice that result resculpt the world into magical landscapes. On the other hand, in the tropics, liquid water is less identifiable owing to its ubiquity. It falls from the sky and streams into standing bodies. It soaks into the ground's aquifers. In swamps, marshes, and oceans, the life cycles of organisms are completely immersed in water. In such contexts, water is less of a thing to be controlled or observed and more of an atmosphere through which beings move.

Even in less aquatic settings, water assumes the qualities of atmosphere. Outside of St. Louis, for example, Dickens experienced how evapotranspiration blurred the boundaries between dark stormy skies, saturated earth, morning mist, and the breath of people and animals. The rains were torrential, said Dickens, and the humidity was oppressive. In such places, to adapt Jack Keroauc's words on the road through San Luis Potosí, the weather is not just something that touches you, that caresses you, or that freezes or sweats you. *It becomes you.* The atmosphere and you become one and the same.[5]

In the Mississippi valley down to the Gulf of Mexico, the steamy heat of midday would build into thunderheads, terrible in their approach. The storm cells spiraled across the mountainless landscape. Flash floods washed through valleys to become deluges that drowned the coast. Then, along that coast, the tropical heat translocated the waters back into amorphous clouds in the upper atmosphere, there to spin out hurricanes that blew through the jungles of the Yucatan Peninsula, pummeled ships in the Gulf, and ripped the roofs off pole-and-thatch homes wherever they might make landfall. From a distance, the great spiraling storms probably looked to Indigenous eyes like monstrous coiled serpents, ready to strike.[6]

Storms are but large-scale examples of the power of water when it is transformed from one state of being (solid, liquid, gas) or one realm (underworld, this world, upperworld) into another. The phenomenal powers of storms—their alternately booming sound effects, freezing magic, soaking liquidity, and shocking electricity—affected all human populations regardless of their cultural dispositions and histories. Storms' universal impacts are undeniable. They lie outside humanity—thunder frightens animals; hail shreds leaves; floods wash away soils.

The impacts of water surely extend to the substance's less dramatic sensory effects, easily perceived by people in most places and in multiple states or dimensions of experience. Psychologists have long discussed these sensorial qualities and their impacts on attitudes and emotions. The cool blueness of a lake, the pleasantly chilled taste of mineral-enhanced spring water, the marine fragrance of waves crashing on a beach, and the quiet trickle of a stream have very real effects.[7] Water has such sensory qualities regardless of a people's particular cultural sensibilities, though in turn those sensibilities mediate the human experience of those sensory qualities.

For most, the color, smells, and sounds of water in its various forms and contexts have positively calming, pleasure-inducing, and awe-inspiring effects. Recordings of running water, falling rain, and thunder are among the most popular today for those seeking soothing background noise. And hot tubs, steamy showers, and steam baths are universally favored ways of relaxing and clearing one's head. Medical researchers agree: the heat and steam of saunas and steam baths have positive therapeutic effects. To pass through one is to open up the lungs, to cleanse the skin, to sweat out aches and fevers, and to emerge completely refreshed and renewed. In an ancient world without modern medicine, there was no greater healing experience.

For the people of Mesoamerica, the positive spiritual and physiological healing power of the steam bath went well beyond general therapeutics to include healing rituals surrounding pregnancy and childbirth. Pregnant women were cared for inside steam baths before, during, and after childbirth. It was common for umbilical cords and afterbirth to be buried inside a family's steam bath as a way of connecting people to place, to heat and steam, and to spirits associated therewith.[8] In other Mesoamerican cases during the colonial era, sexual healing—in the Marvin Gaye sense—was also associated with steam baths. One or more men and women would enter the building together at all hours of the day and night. Colonial Spanish authorities, with Catholic morals, expressed offense and outrage. Of course, from Indigenous points of view, such activities might have been wholly consistent with the healing rituals surrounding pregnancy and childbirth. Certainly, such activities emphasized the uterine or feminine associations of the buildings, associations that were common to circular architecture across North America, according to Robert Hall.[9]

Be that as it may, and as with ontologies generally, it would be a mistake to assume that the widespread, steamy, feminine, and sexual associations were the same everywhere throughout time. For although the human awareness of steam's effects was no doubt almost as old as the discovery of fire itself, the establishment of formal saunas, sweat houses, or steam baths—as opposed to a family's hut in the back yard—is not that old. Understanding the history of such ritual buildings is essential. And there is always a history to such ritual constructions.

Take, for example, the Scandinavian sauna, a sweat house that does not use steam. Today, saunas can be found across Europe in cities, and we can agree that using them must be a time-honored practice. In point of fact, archaeologists have found the remains of ten-thousand-year-old pits dug into the ground where people may have engaged in sauna-style sweats. These morphed into skin-covered tent saunas and, during the first or second millennium BCE in Finland, more permanent buildings with ovens and doors. But the Finnish Iron Age saunas were not a feature of European cities, at least not until they spread to western Europe in the eighteenth century. Other innovations followed, leading up to the formal public saunas of the twentieth century and today.[10]

Let's look at another example: bathhouses. In southern Europe and Asia, bathhouses may have served purposes similar to northern steam rooms. That is, warm water in humid air produces mist and a sensorial atmosphere comparable to steam. Bathhouses are old, of course, with the earliest versions known from the Bronze Age city of Mohenjo-Daro in Pakistan dating to the second millennium BCE. As formalized, public facilities, they are best known among the Iron Age Romans. Across the Roman Empire, politicians met and made decisions in bathhouses, simultaneously relieving the stresses of public life in the warm misty air and water. Even more than Mesoamericans and their steam baths, of course, sexual liaisons were a well-known part of the Roman bathhouse. And, like Scandinavian saunas, bathhouses have a history. Ultimately, both they and saunas fell out of favor across the old empire and the rest of Europe during the Enlightenment, when they became associated with older unenlightened superstitions disdained by the newly enlightened elite.

The history of sweat houses and steam baths in North America has proven a bit more intractable. Both saunas (where hot coals or rocks were used to create dry heat) and steam baths (where water was added to create steam) were in widespread usage by Indigenous Americans when European colonists arrived on the continent's shores. At that time, and as dictated by regional traditions, people across North America used either saunas or steam baths (but seldom both). The existence of these seemingly distinct traditional ways, of course, isn't an explanation in and of itself, as noted at the outset. Rather, they belie a dramatic history of social and religious changes that, from time to time, swept the continent.

Similar to the saunas of the Old World, the earliest North American sweating facilities in one or another region of North America were informal, built by families as part of the small-scale existence of village farmers or itinerant hunters and foragers before the rise of urbanism. Some might have doubled as menstrual huts, special storage sheds, or wintertime sentry shelters, isolated at the edges of settlements. Typically, in the earliest of eras, these would have been basic oval huts or simple pithouses with wigwam frameworks covered over with mats, blankets, and heaped-up earth. Such huts were the simplest and most natural of buildings, constructed in ways dictated by the size and musculoskeletal structure of a human body.

More formal buildings, built under the aegis of some official religious or public authority, entered the picture much later. For example, they are known from Preclassic and Classic Maya cities, such as Tikal, but they are rare, and identified with difficulty. For the most part, the early Maya buildings were merely well-insulated interior rooms, rectangular in shape, with corbelled arches and hearths that might also have been used for purposes other than sweats.[11]

Likewise, some pre-900 CE Basketmaker and Pioneer- or Colonial-period Hohokam pithouses in the American Southwest and North Mexico were probably used as saunas or steam baths, but if so, they doubled for other purposes as well. In neither instance were these buildings strictly set aside for scripted, ritualized bodily purifications. Most were simply the cool-weather homes of ordinary families. In fact, distinctively shaped or formal sweat houses were never part of later Pueblo and Hohokam architectonics, although circular kivas—originally called *estufas* or "stoves" by the Spanish—were likely entangled in medieval America's politico-religious history of circular architecture.[12] In many places in the Southwest, kivas would remain multipurpose clan or community rooms up to the present.

Similarly, perhaps some of the earlier circular buildings of Native Woodland peoples of eastern North America, dating back more than three thousand years, doubled as sweat houses or communal saunas. The oldest of a series of so-called public circular buildings are known at the unusual site Poverty Point, situated on an old southern plantation in northeastern Louisiana populated at first mostly by African American slaves and, later, sharecroppers—hence the name. There, post circles from 80 to over 200 feet in diameter have been found in the 40-acre semi-circular plaza using a magnetometer, which sees under the ground without digging (Figure 11.2).[13] That plaza is surrounded by concentric rows of unusual loaf-shaped mounds and piles of refuse from ceremonial feasts. By the early centuries CE, large monumental circles, up to 375 feet in diameter and made up of piled earth and posts that measured a foot across, were set into place at so-called Hopewell ceremonial complexes in modern-day Ohio and surrounding states.[14] Even larger circular earthworks, over 1,700 feet in diameter, are well known at places that can still be visited today: Newark Earthworks and various pieces of the Hopewell Culture National Historical Park near Chillicothe, Ohio (Figure 11.3).

By the time Europeans began colonizing the eastern seaboard in the 1580s, more modest "dance circles" of posts, probably not unlike the Poverty Point and Hopewell examples or the Sun Circle

Figure 11.2. Modern markers locating posts of timber circles at Poverty Point, Louisiana. Wikimedia: Billy Hathorn, 2013. Creative Commons Attribution-Share Alike 3.0 Unported License.

Figure 11.3. Portion of large circular earthwork in Newark, Ohio. T. Pauketat, 2017.

buildings on the Plains, were seen into the Carolinas. Likewise, large circular communal structures or "townhouses" in the American South were sometimes identified by European and Euro-American explorers as "hot houses" as well. One was seen by Cabeza de Vaca and, a few years later, Hernando de Soto at the center of Apalachee town, in peninsular Florida. Others were sketched by the enlightened Scottish American naturalist William Bartram while visiting Muskogee-Creek towns in the early 1770s. These were circular townhouses complete with interior hearth built atop a circular platform, in turn sitting opposite a rectangular temple.[15] It's the alternating circle and square pattern that we first encountered in Mexico City's Pino Suárez metro station.

Archaeologists generally connect these two dots on their timelines, the old ceremonial post circles or circular buildings and winter homes dating from the end of the so-called Archaic and earliest Woodland eras (ca. 1600–500 BCE) and the more recent round townhouses from the sixteenth through eighteenth centuries. They must be historically related, they reason. And perhaps they were.

But the history of circular architecture in North America is neither a simple story, where people repeatedly innovated such constructions without regard to historical tradition, nor a straight line, where the buildings began some two millennia ago and never went away. To lay out a circle on the ground is a simple enough thing to do. Use a piece of rope tied off to a stake, walk around the stake, and voilà—you have a circle. But the ease of constructing such a plan does not necessarily mean that just anybody would build a circular building. Rather, in recognizing that the "power of the world is in circles," to paraphrase Black Elk, we should assume that formal, perfectly circular architecture would have been constructed only by those sanctioned to do so. As the instance of the Lakota's complex *inipi* ceremony points out, there was a substantial amount of esoteric ritual knowledge that had to be remembered to properly balance, control, or placate the other-than-human powers inherent to the circle and all that it embodied—celestial orbs, the horizon, a 22-degree lunar halo, swirling storm cells,

Figure 11.4. Lunar halo. Wikimedia: Martin Bernardi, 2020. Creative Commons Attribution-Share Alike 4.0 International License.

the ripples emanating from a drop of water in a pool, and the all-knowing goggle-shaped eyes of great spiritual beings (Figure 11.4).

In the Indigenous world of the Americas, such elemental forms, substances, and sensory qualities possessed transformative potential. Spiritual power resided in or emanated from them, and anything made from such a substance and in such a form was powerful. Hence, fundamental materials or pieces thereof—feathers, stones, crystals, skins, special tool kits, and maps of the heavens—were bundled, wrapped in skins or fabrics, and meticulously held in shrines, not to be touched by those lacking the appropriate rites or understandings. Among the Mandan, Hidatsa, Arikara, and others on the Plains, even basic technological skills that anybody *could* have done, such as pottery making, were similarly bundled and restricted to those clans who managed the pottery-making bundles.

As with Plains pottery making, people would not have practiced the ceremonies involving official, circular buildings unless they had inherited or purchased a ceremony—that is, a bundle that contained the instructions for the ceremonies—in which circular architecture was called for. And in any land where circular architecture was absent, one would have had to obtain a bundle before one could build the architecture appropriately. The effect would have been a patchy and potentially discontinuous pan-American history of circular architectural constructions, a function of how knowledge of the sacred buildings was bundled and transferred. Moreover, every bundle transfer or movement would have constituted an opportunity to reinterpret the practices of the forebearer, in turn subject to their whims and fates.

Perhaps the earliest great circular architectonic traditions were linked. It is conceivable, for instance, that the post-circle monuments of Poverty Point and Hopewell peoples two thousand to four thousand years ago may have been connected in some ways to those of the Preclassic Cuicuilco and its circular stormy volcanic mountain Xitle. But if so, there was likely a historical disconnect that ended such constructions across much of the Eastern Woodlands—especially the Mississippi valley proper—by the early centuries of the so-called Late Woodland period, circa 400–600 CE. A similar disconnect producing an irregular, discontinuous history is what one sees by 300 CE in Mesoamerica with the demise of Cuicuilco and the expansion of Teotihuacan. The absence of circular formal architecture, along with ballcourts, defined the great imperial city in the Valley of Mexico.

Meanwhile, Classic-period believers built a civilization around water and circularity—in West Mexico in the form of the *guachimontónes* of the Teuchitlan sites. There, and elsewhere outside of Teotihuacan, people built their own histories and identities around that which gave them joy and satisfaction. Mountains made clouds, clouds brought rain, and rain ensured life. Regional traditions were the norm, especially after the fall of Teotihuacan. And yet starting in the Epiclassic and continuing through the Postclassic, the regionalism was built on a new set of political and architectonic principles, as well as the central significance of the gods—Tlaloc, Ehecatl, Tezcatlipoca, and especially Quetzalcoatl.

Quite possibly, the spread of that Epiclassic-to-Postclassic political ideology was facilitated by the same kind of revitalization or revivalist movements witnessed among the Terminal Classic Maya. Much of North, West, and Central Mexico, after all, was drying out. The Yucatan was seemingly hit the hardest. Across Yucatan's karst lowlands, the reservoirs ran low. The springs dried up. Trips by Maya priests into the watery underworld at places such as Actun Tunichil Muknal and the cenotes of Chichen Itza became more frequent. In those centuries, the cults of gods who inhabited circular buildings zigged into the Terminal Classic Maya and zagged into the Postclassic Huastecan pyramids at Las Flores and Tamtoc.

It seems likely that the plans and practices of such buildings were carried into northeastern Mesoamerica inside bundles by the Maya themselves. Within decades, one such cult was bundled and carried northward to George C. Davis and Crenshaw, perhaps appearing as the original Moon temples managed by the first Tsah Neeshis. In the moonlight, we can see the long shadows of such a religious movement from atop the roofs of Chaco Canyon's kivas and tri-walled circular buildings. And in a mid-medieval-era urbanizing movement, Cahokians reached down south and brought another such cult all the way up into the middle of the Mississippi valley. Given the known facts from archaeology, it is likely that a bundle of Ehecatl-Quetzalcoatl—or some closely related proxy—was unwrapped and reanimated inside round thatched-roof temples atop Cahokia's newly built circular flat-topped pyramids. Another bundle or bundles might have contained pieces of Tezcatlipoca, including outline drawings and encoded instructions for how to make and use broad, double-edged, needle-tipped, chipped-stone daggers. Both spirits seem embodied by Cahokian human-head earpieces.

In the distant land of the American Bottom and Greater Cahokia, the mid-latitude cyclones swirled and electrified humanity in ways that made everyone realize the power of the Thunderers. Great upright poles, cut from watery swamplands south of this city of wood, thatch, and earth, were dragged through black mud, floated upriver, and lifted into place in the new city. Falcon-men flyers or dancers who hung from ropes spoke to the Wind-That-Brings-Rain, who in turn answered in flashes of earthshaking terror. Afterwards, the world was greener and happier.

Places to Visit

Poverty Point, Louisiana

On the west side of modern-day Lake Providence, Louisiana, turn southwest onto Louisiana Highway 134 until you cross the Bayou Maçon, and then turn right/north into a square mile or more of an enigmatic ancient landscape. The great size and arena-style arrangement of the thirty-four-hundred-year-old mounds of Poverty Point remain a singularity, unlike anything anywhere else in the world, as are the artifacts and architecture found by archaeologists at the site. So, too, do the timber circles, arrangements of upright posts each up to 2 feet in diameter.

All indications are that semi-sedentary Late Archaic period hunter-fisher people of this unusual place converged at Poverty Point from all directions, bringing exotic materials here to convert them into zoomorphic fetishes and ritually charged tools and utensils. They built over an even older Middle Archaic mound, some five millennia old, and constructed their earthworks in single events that must have drawn on the labor of thousands. There are later mound complexes nearby as well, including one from the twelfth century CE frequented by Cahokians from the far north.

Newark Earthworks, Newark, Ohio

Taking its place among the great ancient wonders of the world, the Hopewell site of Newark immediately challenges the visitor: "This is amazing. Who built it? Here? In the middle of central Ohio?" If you are driving along I-70 through Ohio, turn off on US Route 79/

Hebron Road north. Seven and a half miles later you drive through the Newark earthworks. Not only are they impressive, but they are a small part of the original elaborate set of embankments, sacred gathering stations, and unseen bent-pole temples and prayer houses of the Hopewell people of a thousand years ago. More than likely, these were ancestors of Algonkian-speaking peoples who participated in an early, widespread religious movement built around gathering the animate spirits of the universe together all in one spot. Amazingly, the remaining Great Circle and Great Octagon—both capable of holding a gathering of ten thousand people during the half-millennium-long classic Hopewell or Middle Woodland period (ca. 100 BCE–400 CE)—are not publicly owned. They are designated a National Historic Landmark but are owned and managed by the Ohio History Connection, concerned citizens who stepped up to preserve this most important of historical locations.

Hopewell Culture National Historical Park, Chillicothe, Ohio

The Hopewell peoples who lived in or made pilgrimages to Newark appear to have made use of the 58-mile-long Great Hopewell Road—actually a ritual avenue. Built by the Hopewell peoples, this road runs to modern-day Chillicothe, Ohio, and traced the Milky Way's Path of Souls on the ground. The Hopewell Culture National Historical Park preserves several critical Hopewell ceremonial centers. The visitors center is located next to one of them (opposite a modern prison). Drive south of Interstate 270, which loops around Columbus, Ohio, using State Highway 23, which takes you through Circleville into Chillicothe. Before reaching the latter, turn right onto Highway 207 four miles to the park entrance.

12

Wind in the Shell

Álvar Núñez Cabeza de Vaca and his three companions, about to travel on their long journey west in 1535, had chided the Avavare people for their story of the Bad Thing, never considering that the story might have been the myth of an evil creator god like Tezcatlipoca, lord of the night winds and underworld counterpart to a bearded beneficent creator god Quetzalcoatl. Yet the Avavares, and subsequent groups met by Cabeza de Vaca, Estevanico, Castillo, and Dorantes, considered the bearded foreigners to be the Children of the Sun—god-men who journeyed west. Cabeza de Vaca himself had carried seashells from group to group during his years as an itinerant middleman in the Texas interior. How often had he placed a shell up to his ear to wonder about the sounds of wind and crashing waves inside?

Now, consider the prominence and number of such shells, along with circular shrines, at archaeological places that you have visited in our tour—Aztec, Cahokia, Chaco, Cherry Valley, Chichen Itza, Crenshaw, Cuicuilco, Calixtlahuaca, Emerald, George C. Davis, Ixtlan del Río, Las Flores, Los Guachimontónes, Paquime, Tamtoc, Tenochtitlan, Trempealeau, and Tula Chico. Those shells meant something profound to descendants of peoples who lived through the Medieval Climate Anomaly. And those shells were often associated with wind, water, and circular temples, shrines, and pyramids that were frequently, in turn, paired with square platforms, buildings, or pyramids. They were connected to temples, sacred fires, and the realm of the dead by causeways or lines of sight sometimes to or through water and occasionally with reference to a great water-bringer spirit, the Moon. And they were connected to or through upright poles and twisted ropes that reached up into the sky to the winds and clouds whence lightning flashed.

Obviously, the various cultures north and south of the Pánuco developed on their own and were not all the same. Cahokian culture and its ontological underpinnings are distinct from Caddo culture and ontology, even if some sizable number of Cahokians hailed from the Caddo region. Caddo ontology was not Huastecan or Puebloan, even if it replicated some of the same imagery from those places. And Pueblo, Hohokam, or Plains cultures were not Mesoamerican, which was itself not one great tradition, but a series of semi-discrete and ever-changing cultural developments—even when integrated by those with imperial aspirations such as the Teotihuacanos. There were a raft of Classic-period Mesoamerican cultures and dialects both inside and outside the great imperial city. The same seems apparent within the boundaries of the balkanized Maya civilization—it was hardly a single civilization at all.

Yet the peoples of these various regional traditions still communicated with each other in one way or another, sharing certain understandings of the world around them, adopting the bundled practices of their neighbors near and far, and arriving in the modern era as distinctive peoples who nevertheless shared deeply enmeshed concepts and engrained practices. Circular shrines and monuments came to be central to the religious and urban complexes of the people in the volatile climatic regime of the Medieval Warm Period. Members of surrounding communities, one might presume, came to water shrines routinely to pray for rain or to be healed.

For farmers, there would have been very little more important in the world than healing the body, soul, community, and cosmos. These were the laborers who did the tilling and planting, the tending and harvesting, the cleaning and processing, and the storage and hauling of all the foodstuffs without which no city could have existed. Their fields were subject to floods and droughts, and their bodies were subject to the aches and pains and illnesses and injuries of the sort that laborers are always disproportionately prone to. They understood the plants they grew and the animals that might raid their fields. But as for how to be healed, or how to control the weather—this was the job of shamans, priests, and elites who had access to the gods and who understood the cosmos.

Farmers needed them. They needed the blessings and healing power of the spirit world. They needed to get right with the gods. And so growers, pilgrims, and the curious from far away came into the sacred shrines and the cities that grew up about them. They carried in their ailing aunts and sick cousins, fathers, and mothers. They came in to the shrines to pray to the gods, to celebrate life, to drink the healing waters, and to be blessed inside the steamy dark chambers. In the process, the histories of Mesoamericans, Chichimecs, Caddos, Cahokians, Chacoans, and so many more to the north became intertwined.

It happened like this. After the collapse of Classic Teotihuacan and the Terminal Classic Maya in the south, Epiclassic and Postclassic replacements were centered on Ehecatl-Quetzalcoatl, his twin nemesis Tezcatlipoca, the brothers Xolotl and Xipe Totec, the water god Tlaloc or Chahk, and versions of feminine goddesses of creation and corn. In the north-central Altiplano of Mexico, Alta Vista and La Quemada thrived until around the year 900, when presumably they were taken out by social and political shifts underwritten by continental climatic trends. Migrants from those centers moved south, even to Tula, where an Epiclassic split between the factions of the Wind-That-Brings-Rain god and those of the night lord of darkness may have led to the abandonment of the old city temples of Tula Chico. Perhaps some when north into Huasteca, which witnessed a resurgence and Maya immigration in the 900s. Circular pyramids and pole-climbing ceremonies honoring Ehecatl-Quetzalcoatl were de rigueur. Crowds cheered, and visitors from the north watched. Back in the Yucatan, the Maya world reoriented itself around Chichen Itza, where the cognate of Ehecatl-Quetzalcoatl known as Kukulkan reigned supreme.

Such religious developments, migrations, bundle transfers, and community theatrics produced cultural impacts as far north as the Colorado Plateau and central Mississippi valley. Pulses of religious and political activity in these places drew inspiration from Mesoamerican wind and water gods. Novel circular architecture appeared—vertical kivas and towers around Chaco and elevated steam baths around Cahokia. Both were connected to supernatural wind and water gods, most notably the Thunderers.

After the demise of Chaco and Cahokia, a series of other communal religious movements coalesced around Mesoamerican gods. In the Southwest it was the Katsina religion.[1] In the Southeast, the so-called Southeastern Ceremonial Complex (formerly known as the Southern Cult) spread near and far, with the Caddos pulling in both Mesoamerican and Southwestern images, practices, and narratives to supplement the usual Mississippian ones from farther east.[2] These same Caddo, at the edge of the southern Great Plains, were the likely conduits for Mesoamerican ceremonies that moved as far north as the Lakota in the Central Plains. Indeed, by 1535, as the stragglers of the Narváez expedition were trudging across Texas, Tamaulipas, Coahuila, and Chihuahua, a new wave of Uto-Aztecan and Huastecan symbols and practices was spreading out across the Plains. There were Morning Star motifs and activities involving ritual combat and human sacrifice. Even the Mesoamerican idea of a heavenly Flower World, known by the 1500s from the Maya up to the Hopi, seems to have swept into the Great Plains and across the upper Midwest around that time. It is still evident today in the flowery beadwork patterns of countless North American tribes.

These were simply the latest in a long history of periodic cultural contacts and exchanges between peoples north and south of the US-Mexico border, some of which—those induced by pan-continental, climatic or geopolitical causes—left indelible signatures on regional histories. None of these original Indigenous cultures, with their overlapping philosophies and ontologies, developed in a vacuum. Mesoamerican relationships with the Pueblo and Hohokam worlds are most easily recognized because there is ample proof of a series of direct contacts and migrations between the peoples and lands north and south of the Mogollon Rim.

Possibly, North Mexico and the Southwest were *less* noticeably affected by medieval-period Mesoamerican influences because contacts were more routine. The Hohokam in particular shared a series of mythical and material attributes with their distant cousins in West and Central Mexico, yet they shied away from buying into Thunderer cults with their circular ritual spaces. The Pueblos of the Anasazi world, on the other hand, developed in contradistinction to the Hohokam and, to a lesser extent, Chichimeca and Mesoamerica. This is especially true of the Chacoan builders of the Place Beyond the Horizon, who from time to time made their own forays into the mythical lands of the old Chalchihuites culture far to the south, perhaps as part of great periodic pilgrimages. They selectively adopted aspects of what they saw.

Mesoamerica's effects on the Eastern Woodlands were even more intermittent but no less dramatic. Up until the 1950s and 1960s, archaeological explanations of the similarities between the Southeast and Mesoamerica rested on an inference that a Southern Cult, with Mesoamerican inspirations, had swept through the forested lands of La Florida west to Texas at or just before European contact.[3] In recent years, archaeologists armed with precise dating methods have stepped back from such scenarios and, in the process, mistakenly attributed the Mississippian phenomenon—beginning with the rise of Cahokia—almost entirely to local cultural roots. Some simply ignore potential Mesoamerican connections, explaining away monumental or artifactual parallels with Mesoamerica as happenstance or historical noise.[4]

Of course, these archaeologists are being myopic and making a historiographical mistake. There *are* multiple lines of evidence to support the claim that a cult-like phenomenon, centered on circular shrines, swept northward out of Mexico. That phenomenon was not primarily or ultimately the product of trade, even though there were established traces connecting both the Rio Grande and Mississippi valleys with central Mexico. Along such established cultural pathways, beginning in the ninth century, the wave of interlinked religious movements spread, stretching from the Yucatan Peninsula up into the widely separated, surprisingly coeval cultural expansions of the early Puebloan, Formative Caddo, and early Cahokia-Mississippian realms. The wave, we now know from actual climate data, happened when farming conditions were more ideal in the north and while portions of Mesoamerica were drying out. In other words, the same global climatic changes that were leading to the Terminal Classic collapse of Maya cities and the early Epiclassic to Postclassic rise of a Toltec-infused ideology were having very different and positive impacts outside Mesoamerica.

At this time, after 900 CE, many of the northern regions of the continent witnessed the appearance of some form of Thunderer god or gods—one or more manifestations of the Wind-That-Brings-Rain deity Ehecatl-Quetzalcoatl and, more than likely, his diabolical alter ego Ehecatl-Tezcatlipoca. Of course, other Mesoamerican gods were entangled in the cults, most importantly a Corn Mother or creator goddess, and the resulting cults of Thunderers happened a little differently in every region because the climatic conditions and historical traditions of each location were dissimilar. But all regions, it now seems apparent, were historically connected, judging by the fact that the various cults happened domino-like within a century and a half of each other, between 900 and 1050 CE, first in the south and last in the north. And they were unified by an emphasis on circular cult buildings, pole-climbing or flying rituals, large chipped-stone daggers, spiral-shaped mollusk shells, and water, especially the kind that fell from the sky.[5]

In those warm and wet medieval years, great rainstorms blew over the tropical lands of lower Mexico and up into the subtropics around the Gulf, sensed by countless generations of people as well as monkeys, felines, birds, frogs, and more, as a source of life, renewal, rebirth, refreshment, and terror. Farmers needed the rain but feared the lightning, thunder, and floods that came with it. Little wonder that prominent shrines to wind and water sat along the Gulf Coast. In fact, exploring the Yucatan coastline, the first Spanish expeditions encountered a number of these shrine sites. These ranged from "a small square with three houses built of masonry, which served as *cues* or prayer-houses" to "some very large buildings of fine masonry . . . the walls of which were painted with the figures of great serpents and evil-looking gods . . . [and] symbols like crosses" in brilliant hues.[6] Here and to the west along the Veracruz coastline, these buildings were the sites of human sacrifices, evident to the impressed Spaniards by "clotted blood" and dismembered bodies.

Seven centuries before Cortés, the Maya shrines along the coast were organized around steam baths, set below the ground, their curvilinear perimeters, arched roofs, and dark interiors mimicking the night sky and drawing on the power of circles. Inside, devotees honored a Wind-That-Brings-Rain god. Outside, the world of the Classic Maya was collapsing, and people prayed for rain. They would be disappointed. At the edges of groundwater pools, in the dark passages of watery caves, atop circular platforms, and inside steam baths, they left behind offerings of shells, water jars, and human beings. The initial wave of medieval weather patterns in the ninth century devastated the Yucatan lowlands.

Had Cortés sailed along the coastline at the time, in the 800s, he may have seen more Maya out on the Gulf waters in boats, some traveling up the coast to new homes in the better-watered land of Huasteca. There, the expatriate Maya mixed with locals, bringing their steam bath ceremonialism with them and melding it with the elevated poles and circular shrines already prominent in other parts of Mexico outside the old imperial city of Teotihuacan. Regionally distinct histories, such as these, along with the ups and downs of agricultural production, would have differentially constrained or enabled the spread of the various cults of Thunderer gods and rain deities. The fall of imperial Teotihuacan around the year 600 stands out as the most significant geopolitical development of the entire pre-Hispanic era, encouraging surrounding peoples to recreate cultural order in their own terms, borrowing a little from here, rejecting a little from there. Hence, with the demise of Teotihuacan, the Hohokam redefined themselves via the Mesoamerican ballgame and large-scale irrigation, making them the economic powerhouse of far North Mexico and the greater Southwest.

Regionally, the mere existence of the Hohokam likely contributed to the rise of Chaco. As a part of that rise, Chacoans pulled other meaningful, vibrant material elements from the south into their emerging canyon complex: macaws, bells, shells, and chocolate out of West Mexico, the Gulf of California, and Huasteca. The last was a possible source of the notion of vertical circular platforms and towers that we see today as the remains of aboveground kivas and tri-walled buildings.

The 800s–900s were also centuries when Huasteca now seems to have been on the receiving end of Maya immigration. The new circular platforms and surmounting steam baths at places such as Tamtoc and Las Flores overlooked both natural lagoons and human-made reservoirs. What was left of the traditional Maya rain god Chahk must have been blended with a vigorous new Toltecan and Huastecan iteration of the wind and storm god Ehecatl-Quetzalcoatl, blown out of nearby Tula like a hurricane. The feathered serpent, here, *was* the beneficent Thunderer, and narratives of the all-powerful deity were sweeping Mexico at the time.

At Tamtoc, Las Flores, and dozens of other Huastec sites, the people climbed the steps to the summits of their earthen, circular temple mounds, some plastered over and others faced with stone. A select few Huastecan acrobats shimmied up poles to commune with the Wind-That-Brings-Rain. Word got around, as it always does, and seems to have reached the Formative Caddo of Texas, sitting there on the crossroads of the Anasazi world to the west, Woodland farmers to the northeast, the Jumanos and Coahuiltecans to the southwest, and the Huastecans to the far south along an early El Camino Real de los Tejas.

The precursors of the Formative Caddo might even have had a historical connection to the Teuchitlan area. Formative Caddo shaft tombs if not circular platforms, after all, are reminiscent of Los Guachimontónes. It is true that mound-building was not new to the Caddo at 900, since their own Fourche Maline ancestors were already burying their dead in accretional mounds. But the flat summits of the tenth-century Formative Caddo mounded constructions were novel, as was the burial in deep vaults similar to the shaft tombs of West Mexico. By 1200, the Caddo were building circular structures atop their circular platforms, possibly thanks to Huastecans.

Certainly, by 1200, the Caddo had adopted some of the artistic traditions of Huasteca, specifically including spiral volute motifs and carved conch shell body ornaments so well-known from the Pánuco. In addition, they revered the Moon and the Milky Way, and realized a rudimentary lunar geometry at least by 900 CE that they either passed to the Chacoans to the west (and the Cahokians to the northeast, perhaps in exchange for corn) or borrowed from the Chacoans, maybe along with the secrets of the maize plant. Seemingly, Caddo culture was a combination of a Woodland (Fourche Maline) heritage, corn agriculture, and imported Puebloan, Mississippian, and Huastecan ceremonialism. Things were happening and fast, in multiple directions. This was a pan-continental movement in the broadest sense, literally and figuratively, and all of the historical parts and players—natural and cultural—seem to have been in motion.

The most momentous happening north of the Rio Grande took place in a stretch of Mississippi River floodplain far to the north, at the future site of the impressive American Indian urban complex of Cahokia. Annual rainfall and average temperatures had increased there at the very inception of the medieval era. And corn and all of its trappings—processing with lye, increased bottomland agricultural orientation, Corn Goddess mythology—were adopted in or shortly after 900 CE. More than likely, corn had arrived in bundles from the Puebloan Southwest, perhaps by way of the Formative Caddo. Cahokians might have then passed strains back to the Caddo, as hinted by genetic studies and confirmed by the many Cahokian objects that turn up in Caddo country.

Either way, maize came bundled with a suite of knowledge, spiritual associations, mythic narratives, and memorized practices about how to properly attend to the needs of the sweet, water-sensitive crop, if not also how to properly process it with lye water. A mid-twentieth-century anthropologist summed up the likely scenario accounting for how maize would have arrived in Cahokian, Caddo, and other Mississippian realms:

> It seems probable that the diffusion of maize within this eastern province would not have represented merely the borrowing of seed corn by the neighbors of agricultural peoples and their handing on seed to their neighbors. In actuality a real maize complex would have been diffused, including specific techniques for the growing and utilization of maize, knowledge of its botanical peculiarities (such as its inability to reproduce itself by self-sowing, and its tendency to grow extra "prop-roots" when dirt is hilled around the base of the plant), a set of magical and ritual precepts and traditions directly concerned with the cultivation and utilization of maize, and mythological and folktale material concerning the origin, nature, history, and use of maize.[7]

However it came to the Cahokians, the historical result of converting to a maize-centric economy for pre-urban (Terminal Late Woodland era) villagers was revolutionary.[8] Instead of experiencing droughts and collapse as seen among the Maya, Cahokians realized a new city and experienced the best of times: ample rainfall, long growing seasons, and bumper crops in a landscape awash in subterranean and atmospheric water. Of course, it was all a result of thunderstorms. The central Mississippi valley—in the middle of the mid-continent's stormy atmospheric convergence of moist, warm Gulf air and cold, dry northern fronts—is at the northern end of a southeastern zone that has more than fifty thunderstorm days per year.

The human population swelled exponentially as the people built Cahokia's three urban precincts. In their lush new reality, the Terminal Late Woodland people of the American Bottom and adjacent hinterlands did what seems almost unimaginable to modern human beings: they birthed urbanity in a single generation. Given the focus on psychedelics, human sacrifice, and lunar observations, and given the ubiquity of Caddo-style pots and ceremonial objects in Cahokian neighborhoods, it seems likely that contingents of Red River Caddo or Southern Plains Caddoans took an active part in Cahokia's construction. Cahokia must have been a diverse, cosmopolitan place where people from multiple ethnic backgrounds spoke very different language dialects in different contexts.

Their urbanizing movement, we can presume, was led by would-be spiritual or political visionaries. Perhaps there was even a prominent outsider or two—a Caddo Tsah Neeshi or a Huastecan traveler, husband, or bride—whose very exoticism, cosmic vision, and inexplicable spiritual powers motivated people to build Cahokia's many monuments. To consolidate the vision, this person or persons, along with their sizeable entourage, would have traveled far and wide to gather knowledge of the known world and its otherworldly powers. There can be no doubt but that they came and went both to and from the far north and to and from the far south. In the north, their lunar shrines still sit atop highly visible bluffs along the Mississippi River, mute testimony to their momentous movement's reach. At one or more far-off northern outposts, powerful Cahokians communed with the spirits of the waters and mists that flowed through the rugged Driftless Area landscape. To and from that shrine, and others like it, they traveled during the warm seasons, raising corn crops on location to feed themselves and the few locals who dared come close to these unusual occupiers.

In the south, they seem to have done likewise, traveling down along the Mississippi and, probably, into Caddo country. The latter might have been reached by walking a relatively easy trail down part of Crowley's Ridge, through Plum Bayou–culture country, and into the ancestral homeland of Cahokia's Caddo clans somewhere out in the Red River's Great Bend region. From there, a vision-seeker may have floated down the Red to the Mississippi or, more simply, trekked overland to the Neches River before hopping back into a dugout at the George C. Davis site and paddling downriver out into the Gulf.

It would have been an exceptional journey, with the better part of an entire warm season devoted just to reaching Caddo country. Boating down the Neches or the Red, the travelers would have passed through thick and dangerous cypress swamps of the Piney Woods region of east Texas and western Louisiana, home to dense populations of frogs, alligators, rattlesnakes, alligator snapping turtles, cottonmouths, beavers, raccoons, and cougars. Possible sightings of the ivory-billed woodpecker, the largest of all avian pole-climbers, extinct today, were made in this country in the mid- to late twentieth century. For travelers in dugout canoes, the passage would have been memorable.

After a couple of weeks paddling down the Neches, they would have reached the Gulf at modern-day Beaumont, Texas. Then, out on the open waters of the Gulf, they would have canoed. If they made some 30 miles a day, it would have taken another three weeks or so for the Cahokian-Caddo flotilla to reach the mouth of the Pánuco. Given the sparsity of game and edible plants along the Texas and Tamaulipas coast, they would have needed to pack commissary canoes full of food.

Unlike the Narváez expedition, they would have known what they were doing and where they were going. They scheduled their trip by counting the full moons. The flotilla would have traveled in the springtime, before the hurricane season, before the month of June. And they would have anticipated traveling unmolested, because of international Indigenous rules that protected religious pilgrims.

Then, given the rules and practices surrounding medicine bundles, it follows that an entourage on a quest to learn sacred bundled knowledge would have stayed on for a time: a year, maybe two, maybe more. They would have participated in the ceremonials inside rounded temples atop circular pyramids overlooking natural lagoons, as at Las Flores, and may well have been invited into the humid tropical interior upriver at a place such as Tamtoc to pay homage to the Huastecan elites and their gods. Upon their departure, they would have taken with them important sacred materials—stones, feathers, seeds, bones, patterns for sacred clothing or daggers, and so on—or copies thereof inside medicine bundles. These materials would have been reanimated back home, used to invoke spirits, predict the future, control the weather, and retell the stories of creation and human origins involving primordial gods named by some Quetzalcoatl or Kukulkan, Tezcatlipoca, Xolotl, Xipe Totec, Tlaltecuhtli, Coatlicue, Coyolxauhqui, and Tlaloc or Chahk.

The whole journey, and so many others like it before and after, might have taken on the cast of a Homeric odyssey, with heroic figures returning not with wealth and trade goods but with visions based on bundled knowledge and universal truths.[9] Back home, that knowledge and those truths might have been secreted away on the altars of temples, to be passed along to subsequent generations of priests and bundle-keepers. And in this way, tradition and oral history were maintained—in actual material packages of substances and things. The stories held within these bundles would be retold through songs, poems, and orations in public ceremonies, animating the imaginations of local farmers. And the truths would be realized back home through the principled designs of new cityscapes, new ritual architecture, new healing ceremonies involving water, steam, and shells, and mythic accounts that place all of the above into a narrative context ultimately derived from Mesoamerica.

★★★

What were those stories?

Among Nahua peoples of Central Mexico, there had been five sequential creations, or "Suns," with the first one inhabited by giants and subsequent creations of human beings sequentially wiped out by storms or floods.[10] Each age was associated with a new Sun, which was subsequently snuffed out and then reborn. In all ages, a great earth mother, Coatlicue, was the source of all life and the mother of the gods. She is depicted in pictorial and sculptural art as headless, with large pendulous breasts, wearing a serpent skirt. Like the original earth monster Tlaltecuhtli (the myths of which overlap), Coatlicue was alternately said to have been slain by Quetzalcoatl and Tezcatlipoca or by a sorceress daughter, the Moon (and sometimes

Milky Way) goddess named Coyolxauhqui, for becoming pregnant with the Aztec Sun god. Before Coatlicue died, she gave birth to the Aztec Sun god (Huitzilopochtli), who was born fully grown and angry. Huitzilopochtli beheaded and dismembered his sister, much as the Moon and night are vanquished by sunlight.

In Aztec lore, Quetzalcoatl and Tezcatlipoca, both bearded gods, were yet said to have created the fifth world from the body of the earth goddess, "sometimes in competition, sometimes in cooperation."[11] These twin or complementary gods, along with other creator gods and siblings Xolotl and Xipe Totec (collectively, the Children of the Sun), variously transformed themselves into serpents or trees to support the new earth or to kill the earth monster deity. Afterward, they descended into the underworld and retrieved the bones of some earlier human beings, who had been wiped out in a flood. In one version of this story from the Mexican state of Oaxaca, the pair of heroes were the sons of a creator god and goddess. One of the hero gods could transform himself into an eagle. The other could change himself into a winged serpent.[12]

As retold among the Quiché Maya, the heroes were twin brothers born to an underworld Moon goddess, named Blood Moon, when she encountered the skull of the father, named One Hunahpu, hanging in a tree in the underworld.[13] One Hunahpu was the Maya personification of the Aztec god Ehecatl-Quetzalcoatl, and one of a pair of brothers who had been killed after losing the Mesoamerican ballgame to the lords of the underworld.[14] When encountered by Blood Moon, the skeletonized head spit into the hand of the maiden and magically impregnated her.

Blood Moon fled, fearing she would be sacrificed by her fellow underworld gods when they discovered her secret pregnancy. While away, she gave birth to twins, and named them Hunahpu (after the father) and Xbalanque. As they grew, the boys, tricksters and monster-slayers extraordinaire, were noticed by the same underworld lords who had killed their father and uncle. The evil lords then also challenged the second-generation twins to a series of contests and ball games, and eventually the boys outmaneuvered and killed the lords of darkness, subsequently reassembling and reanimating the father and making the world safe for humanity.

Similar stories or aspects of them exist across the borderlands to the north of Mesoamerica. They tell of creators and Thunderers, the latter being water spirits from the sky who sometimes took the form of twins and who sometimes were said to be the Children of the Sun or the offspring of a creator god and goddess (if not themselves the creator and his evil twin, a supernatural flint blade or dagger). The female creator was also an Earth or Corn Mother, and her younger sister was the Moon. Invariably, the twins were violent, mischievous, and magical, engaging the other gods—in the Southwest, the Katsinas—in ways reminiscent of a Mesoamerican pantheon.[15]

The traditional Native people of the American Southwest and North Mexico, like those of Mesoamerica, envisioned the emergence of people from the underworld. Among the Zuni, there were four levels or wombs in the underworld, not unlike a typical Mesoamerican notion of four previous creations. It may be no coincidence that the largest masonry or adobe structures of the ancestral Puebloans—from Pueblo Bonito to Paquime—were five stories tall, each story potentially representing one of the creations. And for most Puebloans, the "creator, as far as there is one, is either the Mother who lives underground or mountain-dwelling war spirits, specifically the War Brothers."[16] A Corn Mother deity is common, except among the Uto-Aztecan-speaking Hopi.

The Corn Mother, along with the notion of emergence from the earth, is also common among the Caddo, with certain mounds identified by specific communities as places of emergence, confirming the close historical connections between the Caddo and Pueblo realms. Among the Caddoan-speaking Pawnee, to the north on the Plains, the Corn Mother was closely connected to the feminine character of the Evening Star, the mate of the masculine Morning Star, which is to say the feathered serpent deity Quetzalcoatl.[17] In the Southwest and North Mexico, the Morning Star or his alter ego was a killer of maize: Frost.[18]

A mythical Earth Mother goddess, often seen as an old woman, was also depicted in carved stone and pottery around Greater Cahokia southward into other Mississippian regions. Indeed, across Eastern North America, a mythical old woman had the ability to produce corn from her body. One Cahokian figurine shows her emerging from a funerary casket with outstretched hands, a stalk growing out of each palm. Another carved statuette shows her with large breasts, digging her garden hoe into the back of a great spiral earth serpent, with the resulting vines of gourds growing up and around her back.[19] In narrative accounts of the Cherokee, Muskogee Creek, Natchez, and others, the elderly goddess is said to have produced ears of corn from her body—read, uterus—in a veritable act of birthing.[20] In eleventh- through fourteenth-century pottery art from Missouri, Kentucky, and Tennessee, ceramic bottles that may have been used to store seed corn were often made to look like this bony old woman.[21]

The emergence of people from an underworld is not a common feature of creation narratives or artwork in the Eastern Woodlands, save the heroic acts of a pair of masculine twins in the underworld. However, among the Ho-Chunk and Ioway of the northern Midwest (descendants of Woodland peoples who visited Cahokian shrines at places such as Trempealeau), as well as other Siouan tribes and Caddoans of the eastern Plains and Midwest, origin stories were told in a four-part cycle.[22] These four interconnected narratives appear to be versions of the four primordial Mesoamerican creations as retold by people who lost track of, or chose to modify aspects of, the originals. Among the various northern tribes, as in the final creation of Mesoamerica, the last cycle involved giants vanquished by heroic half-brothers, also called the Children of the Sun, who defeated their enemies in order that human beings might take their place on earth. The Quetzalcoatl, Tezcatlipoca, and other Mesoamerican god parallels—all children of a creator god—are clear.

The supernatural brothers of Ho-Chunk lore were the offspring of the youngest of several demigod brothers from an earlier generation. The youngest brother was known as He-Who-Wears-Human-Heads-as-Earrings. With his name shortened to Human-Head-Earrings by Ioway storytellers, he possessed the power to transform himself into an arrow and to heal with his spittle. He and his oldest brother, Kunu, were often invited on warpaths and to travel in the clouds with thunderbirds. Although they won most challenges against a band of enemy giants, they eventually lost one and were killed, their scalps hung on poles in the enemy village. Fortunately, the sons of Human-Head-Earrings—the hero twins—retrieved the scalps of their father and uncle and resurrected them.[23]

No doubt, the long-nosed god maskettes crafted at Cahokia are the very earpieces worn by the mythical Human-Head-Earrings. Their distribution in the late eleventh and twelfth centuries CE may help to explain the dissemination of this Mesoamerican character across the Plains and Woodlands. There, many myths reference the twin brothers. Like their Mesoamerican counterparts, one is invariably cultured and benevolent, while the other is wild, evil, and dangerous. The latter is sometimes called Thrown-Away, thought by analysts to be named after placental afterbirth, and is usually the character associated with the killing power of flint knives. The good, civilized brother, on the other hand, has healing powers that help people, evident by his ability to spit out mollusk-shell beads. As a pair, they mediate creation, agriculture, and humanity.

Another Mesoamerican-style story, similar to the Ho-Chunk version, was told among the Cherokee and Haudenosaunee (aka Iroquois) peoples of northern Appalachia and New York State. It goes as follows:

> A man and his wife (kanatí, "the hunter," and se·lú, "corn [goddess]") monopolized all of the game and vegetable crops in the world. A son was born to them, and his wild twin was transformed from the thrown-away placenta or from blood. The wild boy was finally captured and the two boys were raised together; the "tame" boy being

> well-behaved, the "wild" boy demonstrating the well-known perversities of the trickster culture hero and taking the lead in their escapades. The twins . . . spied on their mother in the corn house and saw her shaking the corn from her body. The boys, believing that she was tricking them into eating excrement, killed her. When her body was dragged about in the clearing, corn sprang up. . . . The two boys set off in search of their father, who fled to the West when he learned of the death of his wife. In their journey they overcame a number of menaces to humanity, and, finally arriving at their father's abode, assumed their duties as the Thunder[er]s.[24]

Robert Hall has noted that the goddess Selú in the Haudenosaunee account sounds similar to part of the name for a minor Aztec fertility or Corn Goddess, Xilo-nen, a sister of Xipe Totec who sheds her skin like the dried husks of an ear of corn.[25] The corn association continues in another version of the Haudenosaunee story, where

> maize grew from the body of the woman who gave birth to the Creator and his evil-minded twin. This Corn Mother, in turn, was the daughter of a pregnant woman who was let down from heaven, and for whom the earth was formed by the animals (the earth-diver story). The Corn Mother was impregnated by a man from the heavens, who . . . laid a sharp arrow and a blunt arrow on her body, these forming the good and bad brothers. When the twins were ready to be born, the evil-minded one went in the direction of a beam of light, so killing his mother, but the Creator was born naturally. The maize sprang from her body. Flint, the evil-minded brother, and the Creator grew up together, always engaged in struggle. The Creator made man and many useful animals and plants; Flint made carnivorous animals and enemies to man. Finally, the Creator overcame his brother (in the bowl game, according to some variants), and thus ensured the continuance of man and his world. One may note here that the Creator and his brother actually are the twin culture heroes and are equivalents of the Cherokee Thunder[er]s.[26]

These myths are remarkably similar to Mesoamerican stories of creation and emergence. The same elements, characters, meanings, and morals are all here, with some substitutions. There are creator goddesses, masculine twin deities who transform the goddess and save humanity, a journey into mysterious locations, and salvation. No doubt, this is due first and foremost to the fact that these stories originated or were substantially revised in moments of long-distance bundle transfers from Mesoamerica into the Mississippi valley and Eastern Woodlands dating to the Medieval Warm Period.

Secondarily, it is also likely due to the fact that all were rooted in a series of common human experiences. Storms bring needed rain to the people, and yet are accompanied by the terrors of lightening and flooding. The dangers and enemies in this world need to be overcome. Warmth and water allow the maize plants to grow, while cold and frost kills them. Those common experiences affirm historical movements based on visions of danger, violence, medicine, healing, and rebirth. "When a vision comes from the thunder beings of the West," said Oglala Lakota holy man Black Elk, "it comes with terror like a thunder storm; but when the storm of vision has passed, the world is greener and happier."[27] Echoes of these same concerns reverberate in the stories, ceremonies, and images that emerged in the medieval era across the continent. They culminated in the post-Chacoan and post-Cahokian reorientation of Puebloans, Caddos, and Mississippians toward Mexico, exemplified in key rituals of life and death.

The story of the killer Bad Thing among the Avavares, relayed to Cabeza de Vaca in south Texas or Tamaulipas as the embodiment of a flint dagger, was one such echo of a Mesoamerican myth. This bearded, disemboweling being from beneath the earth was likely a local rendition of one of the Toltec-Aztec creator gods, the lord of the dark winds named Tezcatlipoca. And the fact that Cabeza de Vaca, Estevanico, Castillo, and Dorantes—bearded and pale-skinned—fit the description of the mythical Children of the Sun brothers, led by Quetzalcoatl, who were to return from the east and travel west, accounts for the respect given them as healers and their subsequent ability to move uninhibited up along the Rio Grande, across North Mexico and the Southwest, and then south to Culiacan, curing as they went.

Another late-appearing practice described among Caddoan speakers on the Plains, the Arrow Sacrifice, was also an echo of Mesoamerica.[28] As depicted in several central Mexican codices, a woman or a man is tied to a vertical rack, arms and legs splayed out in an X-shape, not unlike the carved rock panel of goddesses known at Monument 32 at Tamtoc. While she or he hung there, the *voladores* would reenact the great spiral storm serpent, the Wind-That-Brings-Rain god Ehecatl-Quetzalcoatl who was also, of course, embodied by marine conch shells. When the flyers touched down, the action shifted back to the rack, where a bowman would shoot the first of a series of arrows into the person tethered there. No doubt it was a medicinal arrow intended to bring about cosmic healing. As drawn in Mesoamerican codices, copied in the 1540s from even earlier Indigenous books, the spectacle was extreme, exciting, and memorable (Figure 12.1).[29] Presumably, the crowd cheered.

Figure 12.1. *Voladores* pole, with framework and ropes, and arrow sacrifice rack. Codex Porfirio Díaz, ca. 1540. Public domain.

This same Mexican arrow ritual sacrifice ended up on the Plains among the Caddo and their Caddoan-speaking cousins to the north, the Pawnee.[30] It had probably been carried north of the US-Mexico border inside a sacred medicine bundle by a Caddo entourage on a quest, perhaps via the Gulf or perhaps along the Indigenous trace later to become El Camino Real de los Tejas. There must have been an earlier journey out of Cahokia as well, since that city's great poles appeared in 1050 CE in association with the ritual sacrifice of children and young maidens. Clearly, we know that Chacoans made pilgrimages south, and that the Hohokam and Mogollon peoples were on the receiving end of materials flowing northward out of Mesoamerica. So, too, did and were the Caddo and Cahokians, if less frequent.

Far from being aspects of common Native lore supposedly diffused slowly over the millennia, these narratives are the rich remains of a series of actual historical linkages between peoples south and north of a so-called sea of Chichimecs. Flint daggers wide at the top and narrow at the base are another. Pole ceremonialism is still another. The imagery of goggle-eyed water spirits, another. The ruins of circular temples to the wind and rain, and their association with seashells, are more. The maize plant itself is yet another.

These remains and more are evidence of the extent to which the Medieval Climatic Anomaly altered the course of North American history between 800 and 1300 CE. In some ways, this alteration was comparable to other parts of the world, where the effects of agricultural production, political reshuffling, religious movements, and long-distance quests and pilgrimages were exacerbated under the warmer weather of the era.

That is, the expansion of cults of Wind-That-Brings-Rain or Thunderer gods in North America shares some political, economic, and demographic attributes with the spread of Christianity, Hinduism, and Islam across Europe, North Africa, and Asia. In Europe and Asia, the medieval warming facilitated agricultural expansion and economic development. Thus, Viking raids and colonies reshaped the political and demographic landscape while agricultural production boomed across the continent and European states to the south began to consolidate. About the same time, starting in the late 700s, South and Southeast Asian empires emerged thanks to global monsoonal changes. Such consolidations and expansions of Old World states and empires, from Europe to Southeast Asia, happened simultaneously with the climate-driven collapse of the Maya and the subsequent climate-induced consolidations of the Toltecs, Huastecs, Pueblos, Caddos, and Mississippians after 800 CE.

But there was something unique about the ontological dimension of human experience or the spirituality of the times in North America. That is, the way Indigenous peoples related to wind, rain, earth, and sky, and all of the moving parts and beings thereof and therein, was different in degree if not kind from the Old World. A substance such as water, with its ability to change physical states and to permeate both air and earth was understood to be infused with spiritual energy, to embody a god such as Tlaloc or Chahk. The earth and its fertility, or the maize plant, was the embodiment of the Aztec goddess Coatlicue, the Mississippian Grandmother or Corn Mother, and the Haudenosaunee goddess Selú. Her daughter was often the Moon who lived in the night sky. The darkness and earth below one's feet was the abode of Tezcatlipoca, Xolotl, Thrown-Away, and Flint or Flint Knife, among others. These were brothers or counterparts of Quetzalcoatl, One Hunahpu, or Human-Head-Earrings. And Quetzalcoatl, or Ehecatl-Quetzalcoatl, was the Wind-That-Brings-Rain (aka Kukulkan), one of the Thunder Beings sometimes to be seen as a sidewinder rattlesnake or a star in the early morning sky.

All of these gods were experienced directly by people as weather, weather-related crops, water-related materials, and celestial phenomena or orbs, such as the Moon. They were not fanciful or abstract beliefs conceptualized only in one's mind. They were real, visible or palpable phenomena that affected the lives of human beings. Corn grew from the body of the great lifegiving goddess. The night-time wind or a chipped-stone dagger was Ehecatl-Tezcatlipoca. The

Evening Star was Xolotl. The Morning Star was Quetzalcoatl, who visited people as Ehecatl-Quetzalcoatl in thunderstorms and hurricanes, come to bring both terror and happiness via much-needed rains to those below. His spirit lived inside mollusk shells and could be heard as the wind in the shell.

Thus, a change in the weather, a dramatic climatic event, or a celestial moment—a maximum or minimum moonrise, an eclipse, or the appearance of a comet or supernova—were the gods intervening in the affairs of people. And people paid attention. Ample rainfall, on the one hand, or droughts, on the other, were direct messages from the gods, led by Ehecatl-Quetzalcoatl or his local cognates. People heard the messages; they recognized the signs; they heeded the rumbled words of distant thunder; they traveled for knowledge to understand what it was they were hearing. In such ways, local weather—played out over the long term as climate—changed the history of people. And climate change, travel, and spirituality were so thickly entangled as to be practically inseparable.

Cabeza de Vaca and his three bearded companions had become enmeshed in this same world after the fact, acting as intermediaries for the meaningful Native exchanges of ocean shells and flint while healing the sick, attaining the status of the mythical Children of the Sun creator lords as they traveled west. Perhaps they too, having walked out of the ancient world somewhere in Nuevo Galicia back to Mexico City, had begun to understand something that we have long since overlooked.

Margaret Mead proclaimed that a "small group of committed citizens can change the world." But she was only partially correct to conclude, by extension, that "it's the only thing that ever has." Cabeza de Vaca might have better understood, in the end, a truth that the Indigenous history of medieval America teaches, and which Mead overlooked. People were not distinct from water, wind, earth, other beings, and the physical experience of the world. Myth was not always distinct from historical events. And climate change was not simply something that happened *to* people.

Rather, across North America, history swirled around medieval climatic shifts like the wind in a conch shell. If you listen carefully, you can still hear it. The atmosphere and the people were one and, so, climate happened through people, and climate history was human history. It's the central lesson of America's medieval period and its gods of thunder, from the Maya westward into Central Mexico, northward into the American Southwest and Southern Plains and, finally, up the Mississippi.

Glossary

WITH INDIGENOUS WORD PRONUNCIATIONS

Acoma (a'-kō-ma), pueblo in New Mexico.

Actun Tunichil Muknal (ak-tün' tü-nēsh'-ēl mük-nal'), a Maya ritual cave in Belize.

Ahuitzotl (a-wēt'-zot^{l}), Aztec emperor before Moctezuma II.

Alta Vista, Epiclassic site in Zacatecas.

Altiplano, North and West Mexico's high plains.

Alvarado, Pedro de, primary subcommander under Cortés.

American Bottom, named 150-mile-long stretch of Mississippi River floodplain adjacent to St. Louis, Missouri.

Anasazi (a-na-sa'-zē), generic term for Puebloan and Navajo "ancient ones."

Apalachee (a-pa-la'-chē), Mississippian ethnicity and town site in northwestern Florida.

Arapaho (a-ra'-pa-hō), Algonkian-speaking Plains tribal nation.

Arikara (a-rē'-kar-a), Caddoan-speaking Plains tribal nation.

Atl-atl (at^{l}'-at^{l}), spearthrowing stick.

Aute (a-ü'-tā), village of Indians in La Florida encounted by Narváez.

Avavares (a-va-var'-ās), forager Indian band encountered by Narváez expedition survivors in south Texas or northern Tamaulipas.

Axis mundi, the point where vertical order meets horizontal order.

Aztec (az'-tek), ruins, a misnamed Puebloan great house complex in Colorado.

Aztecs (az'-teks), also known as the Mexica, Chichimec group who migrated into Central Mexico and founded empire.

Bajo, shallow pit or sinkhole that fills with water.

Bejucal (bā-hü-kal'), Classic Maya city that shows Teotihuacan influences.

Belize, nation-state in the Yucatan.

Black Drink, caffeinated tea made from the yaupon holly.

Cabeza de Vaca, Álvar Núñez, survivor of the Narváez expedition.

Caddo (ka'-dō), tribal nations and language family originally in Texas, Lousiana, Oklahoma, and southwest Arkansas.

Caddo Mounds State Historic Site, southern Caddo site on the Neches River and the old Spanish road into Mexico. Also called George C. Davis site.

Cahokia (ka-hō'-kē-a), largest, earliest Mississippian site, major precinct of an urban complex also known as Cahokia.

Calakmul (ka-lak-mül'), Classic Maya city.

Calixtlahuaca (Ka-lish-tla-hwa'-ka), Postclassic city west of Tenochtitlan.

Caracol (ka-ra-kōl'), Classic Maya city.

Carson Mounds, large Mississippian mounded complex in the Delta of northwestern Mississippi.

Casa Grande, also known as the Grewe site, Classic Hohokam town in Arizona.

Casa Rinconada, great kiva in the middle of Chaco Canyon.

Casas Grandes, precontact culture associated with Paquime in Chihuahua.

Castillo Maldonado, Alonso del, survivor of the Narváez expedition.

Ceboruco, volcano in West Mexico.

Cenote, water-filled limestone cavern with a collapsed roof.

Chacmool, pre-Hispanic stone altar carved in humanoid shape.

Chaco, Puebloan cultural phenomenon centered on Chaco Canyon.

Chahk (chak), Maya water or rain deity, counterpart to Aztecs' Tlaloc.

Chalchihuites (chal-chē-hwē'-tēs), a regional culture that subsumes the Alta Vista and La Quemada sites in Zacatecas.

Chalchiuhtilcue (chal-chē-ü-tēl'-kwü), goddess of groundwater among the Aztecs, feminine counterpart to Tlaloc.

Cherry Valley, mound site on Crowley's Ridge in northeastern Arkansas.

Chetro Ketl, Chaco Canyon great house.

Cheyenne (shī-en'), Algonkian-speaking Plains tribal nation.

Chiapas, state in Mexico.

Chichen Itza (chē'-chen ēt'-za), Postclassic Maya city in the Yucatan.

Chichimec (chē'-chi-mek), generic Indigenous North Mexican cultural identity.

Chihuahua, state in Mexico.

Chimney Rock, Chaco great house in Colorado.

Coahuila, state in Mexico.

Coahuiltecan (kō-a-hwēl-tek'-an), group of Indigenous forager bands in Texas.

Coatlicue (kō-at'-lē-kyü), Aztec grandmother goddess of agricultural fertility and serpents.

Colima, state in Mexico.

Conquistador, group of elite Spanish men who conquered Native peoples.

Copan (kō-pan'), Classic Maya city in Guatemala that shows Teotihuacan influences.

Coronado, Francisco Vázquez de, principal conquistador of the American Southwest.

Cortés, Hernán, principal conquistador of Mexico.

Coyolxauhqui (kōy-ōl-shaw'-kē), daughter of Aztec goddess Coatlicue associated with the Moon.

Crenshaw, Caddo town on the Red River, southwest Arkansas.

Crow (krō), Siouan-speaking northern Plains tribal nation.

Crowley's Ridge, 150-mile long, 200- to 500-foot-high Miocene-age landform that bows across southeast Missouri and northeast Arkansas.

Cuauhtemoc (kwa-ü-tā'-mōk), last Aztec king, ruled for a short period during the conquest.

Cuéllar, Diego Velázquez de, governor of Cuba at time of conquest.

Cuicuilco (kwē-kwēl'-kō), Preclassic city in Central Mexico.

Culiacan (kü'-lē-a-kan), coastal colonial city in northwestern Mexico.

De Soto, Hernando, principal conquistador of the American Southeast.

Dorantes, Andrés, survivor of the Narváez expedition.

Driftless Area, a 24,000-square-mile area left unglaciated during the Pleistocene.

Ehecatl (ā-hā'-kat^{l}), Nahuatl name for Mesoamerican god of wind.

Ehecatl-Quetzalcoatl (ā-hā'-kat^{l} ket-zal-kō'-at^{l}), Nahuatl name for combined Wind-That-Brings-Rain or storm god.

Ehecatl-Tezcatlipoca (ā-hā'-kat^{l} tesh-kat-lē-pō'-ka), Nahuatl name for combined night-wind god.

El Camino Real de los Tejas, the royal road from Mexico City through Texas.

El Caracol, gastropod-shell-shaped circular monument at Chichen Itza.

El Castillo, the Temple of Kukulkan at Chichen Itza.

El Mixtón, fortified cliff where resistant Altiplano warriors jumped to their deaths.

El Niño, period every three to five years when ocean surface water heats above average in the equatorial Pacific.

Emerald Mound (of Illinois), Cahokian shrine complex of twelve circular and square mounds.

Encomienda (ān-kō-mē-ān'-da), a forced labor system based on estates awarded to conquistadores.

Estevanico the Moor, black slave of Dorantes, also known as Esteban de Dorantes or Mustafa Azemmouri.

Fajada Butte, the large pillar-shaped mesa in the middle of Chaco Canyon.

Fourche Maline, pre-Caddo cultural complex.

George C. Davis site, *see* Caddo Mounds State Historic Site.

Gilmore Corridor, the open coastal plain between Texas and Mexico.

Grijalva, Juan de, Spanish conquistador who explored the Gulf Coast of Mexico.

Guachimontónes, circular mounds or pyramids in West Mexico.

Guzmán, Nuño Beltrán de, ruthless administrator of Nuevo Galicia.

Hasinai (has'-i-nī), a Caddo tribe or ethnicity.

Hawikuh (ha'-wi-kyü), one of the Zuni pueblos.

Heháka Sápa, also known as Black Elk, Lakota holy man.

Hidalgo, state in Mexico.

Hidatsa (hi-dat'-sa), Siouan-speaking Plains tribal nation.

Ho-Chunk (hō'-chunk), Siouan-speaking tribal nation.

Hohokam, precontact agricultural peoples of southern Arizona.

Hopi (hō'-pē), Uto-Aztecan-speaking Puebloan people.

Huastec (hwas'-tek), northeastern Mesoamericans.

Huasteca (hwas-tek'-a), Mesoamerican cultural region centered in San Luis Potosí, Mexico.

Huitzilopochtli (hwētz-lē-pōch'-tlē), Aztec Sun god.

Hunahpu (hün'-a-pü), Maya hero, son of One Hunahpu.

Inipi (i-nē'-pē), Lakota sweat lodge ritual.

Ioway (Ī'-ō-wā), Chiwerean-Siouan-speaking tribal nation.

Ixtlan del Río, Postclassic site near Ceburco volcano, West Mexico.

Jalisco, state in Mexico.

Kadohadacho (ka-dō-ha-da'-kō), a Caddo tribe or ethnicity.

Katsina (kat-sē'-na), religious movement in late Ancestral Puebloan society.

Kin Kletso (kēn klet'-sō), late Chacoan great house with kiva built atop fossiliferous rock.

Kuaua (kwa'-wā), late pueblo visited by Coronado.

Kukulkan (kü-kül-kan'), Maya cognate of Ehecatl-Quetzalcoatl.

Kunu (kü'-nü), brother of Human-Head-Earrings among the Ioway and Ho-Chunk.

La Noche Triste, night of sorrows, when Cortés and his army were nearly defeated while escaping Tenochtitlan.

La Quemada, Epiclassic site in Zacatecas.

Lakota (la-kō-ta), Siouan-speaking Plains tribal nation.

Las Flores, Huastecan site in Tampico, Mexico.

Looking Glass Prairie, expanse of tall grass prairie in Illinois visited by Charles Dickens.

Los Guachimontónes (lōs hwa-chē-mōn-tō'nās), largest of circular mound sites in West Mexico.

Maize, corn.

Maya (mī'-ya), the people and culture of the Yucatan and surrounding highlands.

Mayan (mī'-yan), the language of the Maya.

Mexica (me-shē'-ka), Aztec ethnicity.

Miami (mī-a'-ma), Algonkian-speaking tribal nation.

Missouria (mi-sör'-ē-a), Chiwerean-Siouan-speaking tribal nation.

Moctezuma II (mōk-tā-zō'-ma), Aztec ruler when Cortés entered Tenochtitlan. Also called Motecuhzoma Xocoyotzin.

Mogollon (mu-ga-yōn'), major culture area of the American Southwest.

Monks Mound, Cahokia's principal pyramid.

Nahuatl (na'-hwat[l]), language of the Aztecs.

Narváez, Pánfilo de, brutal would-be conquistador of La Florida.

Navajo (na'-va-hō), non-Puebloan Athapaskan-speaking peoples in the Great Basin and Southwest. Also called Diné.

Nayarit, state in Mexico.

Neches, river in central Texas.

O'odham (ō-ō-dam'), Indigenous peoples descended from the Hohokam.

Olid, Cristóbal de, one of Cortés's subcommanders.

Oñate, Juan de, brutal conquistador of the Southwest.

One Hunahpu (hün'-a-pü), Maya personification of the Aztec god Ehecatl-Quetzalcoatl, comparable to the Ioway and Ho-Chunk character Human-Head-Earrings.

Osage (ō-sāj'), Dhegihan-Siouan-speaking tribal nation.

Otoe (Ō'-tō), Chiwerean-Siouan-speaking tribal nation.

Ouachita Mountains (wash'-i-taw), low range in Arkansas.

Pánuco, river that flows to the Gulf from Huasteca and Central Mexico.

Paquime, urban pueblo at the core of the Casas Grandes, Chihuahua, Mexico.

Pawnee (paw-nē'), Caddoan-speaking Plains tribal nation(s).

Peñasco Blanco, Chaco Canyon great house.

Peoria (pē-or'-ē-a). Algonkian-speaking tribal nation in the Midwest.

Picuris (pi-kyur'-ē), pueblo in the Southwest.

Ponca (pon'-ka), Dhegihan-Siouan-speaking tribal nation in the Midwest.

Popocatepetl (pō-pō-ka-te'-pet[l]), volcano rimming the Valley of Mexico.

Potawatomi (po-ta-wa'-tō-mē), Algonkian-speaking tribal nation.

Pueblo Alto, Chaco Canyon great house.

Pueblo Bonito, Chaco Canyon great house.

Pueblo del Arroyo, Chaco Canyon great house with a tri-walled kiva.

Puebloan, culture area consisting of multiple organized towns and languages.

Quapaw (kwa'-pa), Dhegihan-Siouan-speaking tribal nation in the Midwest and Mid-South.

Quetzalcoatl (ket-zal-kō'-at^{l}), Nahuatl name for the principal Wind-That-Brings-Rain deity of the Epiclassic and Postclassic Mesoamerican world.

Quivira, legendary city sought by Coranado in the Great Plains.

Ramey, type of knife, scroll, and pottery associated with Cahokia.

Ridge Ruin, a Sinagua ruin south of Wupatki.

Rio Azul, Classic Maya city that shows Teotihuacan influences.

Sacbe (sak'-bā), Maya elevated causeway or road.

Salado, post-Chaco movement featuring early Katsina-style motifs on polychrome pots.

San Luis Potosí, state in Mexico.

Sand Canyon, a Pueblo III site in Colorado.

Selú (sā-loó), Haudenosaunee goddess of maize.

Sierra Madre, ranges of mountains running through Mexico.

Sihyaj K'ahk (sē-yazh k-ak), Teotihuacan emperor commemorated at Tikal. Also called Fire Born.

Sinaloa, state in Mexico.

Snaketown, a Colonial- and Sedentary-period Hohokam town.

Sonora, state in Mexico.

Spiro, northern Caddo mounded complex.

Tamaulipas, state in Mexico.

Tampico, modern city at the mouth of the Pánuco River.

Tampaon, river that runs through Tamtoc into the Pánuco.

Tamtoc, large Huastecan urban settlement.

Taos (taös), contemporary pueblo in northern New Mexico.

Tecpatl (tāk'-pat^{l}), Postclassic central Mexican chipped-stone dagger with an elongate, double-edged form, wide at the top with a needle-like tip.

Téenek (tē'-e-nēk), Maya-speaking Huastecans.

Tenochtítlan (tā-nōsh-tēt'-lan), Aztec capital city in Lake Texcoco.

Teocentli (tā-ō-sen'-tlē), wild grass ancestor of maize.

Teotihuacan (tā-ō-tē-hwa'-kan), Classic-period imperial city in Central Mexico.

Tequila, volcano in West Mexico from which the alcoholic drink takes its name.

Teuchitlan (tā-ü-shēt'-lan), Classic-period culture area in West Mexico associated with *guachimotónes*.

Texcoco (tesh-kō'-kō), lake in the middle of the Valley of Mexico on which was built Tenochtitlan.

Tezcatlipoca (tesh-kat-lē-pō'-ka), Aztec creator god and underworld lord of nighttime winds, associated with black obsidian glass.

Thebes Gap, a constriction in the Mississippi River south of Cape Girardeau formed where the water pushes through Miocene deposits.

Thule (tü'-lā), ancestral Inuit Arctic peoples.

Tikal (tē-kal'), large Preclassic and Classic Maya city in Guatemala.

Tiwanaku (tē-wa-na'-kü), Middle Horizon city near Lake Titicaca in the Bolivian Andes.

Tlaloc (tla'-lōk), primeval Aztec god of rain and water.

Tlaltecuhtli (tla-tā-kü'-tlē), monstrous earth being of the Aztecs present at the very beginning.

Tlatelolco (tla-tā-lōl'-cō), sister city to and later suburb of Tenochtitlan.

Tlililtzin (tlē-lēlt'-zēn), psychoactive morning-glory-based beverage.

Tollan (tō-lan'), mythical city of origins for Aztecs and other Mesoamericans.

Toltec (tōl'-tek), Epiclassic and Postclassic people associated with Tula and Central Mexico before the Aztecs.

Toltec site, misnamed Late Woodland cultural site in Arkansas.

Topiltzin (tō-pēlt-zēn'), legendary king of the Toltecs.

Trempealeau, northern Cahokian shrine complex in western Wisconsin.

Tsah Neeshi (tsa nēsh'-ē), Caddo term for local ruler, meaning Lord Moon.

Tula (tü'-la), primary city of the Toltecs, in Hidalgo.

Tzompantli (zōm-pan'-tlē), Aztec name for a rack of human skulls.

Uaxactun (Wa-shak-tün'), Classic Maya city that shows Teotihuacan influences.

Umiak (ü'-mē-ak), large ocean-going whale-hunting boat of the Arctic.

Uto-Aztecan, language family that includes Nahuatl in the south to Hopi in the north.

Veracruz, state in Mexico.

Voladore, human acrobatic flyer associated with pole ceremonialism in Mexico.

Wakan (wa-kan'), Lakota name for holy or spiritual power.

Wakan-Tanka (wa'-kan tan'-ka), Lakota name for Great Spirit.

Wari, Middle Horizon city in Peru.

Wichita (wi'-chi-taw), Caddoan-speaking Plains tribal nation.

Wupatki (wü-pat'-kē), Sinagua great house complex in northern Arizona.

Xbalanque (Shba-lan'-kā), brother of Maya hero Hunahpu.

Xilo-nen (shē-lō'-nen), Aztec corn goddess, sister of Xipe Totec.

Xipe Totec (shē'-pā tō'-tec), Aztec god associated with rebirth and flayed skins of sacrificial victims.

Xitle (shēt'-lā), volcano in Central Mexico near Cuicuilco.

Xochimilco (sō-chē-mēl'-kō), suburb of Tenochtitlan famous for its waterways and floating gardens.

Xolotl (shō'-lōt[l]), anthropomorphized canine god of death and lord of the underworld among the Aztecs, an alter ego of Quetzalcoatl.

Xunantunich (shü-nan-tü-nēk'), Classic Maya city in the Yucatan.

Yax Ku'k Mó (yash kük mō'), ruler of Copan who modeled himself after Tlaloc and Teotihuacan rulers.

Yax Nuun Ahiin (yash nü-ün ahē-ēn), vassal of Sihyaj K'ahk installed at Tikal. Also called Curl Snout.

Yucatan, peninsula shared by Mexico, Belize, and Guatemala.

Yupqoyvi (yüp-kōi-vē), Hopi term for Place Beyond the Horizon, or Chaco Canyon.

Zacatecas, state in Mexico.

Zócalo, plaza in the middle of a Mexican city, including Mexico City.

Zuni (zü'-nē), colonial and contemporary pueblo and people in east-central New Mexico.

Notes

PRELIMS

1. Hall, Robert L. 2012. "Some Commonalities Linking North America and Mesoamerica." In *The Oxford Handbook of North American Archaeology*, edited by Timothy R. Pauketat, pp. 52–63. Oxford: Oxford University Press.

INTRODUCTION

1. Fagan, Brian. 2008. *The Great Warming: Climate Change and the Rise and Fall of Civilizations.* New York: Bloomsbury. Mann, Michael E., Zhihua Zhang, Scott Rutherford, Raymond S. Bradley, Malcolm K. Hughes, Drew Shindell, Caspar Ammann, Greg Faluvegi, and Fenbiao Ni. 2009. "Global Signatures and Dynamical Origins of the Little Ice Age and Medieval Climate Anomaly." *Science* 326: 1256–1260. https://doi.org/10.1126/science.1177303.
2. Lieberman, Benjamin, and Elizabeth Gordon. 2018. *Climate Change in Human History: Prehistory to the Present.* London: Bloomsbury Academic.
3. Lieberman and Gordon, *Climate Change*, pp. 83–84.
4. Helms, Mary W. 1988. *Ulysses' Sail: An Ethnographic Odyssey of Power, Knowledge, and Geographical Distance.* Princeton, NJ: Princeton University Press.
5. Lieberman and Gordon, *Climate Change.*
6. Janusek, John W. 2008. *Ancient Tiwanaku.* Cambridge: Cambridge University Press.
7. Arnold, Jeanne E., and Michael R. Walsh, 2010. *California's Ancient Past: From the Pacific to the Range of Light.* Washington, DC: Society for American Archaeology Press.
8. Maschner, Herbert D. G. 2012. "Archaeology of the Northwest Coast." In *The Oxford Handbook of North American Archaeology*, edited by Timothy R. Pauketat, pp. 160–172. Oxford: Oxford University Press. Prentiss,

Anna Marie, and Ian Kuijt. 2012. *People of the Middle Fraser Canyon: An Archaeological History.* Vancouver: University of British Columbia Press.

CHAPTER 1

1. Sahagún, Fray Bernardino de. 1981. *Florentine Codex: General History of the Things of New Spain, Book 1—The Gods.* 2nd ed. Translated by Arthur J. O. Anderson and Charles E. Dibble. Salt Lake City: School of American Research and University of Utah Press.
2. The language of the Aztec (or Mexica) people of central Mexico is known as Nahuatl. Typically, in Nahuatl, the penultimate syllable is accented, as in Teotihuacan (pronounced Tā-ō-tē-hwæ′-kæn), Tenochtítlan (Tā-nōsh-tēt′-læn), Ehécatl (Ā-hā′-căt^{l}), or Quetzalcóatl (Ket-zæl-kō′-ăt^{l}). The "l" sound at the end of the final syllable (-atl, -otl) of some words such as Ehécatl, Quetzalcóatl, or Náhuatl is meant to end the word with the tongue on the roof of the mouth. Knowing this, and to avoid confusion with Spanish accent patterns (which often place emphasis on the final syllables in place names), I will not add accent marks above the penultimate syllables of Nahuatl words throughout the rest of the book.
3. Sahagún, *Florentine Codex.*
4. Olivier, Guilhem. 2014. "Enemy Brothers or Divine Twins? A Comparative Approach Between Tezcatlipoca and Quetzalcoatl, Two Major Deities from Ancient Mexico." In *Tezcatlipoca: Trickster and Supreme Deity*, edited by Elizabeth Baquedano, pp. 59–82. Boulder: University of Colorado Press.
5. Reuters, "Ancient Aztec Temple and Ball Court Unearthed in Heart of Mexico City," *The Guardian*, June 8, 2017, https://www.theguardian.com/world/2017/jun/08/mexico-city-ancient-aztec-temple-ball-court.
6. Guilliem Arroyo, Salvador. 1999. *Ofrendas a Ehécatl-Quetzalcóatl en Mexico-Tlatelolco: Proyecto Tlatelolco, 1987–1996.* Serie Arqueología. México, DF: Instituto Nacional de Antropología e Historia.
7. Pauketat, Timothy R. 2009. *Cahokia: Ancient America's Great City on the Mississippi.* New York: Viking-Penguin.
8. Pepper, George H., and Gilbert L. Wilson. 1974. *An Hidatsa Shrine and the Beliefs Respecting It.* American Anthropological Association Memoir 2. Millwood, NY: Kraus.
9. DiPeso, Charles C. 1974. *Casas Grandes: A Fallen Trading Center of the Gran Chichimeca.* 3 vols. Dragoon and Flagstaff, AZ: Amerind Foundation

and Northland Press. Minnis, Paul E., and Michael E. Whalen, eds. 2015. *Ancient Paquimé and the Casas Grandes World*. Tucson: University of Arizona Press. Mathiowetz, Michael D. 2011. "The Diurnal Path of the Sun: Ideology and Interregional Interaction in Ancient Northwest Mesoamerica and the American Southwest." PhD dissertation, Department of Anthropology, University of California, Riverside. Pitezel, Todd A. 2011. "From Archaeology to Ideology in Northwest Mexico: Cerro de Moctezuma in the Casas Grandes Ritual Landscape." PhD dissertation, Department of Anthropology, University of Arizona. Swanson, Steven. 2003. "Documenting Prehistoric Communication Networks: A Case Study in the Paquime Polity." *American Antiquity* 68: 753–767.

10. Whalen, Michael E. 2013. "Wealth, Status, Ritual, and Marine Shell at Casas Grandes, Chihuahua, Mexico." *American Antiquity* 78, no. 4: 624–639.
11. López Austin, Alfredo, and Leonardo López Luján. 2000. "The Myth and Reality of Zuyúa: The Feathered Serpent and Mesoamerican Transformations from the Classic to the Postclassic." In *Mesoamerica's Classic Heritage: From Teotihuacán to the Aztecs*, edited by David Carrasco, Lindsay Jones, and Scott Sessions, pp. 21–84. Boulder: University Press of Colorado.
12. Reilly, F. Kent, III. 2007. "The Petaloid Motif: A Celestial Symbolic Locative in the Shell Art of Spiro." In *Ancient Objects and Sacred Realms*, edited by F. Kent Reilly III and James F. Garber, pp. 39–55. Austin: University of Texas Press.
13. Hall, Robert L. 1997. *An Archaeology of the Soul: Native American Indian Belief and Ritual*. Urbana: University of Illinois Press, p. 163. Lankford, George E. 2007. *Reachable Stars: Patterns in the Ethnoastronomy of Eastern North America*. Tuscaloosa: University of Alabama Press, p. 253.
14. Kerouac, Jack. 2007. *On the Road: The Original Script*. New York: Penguin, pp. 391, 396.
15. Mauss, Marcel. 1985. "The Category of the Human Mind: The Notion of Person; the Notion of Self." Translated by W. D. Halls. In *The Category of the Person: Anthropology, Philosophy, History*, edited by Michael Carrithers, Steven Collins, and Steven Lukes, pp. 1–45. Cambridge: Cambridge University Press. Strathern, Marilyn. 1988. *The Gender of the Gift: Problems with Women and Problems with Society in Melanesia*. Berkeley: University of Califorina Press. Deloria, Vine, Jr. 2003. *God Is Red: A Native View of Religion*. Golden, CO: Fulcrum.
16. Alt, Susan M., and Timothy R. Pauketat, eds. 2019. *New Materialisms Ancient Urbanisms*. New York: Routledge.

17. Pauketat, Timothy R. 2013. *An Archaeology of the Cosmos: Rethinking Agency and Religion in Ancient America.* London: Routledge.
18. Lieberman, Benjamin, and Elizabeth Gordon. 2018. *Climate Change in Human History: Prehistory to the Present.* London: Bloomsbury Academic. The state has been defined differently by various researchers, and there are clear distinctions between the states of Europe, Asia, and Africa and those of the Americas. The important qualities that all share include the development of governmental bodies that administer territories larger than natal communities, if not multiple communities, which significantly alter the social identities and cultural practices of the people who comprise them.
19. Lekson, Stephen H. 2008. *A History of the Ancient Southwest.* Santa Fe, NM: School for Advanced Research Press, p. 8.
20. Helms, Mary W. 1988. *Ulysses' Sail: An Ethnographic Odyssey of Power, Knowledge, and Geographical Distance.* Princeton, NJ: Princeton University Press.
21. Today's US-Mexico border has most definitely been an impediment to the telling of this big, preconquest, pan-American story. In part this is because the international political border has hardened into a language barrier and, with it, an invisible cultural and publication-distribution wall. That wall keeps Mexican presses from circulating their Spanish-language books to the north, and vice versa. There are even separate professional journals and text books for Mesoamerica, which is part of North America, and North America north of the Chihuahua desert.
22. VanPool, Christine S., and Todd L. VanPool. 2007. *Signs of Casas Grandes Shamans.* Salt Lake City: University of Utah Press.

CHAPTER 2

1. Diaz, Bernal, 1963 *The Conquest of New Spain.* Translated by J. M. Cohen. New York: Penguin, p. 215.
2. Diaz, *Conquest*, p. 282.
3. "Álvar Núñez Cabeza de Vaca: Pioneer Historian, Ethnologist, Physician." Center for the Study of the Southwest, Texas State University. https://www.txstate.edu/cssw/research-and-programming/cdvresources/windows/pionhist.html. Accessed November 27, 2020.
4. Cabeza de Vaca, Álvar Núñez. 2002. *Chronicle of the Narváez Expedition.* Translated by Fanny Bandelier and Harold Augenbraum. New York: Penguin, p. 68.

5. Hassig, Ross. 2006. *Mexico and the Spanish Conquest.* Norman: University of Oklahoma Press.
6. Carson, David. 2018. *The Account of Cabeza De Vaca: A Literal Translation with Analysis and Commentary.* Friendswood, TX: Living Water Specialties.
7. Cabeza de Vaca, Álvar Núñez. 2002. *Chronicle of the Narváez Expedition.* Translated by Fanny Bandelier and Harold Augenbraum. New York: Penguin, p. 61.
8. "Artifacts, Archaeology, and Cabeza de Vaca in Southern Texas and Northeastern Mexico." Center for the Study of the Southwest, Texas State University. Accessed November 27, 2020. https://www.txstate.edu/cssw/research-and-programming/cdvresources/windows/artifactarch.html.
9. Almere Read, Kay, and Jason J. Gonzolez. 2000. *Mesoamerican Mythology: A Guide to the Gods, Heroes, Rituals, and Beliefs of Mexico and Central America.* Oxford: Oxford University Press.
10. Cabeza de Vaca, *Chronicle*, pp. 60–61.
11. "Caddoan" is usually used to describe the languages and peoples (such as the Pawnee, Wichita, and Arikara) historically related to but distinct from the Caddo languages and the settled agricultural peoples of southeastern Oklahoma, southwestern Arkansas, and northeastern Texas.

CHAPTER 3

1. LeBrun, David, dir. 2008. *Breaking the Maya Code: The 200-Year Quest to Decipher the Hieroglyphs of the Ancient Maya.* Night Fire Films, in association with Arte France (www.nightfirefilms.org).
2. Lentz, David L., Nicholas P. Dunning, and Vernon L. Scarborough, eds. 2015. *Tikal: Paleoecology of an Ancient Maya City.* Cambridge: Cambridge University Press.
3. Fletcher, Roland. 2009. "Low-Density, Agrarian-Based Urbanism: A Comparative View." *Insights (Institute of Advanced Study, Durham)* 2, no. 4: 2–19.
4. Martin, Simon, and Nikolai Grube. 2008. *Chronicle of the Maya Kings and Queens.* 2nd ed. London: Thames and Hudson. Stuart, David. 2002. "'The Arrival of Strangers': Teotihuacan and Tollan in Classic Maya History." In *Mesoamerica's Classic Heritage: From Teotihuacan to the Aztecs,* edited by David Carrasco, Lindsay Jones, and Scott Sessions, pp. 465–513. Boulder, CO: Westview Press.
5. Martin, Simon. 2003. "In Line of the Founder: A View of Dynastic Politics at Tikal." In *Tikal: Dynasties, Foreigners, and Affairs of State*, edited

by Jeremy A. Sabloff, pp. 3–45. Santa Fe, NM: School of American Research Press, p. 12. See also Houston, Stephen D., and Takeshi Inomata. 2009. *The Classic Maya*. Cambridge: Cambridge University Press, pp. 106–108.

6. These Maya realms never unified. The K'iché Maya hated their Maya neighbors to the west; the Kaqchikel Maya were at war with the Tz'utujil Maya; and the Pipil Maya were organized into a number of separate provinces that took Alvarado's central-Mexican Indian army years to vanquish. Indeed, the area around Tikal wasn't conquered entirely until 1697. Being Maya, in other words, did not translate into political unity.
7. Alberti, Benjamin. 2016. "Archaeologies of Ontology." *Annual Review of Anthropology* 45: 163–179. Viveiros de Castro, Eduardo. 2004. "Exchanging Perspectives: The Transformation of Objects into Subjects in Amerindian Ontologies." *Common Knowledge* 10, no. 3: 463–484.
8. Stephens, John Lloyd. 1996. *Incidents of Travel in Central America, Chiapas, and Yucatan*. Originally published 1843. Washington, DC: Smithsonian Institution Press, p. 217.
9. Lucero, Lisa J. 2006. *Water and Ritual: The Rise and Fall of Classic Maya Rulers*. Austin: University of Texas Press, p. 186.
10. Lucero, Lisa J., and Sherry A. Gibbs. 2007. "The Creation and Sacrifice of Witches in Classic Maya Society." In *New Perspectives on Human Sacrifice and Ritual Body Treatments in Ancient Maya Society*, edited by V. Tiesler and A. Cucina, pp. 45–73. New York: Springer.

CHAPTER 4

1. Ekholm, Gordon F. 1944. *Excavations at Tampico and Panuco in the Huasteca, Mexico*. Anthropological Papers of the American Museum of Natural History, volume 38, part 5. New York: American Museum of Natural History, p. 502.
2. Widely attributed to Margaret Mead, source unknown.
3. Ahern, Maureen. 2007. "Martyrs and Idols: Performing Ritual Warfare on Early Missionary Frontiers in the Northwest." In *Religion in New Spain*, edited by Susan Schroeder and C. M. Stafford Poole, pp. 279–298. Albuquerque: University of New Mexico Press. Altman, Ida. 2010. *The War for Mexico's West: Indians and Spaniards in New Galicia, 1524–1550*. Albuquerque: University of New Mexico Press.
4. Child, Mark B. 2006. "The Archaeology of Religious Movements: The Maya Sweatbath Cult of Piedras Negras." PhD dissertation, Yale University.

5. Harrison-Buck, Eleanor. 2012. "Architecture as Animate Landscape: Circular Shrines in the Ancient Maya Lowlands." *American Anthropologist* 114, no. 1: 64–80.
6. McAnany, Patricia A. 2012. "Terminal Classic Maya Heterodoxy and Shrine Vernacularism in the Sibun Valley, Belize." *Cambridge Archaeological Journal* 22, no. 1: 115–134.
7. Zaragoza Ocaña, Diana. 2015. "The Maya Presence in the Huastec Region: An Archaeological Perspective." In *The Huasteca: Culture, History, and Interregional Exchange*, edited by Katherine A. Faust and Kim N. Richter, pp. 59–74. Norman: University of Oklahoma Press.
8. Robertson, John, and Stephen D. Houston. 2015. "The Huastec Problem: A Linguistic and Archaeological Perspective." In *The Huasteca: Culture, History, and Interregional Exchange*, edited by Katherine A. Faust and Kim N. Richter, pp. 19–36. Norman: University of Oklahoma Press.
9. In fact, the Cortés expedition's Bernal Díaz del Castillo, as well as Christopher Columbus and Columbus's son, Ferdinand, all described native dugout canoes and pirogues with paddles and perhaps sails navigating the waters of the Gulf of Mexico and Caribbean between Hispaniola, Cuba, and the Yucatan in the late 1400s and early 1500s. Ferdinand stopped one large Maya dugout in 1502, piled full of cargo, and discovered cacao, the bean used to make chocolate, previously unknown to the Spanish.
10. Hester, Thomas R. 2004. "The Prehistory of South Texas." In *The Prehistory of Texas*, edited by Timothy K. Perttula, pp. 127–151. College Station: Texas A&M University Press.
11. Kubler, George. 1962. *The Art and Architecture of Ancient America: The Mexican, Maya and Andean Peoples.* New York: Penguin.
12. Kubler, *Art and Architecure*, 220–222.
13. Kubler, *Art and Architecure*, 220–222.
14. Olivier, Guilhem. 2014. "Enemy Brothers or Divine Twins? A Comparative Approach Between Tezcatlipoca and Quetzalcoatl, Two Major Deities from Ancient Mexico." In *Tezcatlipoca: Trickster and Supreme Deity*, edited by Elizabeth Baquedano, pp. 59–82. Boulder: University of Colorado Press.
15. Nicholson, H. B. 2001. *Topiltzin Quetzalcoatl: The Once and Future Lord of the Toltecs.* Boulder: University of Colorado Press.
16. López Austin, Alfredo, and Leonardo López Luján. 2000. "The Myth and Reality of Zuyúa: The Feathered Serpent and Mesoamerican Transformations from the Classic to the Postclassic." In *Mesoamerica's Classic Heritage: From Teotihuacán to the Aztecs*, edited by David Carrasco,

Lindsay Jones, and Scott Sessions, pp. 21–84. Boulder: University Press of Colorado.

17. That said, one study in the La Quemada region has shown that aridity does not seem to have been the cause of either the rise or fall of this par ticular center. See Elliott, Michelle, Christopher T. Fisher, Ben A. Nelson, Roberto S. Molina Garza, Shawn K. Collins, and Deborah M. Pearsall. 2010. "Climate, Agriculture, and Cycles of Human Occupation over the Last 4000 Yr in Southern Zacatecas, Mexico." *Quaternary Research* 74: 26–35.
18. Jimenez, Peter F. 2020. *The Mesoamerican World System, 200–1200 ce: A Comparative Approach Analysis of West Mexico.* Cambridge: Cambridge University Press.
19. Guadalupe Mastache, Alba, Robert H. Cobean, and Dan M. Healan. 2002. *Ancient Tollan: Tula and the Toltec Heartland.* Boulder: University of Colorado Press. See also Healan, Dan M., and Robert H. Cobean. 2012. "Tula and the Toltecs." In *The Oxford Handbook of Mesoamerican Archaeology*, edited by Deborah L. Nichols and Christopher A. Pool, pp. 372–384. Oxford: Oxford University Press.
20. Marley, David F. 2010. *Pirates of the Americas, Volume 1: 1650–1685.* Santa Barbara, CA: ABC-CLIO.
21. Ekholm, *Excavations.*
22. Vivó Escoto, Jorge A. 1964. "Weather and Climate of Mexico and Central America." In *Handbook of Middle American Indians, Volume One: Natural Environment and Early Cultures*, edited by Robert C. West, pp. 187–215 and fig. 10. Austin: University of Texas Press.
23. Alarcón, Gerardo, and Guillermo Ahuja. 2015. "The Materials of Tamtoc." In *The Huasteca: Culture, History, and Interregional Exchange*, edited by Katherine A. Faust and Kim N. Richter, pp. 37–58. Norman: University of Oklahoma Press.
24. Willis, John, Shaunna Oteka-McCovey, and Terry Tempest Williams. 2019. *Mni Wiconi/Water Is Life: Honoring the Water Protectors at Standing Rock and Everywhere in the Ongoing Struggle for Indigenous Sovereignty.* Staunton, VA: George F. Thompson.
25. Sahagún, Fray Bernardino de. 1981. *Florentine Codex: General History of the Things of New Spain, Book 1—The Gods.* 2nd ed. Translated by Arthur J. O. Anderson and Charles E. Dibble. Salt Lake City: School of American Research and University of Utah Press.
26. Kowalski, Jeff Karl, and Cynthia Kristan-Graham, eds. 2011. *Twin Tollans: Chichen Itza, Tula, and the Epiclassic to Early Postclassic Mesoamerican World.* Rev. ed. Dumbarton Oaks Pre-Columbian Symposia and Colloquia. Cambridge, MA: Harvard University Press.

27. Riley, Carroll L., and Basil C. Hedrick, eds. 1978. *Across the Chichimec Sea: Papers in Honor of J. Charles Kelley.* Carbondale: Southern Illinois University Press.

CHAPTER 5

1. Cabeza de Vaca, Álvar Núñez. 2002. *Chronicle of the Narváez Expedition.* Translated by Fanny Bandelier and Harold Augenbraum. New York: Penguin, p. 86.
2. Carson, David. 2018. *The Account of Cabeza de Vaca: A Literal Translation with Analysis and Commentary.* Friendswood, TX: Living Water Specialties, p. 181 n. 1.
3. Neihardt, John G. 2008. *Black Elk Speaks: Being the Life Story of a Holy Man of the Oglala Sioux.* Albany: State University of New York Press. Brown, Joseph Epes. 1953. *The Sacred Pipe: Black Elk's Account of the Seven Rites of the Oglala Sioux.* Norman: University of Oklahoma Press.
4. Hall, Robert L. 1997. *An Archaeology of the Soul: Native American Indian Belief and Ritual.* Urbana: University of Illinois Press.
5. "This Dance Will Give You Vertigo (Traditional and Prehispanic Dance from Mexico)." YouTube, posted by Estudio Arkano, October 18, 2018. https://www.youtube.com/watch?v=Xi1KJVRv_AY.
6. Neihardt, *Black Elk Speaks*, pp. 32–33.
7. Archambault, JoAllyn. 2001. "Sun Dance." In *Handbook of North American Indians, Volume 13, Plains, Part 2*, edited by Raymond J. DeMallie, pp. 983–995. Washington, DC: Smithsonian Institution.
8. Hall, Robert L. 1991. "Cahokia Identity and Interaction Models of Cahokia Mississippian." In *Cahokia and the Hinterlands: Middle Mississippian Cultures of the Midwest*, edited by Thomas E. Emerson and R. Barry Lewis, pp. 3–34. Urbana: University of Illinois Press.
9. Mooney, James 1973. *The Ghost-Dance Religion and Wounded Knee.* New York: Dover.
10. Hall, Robert L. 1985. "Medicine Wheels, Sun Circles, and the Magic of World Center Shrines." *Plains Anthropologist* 30, no. 109: 181–193. Hall, *Archaeology of the Soul.*
11. Beekman, Christopher S. 2012. "Current Views on Power, Economics, and Subsistence in Ancient Western Mexico." In *The Oxford Handbook of Mesoamerican Archaeology*, edited by Deborah L. Nichols and Christopher A. Pool, pp. 495–512. Oxford: Oxford University Press.
12. Diaz del Castillo, Bernal, 1963 *The Conquest of New Spain.* Translated by J. M. Cohen. New York: Penguin, p. 182.

13. Vivó Escoto, Jorge A. 1964. "Weather and Climate of Mexico and Central America." In *Handbook of Middle American Indians, Volume One: Natural Environment and Early Cultures*, edited by Robert C. West, pp. 187–215, fig. 6. Austin: University of Texas Press.
14. Cummings, Byron. 1933. *Cuicuilco and the Archaic Culture of Mexico.* Bulletin 4. Tucson: University of Arizona.
15. Cowgill, George L. 2015. *Ancient Teotihuacan: Early Urbanism in Central Mexico.* Cambridge: Cambridge University Press, pp. 41–46.
16. Sieron, K., and C. Siebe. 2008. "Revised Stratigraphy and Eruption Rates of Ceboruco Stratovolcano and Surrounding Monogenetic Vents (Nayarit, Mexico) from Historical Documents and New Radiocarbon Dates." *Journal of Volcanology and Geothermal Research* 176: 241–264. doi:10.1016/j.jvolgeores.2008.04.006.
17. Cowgill, *Ancient Teotihuacan.*
18. Hassig, Ross. 1985. *Trade, Tribute, and Transportation: The Sixteenth-Century Political Economy of the Valley of Mexico.* Norman: University of Oklahoma Press.

CHAPTER 6

1. Cabeza de Vaca, Alvar Núñez. 2002. *Chronicle of the Narváez Expedition.* Translated by Fanny Bandelier and Harold Augenbraum. New York: Penguin, p. 86.
2. For a discussion of cultural nomenclature, see Lekson, Stephen H. 2008. *A History of the Ancient Southwest.* Santa Fe, NM: School for Advanced Research Press.
3. McGuire, Randall H. 2012. "Mesoamerica and the Southwest/Northwest." In *The Oxford Handbook of Mesoamerican Archaeology*, edited by Deborah L. Nichols and Christopher A. Pool, pp. 513–524. Oxford: Oxford University Press, p. 515.
4. Bostwick, Todd W., Stephanie M. Whittlesey, and Douglas R. Mitchell. 2010. "Reconstructing the Sacred in Hohokam Archaeology: Cosmology, Mythology, and Ritual." *Journal of Arizona Archaeology* 1, no. 1: 87–99.
5. Jimenez, Peter F. 2020. *The Mesoamerican World System, 200–1200 ce: A Comparative Approach Analysis of West Mexico.* Cambridge: Cambridge University Press.
6. Fish, Suzanne K., and Paul R. Fish, eds. 2007. *The Hohokam Millennium.* Santa Fe, NM: School for Advanced Research Press.
7. Stahle, David W., J. Villanueva Diaz, D. J. Burnette, J. Cerano Pareds, R. R. Heim Jr., F. K. Fuey, R. Acuna Soto, M. D. Therrell, M. K. Cleaveland,

and D. K. Stahle. 2011. "Major Mesoamerican Droughts of the Past Millennium." *Geophysical Research Letters* 38, no. L05703: 1–4. https://doi.org/10.1029/2010GL046472.

8. Kelley, J. Charles. 1991. "The Known Archaeological Ballcourts of Durango and Zacatecas, Mexico." In *The Mesoamerican Ballgame*, edited by Vernon L. Scarborough and David R. Wilcox, pp. 87–100. Tucson: University of Arizona Press.
9. Jimenez, Peter F. 2020. *The Mesoamerican World System, 200–1200 ce: A Comparative Approach Analysis of West Mexico.* Cambridge: Cambridge University Press.
10. Torvinen, Andrea, and Ben A. Nelson. 2020. "Refinement of the Chronology of La Quemada, Zacatecas, Mexico, Using Ceramic Seriation." *Latin American Antiquity* 31, no. 1: 61–80. https://doi.org/10.1017/laq.2019.106.
11. Nelson, Ben A., and Debra L. Martin. 2015. "Symbolic Bones and Interethnic Violence in a Frontier Zone, Northwest Mexico, ca. 500–900 CE." *PNAS* 112: 9196–9201.
12. Armillas, Pedro. 1969. "The Arid Frontier of Mexican Civilization." *Transactions of the New York Academy of Sciences* 31: 697–704.
13. Whittlesey, Stephanie M. 2007. "Hohokam Ceramics, Hohokam Beliefs." In *The Hohokam Millennium*, edited by Suzanne K. Fish and Paul R. Fish, pp. 65–73. Santa Fe, NM: School for Advanced Research Press.
14. Bostwick, Whittlesey, andMitchell. "Reconstructing the Sacred in Hohokam Archaeology."
15. LeBlanc, Steven A. 1999. *Prehistoric Warfare in the American Southwest.* Salt Lake City: University of Utah Press.

CHAPTER 7

1. Lekson, Stephen H., ed. 2007. *The Architecture of Chaco Canyon, New Mexico.* Salt Lake City: University of Utah Press.
2. Martin, Deborah L., Nancy J. Akins, Bradley J. Crenshaw, and Pamela K. Stone. 2008. "Inscribed in the Body, Written in the Bones: The Consequences of Social Violence at La Plata." In *Social Violence in the Prehispanic American Southwest*, edited by Deborah L. Nichols and Patricia L. Crown, pp. 98–122. Tucson: University of Arizona Press.
3. Benson, Larry V., and Michael S. Berry. 2009. "Climate Change and Cultural Response in the Prehistoric American Southwest." *Kiva* 75, no. 1: 89–119.

4. Stein, John, Richard Friedman, Taft Blackhorse, and Richard Loose. 2007. "Revisiting Downtown Chaco." In *The Architecture of Chaco Canyon, New Mexico*, edited by Stephen H. Lekson, pp. 199–223. Salt Lake City: University of Utah Press. Weiner, Robert S. 2015. "A Sensory Approach to Exotica, Ritual Practice, and Cosmology at Chaco Canyon." *Kiva* 81, nos. 3–4: 220–246.
5. Kennett, Douglas J., Stephen Plog, Richard J. George, Brendan J. Culleton, Adam S. Watson, Pontus Skogland, Nadin Rohland, Swapan Mallick, Kristin Stewardson, Logan Kistler, Steven A. LeBlanc, Peter M. Whiteley, David Reich, and George H. Perry. 2017. "Archaeogenomic Evidence Reveals Prehistoric Matrilineal Dynasty." *Nature Communications 8: 14115*. doi: 10.1038/ncomms14115. Plog, Stephen, and Carrie Heitman. 2010. "Hierarchy and Social Inequality in the American Southwest, A.D. 800–1200." *Proceedings of the National Academy of Sciences* 107, no. 46: 19619–19626. doi: 19610.11073/pnas.1014985107.
6. Pepper, George H. 1996. *Pueblo Bonito.* Albuquerque: University of New Mexico Press.
7. Judd, Neil Merton. 1954. *The Material Culture of Pueblo Bonito.* Smithsonian Miscellaneous Collections, volume 124. Washington, DC: Smithsonian Institution.
8. Stein et al., "Revisiting Downtown Chaco."
9. Sofaer, Anna. 2008. *Chaco Astronomy: An Ancient American Cosmology.* Santa Fe, NM: Ocean Tree Books.
10. Hively, Ray, and Robert Horn. 2010. "Hopewell Cosmography at Newark and Chillicothe, Ohio." In *Hopewell Settlement Patterns, Subsistence, and Symbolic Landscapes*, edited by A. Martin Byers and DeeAnne Wymer, pp. 128–164. Gainesville: University Press of Florida. Romain, William F. 2020. "Lunar Alignments at Ur: Entanglements with the Moon God Nanna." *Journal of Skyscape Archaeology* 5, no. 2: 151–176. https://doi.org/https://doi.org/10.1558/jsa.39074.
11. Malville, J. McKim, ed. 2004. *Chimney Rock: The Ultimate Chacoan Outlier.* Lanham, MD: Lexington Books. See also Appendix C in Lekson, Stephen H. 2015. *The Chaco Meridian: One Thousand Years of Political and Religious Power in the Ancient Southwest.* 2nd ed. Lanham, MD: Rowman and Littlefield.
12. Fowles, Severin M. 2013. *An Archaeology of Doings: Secularism and the Study of Pueblo Religion.* Santa Fe, NM: School for Advanced Research Press.
13. Sofaer, Anna, dir. 2003. *The Mystery of Chaco Canyon.* Bullfrog Films.
14. Windes, Thomas C. 2004. "The Rise of Early Chacoan Great Houses." In *In Search of Chaco: New Approaches to an Archaeological Enigma*, edited

by David Grant Noble, pp. 14–21. Santa Fe, NM: School of American Research Press. Van Dyke, Ruth M. 2007. "Great Kivas in Time, Space, and Society." In *The Architecture of Chaco Canyon, New Mexico*, edited by Stephen H. Lekson, pp. 93–126. Salt Lake City: University of Utah Press.

15. Mills, Barbara J., and T. J. Ferguson. 2008. "Animate Objects: Shell Trumpets and Ritual Networks in the Greater Southwest." *Journal of Archaeological Method and Theory* 15, no. 4: 338–361.
16. Stein et al., "Revisiting Downtown Chaco.".
17. Agostini, Mark R., and Ivy Notterpek. 2020. "Cosmological Expressions and Medicine Stones in the Ancestral Pueblo World." *Kiva* 86, no. 4: 403–427. https://doi.org/10.1080/00231940.2020.1832406. Weiner, "Sensory Approach."
18. Lekson, *Chaco Meridian*. Lekson, *Architecture of Chaco Canyon*.
19. Dove, David M. 2021. "Greathouse Formation: Agricultural Intensification, Balanced Duality, and Communal Enterprise at Mitchell Springs." *Southwestern Lore* 87, no. 1: 5–49. Kuckelman, Kristin A. "Architecture." In *The Archaeology of Yellow Jacket Pueblo: Excavations at a Large Community Center in Southwestern Colorado*, edited by Kristin A. Kuckelman, 1–49. Cortez, CO: Crow Canyon Archaeological Center, 2003. https://www.crowcanyon.org/ResearchReports/YellowJacket/Text/yjpw_architecture.asp.
20. Nelson, Ben A. 2006. "Mesoamerican Objects and Symbols in Chaco Canyon Contexts." In *The Archaeology of Chaco Canyon: An 11th Century Pueblo Regional Center*, edited by Stephen H. Lekson, pp. 339–371. Santa Fe, NM: School for Advanced Research Press.
21. Guiterman, Christopher H., Christopher H. Baisan, Nathan B. English, Jay Quade, Jeffrey S. Dean, and Thomas W. Swetnam. 2020. "Convergence of Evidence Supports a Chuska Mountains Origin for the Plaza Tree of Pueblo Bonito, Chaco Canyon." *American Antiquity* 85, no. 2: 331–346. https://doi.org/doi:10.1017/aaq.2020.6.
22. Van Dyke, Ruth M. 2004. "Memory, Meaning, and Masonry: The Late Bonito Chacoan Landscape." *American Antiquity* 69: 413–431. Van Dyke, Ruth M. 2009. "Chaco Reloaded." *Journal of Social Archaeology* 9, no. 2: 220–248.
23. Crown, Patricia L., and W. Jeffrey Hurst. 2009. "Evidence of Cacao Use in the Prehispanic American Southwest." *Proceedings of the National Academy of Sciences* 106, no. 7: 2110–2113.
24. Crown, Patricia L. 2018. "Drinking Performance and Politics in Pueblo Bonito, Chaco Canyon." *American Antiquity* 83, no. 3: 387–406.

25. O'Hara, F. Michael. 2012. "Hohokam and Chaco in the Sierra Sin Agua." In *Hisat'sinom: Ancient Peoples in a Land Without Water*, edited by Christian E. Downum, pp. 59–67. Santa Fe, NM: School for Advanced Research Press.
26. Kuwanwisiwma, Leigh J. 2004. "Yupköyvi: The Hopi Story of Chaco Canyon." In *In Search of Chaco: New Approaches to an Archaeological Enigma*, edited by D. G. Noble, pp. 41–47. Santa Fe, NM: School for Advanced Research Press. Swentzell, Rina. 2004. "A Pueblo Woman's Perspective on Chaco Canyon." In *In Search of Chaco: New Approaches to an Archaeological Enigma*, edited by David Grant Noble, pp. Santa Fe, NM: School of American Research Press. Begay, Richard M. 2004. "Tsé Bíyah 'Anii'áhí: Chaco Canyon and Its Place in Navajo History." In *In Search of Chaco: New Approaches to an Archaeological Enigma*, edited by D. G. Noble, pp. 54–60. Santa Fe, NM: School for Advanced Research Press. Weiner, Robert S. 2018. "Sociopolitical, Ceremonial, and Economic Aspects of Gambling in Ancient North America: A Case Study of Chaco Canyon." *American Antiquity* 83, no. 1: 34–53.
27. Kuckelman, Kristin A. 2008. "An Agent-Centered Case Study of the Depopulation of Sand Canyon Pueblo." In *The Social Construction of Communities: Agency, Structure, and Identity in the Prehispanic Southwest*, edited by Mark D. Varien and James M. Potter, pp. 109–121. Walnut Creek, CA: AltaMira Press.
28. Downum, Christian E., ed. 2012. *Hisat'sinom: Ancient Peoples in a Land without Water*. Santa Fe, NM: School for Advanced Research Press.
29. Gruner, Erina. 2018. "The Mobile House: Religious Leadership at Chacoan and Chacoan Revival Centers." In *Religion and Politics in the Ancient Americas*, edited by Sarah B. Barber and Arthur A. Joyce, pp. 27–50. London: Routledge.
30. McGuire, Randall H. 2011. "Pueblo Religion and the Mesoamerican Connection." In *Religious Transformation in the Late Pre-Hispanic Pueblo World*, edited by Donna M. Glowacki and Scott Van Keuren, pp. 23–49. Tucson: University of Arizona Press.
31. Fowles, Severin M. 2013. *An Archaeology of Doings: Secularism and the Study of Pueblo Religion*. Santa Fe, NM: School for Advanced Research Press.
32. Mathiowetz, Michael D. 2011. "The Diurnal Path of the Sun: Ideology and Interregional Interaction in Ancient Northwest Mesoamerica and the American Southwest." PhD dissertation, Department of Anthropology, University of California, Riverside. Schaafsma, Polly. 1994. *Kachinas in the Pueblo World*. Albuquerque: University of New Mexico Press.

Schaafsma, Polly. 1999. "Tlalocs, Kachinas, Sacred Bundles, and Related Symbolism in the Southwest and Mesoamerica." In *The Casas Grandes World*, edited by Curtis F. Schaafsma and Carroll L. Riley, pp. 164–193. Salt Lake City: University of Utah Press.

CHAPTER 8

1. Kelley, J. Charles. 1955. "Juan Sabeata and Diffusion in Aboriginal Texas." *American Anthropologist* 57, no. 5: 981–995.
2. Perttula, Timothy K. 1992. *"The Caddo Nation": Archaeological and Ethnohistoric Perspectives.* Austin: University of Texas Press.
3. Smith, Bruce D. 1984. "Mississippian Expansion: Tracing the Historical Development of an Explanatory Model." *Southeastern Archaeology* 3, no. 1: 13–32.
4. Girard, Jeffrey S., Timothy K. Perttula, and Mary Beth Trubitt. 2014. *Caddo Connections: Cultural Interactions Within and Beyond the Caddo World.* Lanham, MD: Rowman and Littlefield.
5. Story, Dee Ann. 1997. "1968–1970 Archaeological Investigations at the George C. Davis Site, Cherokee County, Texas." *Bullein of the Texas Archeological and Paleontological Society* 68: 1–103.
6. Webb, Clarence H. 1959. *The Belcher Mound: A Stratified Caddoan Site in Caddo Parish, Louisiana.* Memoirs of the Society for American Archaeology 16. Salt Lake City: Society for American Archaeology.
7. Harrington, M. R. 1920. *Certain Caddo Sites in Arkansas.* Indian Notes and Monographs. New York: Museum of the American Indian, Heye Foundation, p. 135.
8. Kelley, "Juan Sabeata." Phillips, Philip. 1940. "Middle American Influences on the Archaeology of the Southeastern United States." In *The Maya and Their Neighbors*, edited by Clarence L. Hay, Ralph L. Linton, Samuel K. Lothrop, Harry L. Shapiro, and George C. Vaillant, pp. 349–367. New York: Appleton-Century (Dover reprint, 1977).
9. Crown, Patricia L., Thomas E. Emerson, J. Gu, William J. Hurst, Timothy R. Pauketat, and Timothy Ward. 2012. "Ritual Black Drink Consumption at Cahokia." *Proceedings of the National Academy of Sciences* 109, no. 35: 13944–13949.
10. Carson, David. 2018. *The Account of Cabeza de Vaca: A Literal Translation with Analysis and Commentary.* Friendswood, TX: Living Water Specialties, pp. 150–151.
11. Hudson, Charles M., ed. 1979. *Black Drink: A Native American Tea.* Athens: University of Georgia Press.

12. King, Adam, Terry G. Powis, Kong F. Cheong, Bobi Deere, Robert B. Pickering, Eric Singleton, and Nilesh W. Giakwad. 2018. "Absorbed Residue Evidence for Prehistoric *Datura* Use in the American Southeast and Western Mexico." *Advances in Archaeological Practice* 6, no. 4: 312–327. https://doi.org/10.1017/aap.2018.30. Parker, Kathryn E., and Mary L. Simon. 2018. "Magic Plants and Mississippian Ritual." In *Archaeology and Ancient Religion in the American Midcontinent*, edited by Brad Koldehoff and Timothy R. Pauketat, pp. 117–166. Tuscaloosa: University of Alabama Press. Lambert, Shawn P., Timothy K. Perttula, and Nilesh W. Giakwad. 2021. "Organic Residue Evidence for Late Precolumbian *Datura*-Making in the Central Arkansas River Valley." *Advances in Archaeological Practice* 10, no. 2: 1–11. https://doi.org/10.1017/aap.2021.15.
13. Archaeobotanist Kathryn Parker, an authority on ancient psychotropic plants, pointed out this interview to me. See "John Waters Hitchhikes Across America, and Lives to Write About It." *All Things Considered*, NPR, August 29, 2014. https://www.kvpr.org/post/john-waters-hitchhikes-across-america-and-lives-write-about-it-0.
14. Schultes, Richard Evans, Albert Hofmann, and Christian Ratsch. 1992. *Plants of the Gods: Their Sacred, Healing, and Hallucinogenic Powers.* Rochester, VT: Healing Arts Press.
15. Krieger, Alex D. 1948. "Importance of the 'Gilmore Corridor' in Culture Contacts Between Middle America and the Eastern United States." *Bulletin of the Texas Archeological and Paleontological Society* 19: 155–178.
16. Kelley, "Juan Sabeata."
17. Phillips, "Middle American Influences."
18. Carpenter, Stephen M. 2020. "Mesoamerican-Mississippian Interaction Across the Far Southern Plains by Long-Range Toyah Intermediaries." *Plains Anthropologist* 65: 325–356. doi: 10.1080/00320447.2020.1779910
19. Vigouroux, Yves, Jeffery C. Glaubitze, Yoshihiro Matsuoka, Major M. Goodman, Jesus G. Sanchez, and John Doebley. 2008. "Population Structure and Genetic Diversity of New World Maize Races Assessed by DNA Microsatellites." *American Journal of Botany* 95: 1240–1253.
20. Ford, Richard I. 1997. "Appendix 1: Preliminary Report on the Plant Remains from the George C. Davis Site, Cherokee County, Texas, 1968–1970 Excavations." *Bulletin of the Texas Archeological and Paleontological Society* 68: 104–107.
21. Hart, John, H. J. Brumbach, and R. Lusteck. 2007. "Extending the Phytolith Evidence for Early Maize (*Zea mays* ssp. *mays*) and Squash (*Curcurbita* sp.) in Central New York." *American Antiquity* 72: 563–583.

22. Emerson, Thomas E., Kristin M. Hedman, Mary L. Simon, Matthew A. Fort, and Kelsey E. Witt. 2020. "Isotopic Confirmation of the Timing and Intensity of Maize Consumption in Greater Cahokia." *American Antiquity* 85, no. 2: 241–262. https://doi.org/10.1017/aaq.2020.7.
23. Smith, Bruce D., and C. Wesley Cowan. 2003. "Domesticated Crop Plants and the Evolution of Food Production Economies in Eastern North America." In *People and Plants in Ancient Eastern North America*, edited by Paul E. Minnis, pp. 105–125. Washington, DC: Smithsonian Books.
24. Benson, Larry V., Michael S. Berry, Edward A. Jolie, Jerry D. Spangler, David W. Stahle, and Eugene M. Hattori. 2007. "Possible Impacts of Early-11th, Middle-12th, and Late-13th-Century Droughts on Western Native Americans and the Mississippian Cahokians." *Quaternary Science Reviews* 26: 336–350. Benson, Larry V., Timothy R. Pauketat, and Edward Cook. 2009. "Cahokia's Boom and Bust in the Context of Climate Change." *American Antiquity* 74: 467–483. Cook, Edward R., D. M. Meko, D. W. Stahle, and M. K. Cleaveland. 1999. "Drought Reconstructions for the Continental United States." *Journal of Climate* 12: 1145–1162. Cook, Edward R., R. Seager, R. R. Heim, R. S. Vose, C. Herweijer, and C. W. Woodhouse. 2010. "Megadroughts in North America: Placing IPCC Projections of Hydroclimatic Change in a Long-Term Paleoclimate Context." *Journal of Quaternary Science* 25, no. 1: 48–61.
25. Swanton, John R. 1942. *Source Material on the History and Ethnology of the Caddo Indians.* Bureau of American Ethnology, Bulletin 132. Washington, DC: Smithsonian Institution, p. 27.
26. Samuelsen, John R. 2016. "A Reanalysis of Strontium Isotopes from a Skull and Mandible Cemetery at the Crenshaw Site: Implications for Caddo Interregional Warfare." *Journal of Archaeological Science: Reports* 5: 119–134.
27. Lankford, George E. 2007. *Reachable Stars: Patterns in the Ethnoastronomy of Eastern North America.* Tuscaloosa: University of Alabama Press.
28. Miller, Jay. 1996. "Changing Moons: A History of Caddo Religion." *Plains Anthropologist* 41, no. 157: 243–259.
29. Weinstein, Richard A., David B. Kelley, and Joe W. Saunders, eds. 2003. *The Louisiana and Arkansas Expeditions of Clarence Bloomfield Moore.* Tuscaloosa: University of Alabama Press, p. 69.
30. Schambach, Frank. 2002. "Fourche Maline: A Woodland Period Culture of the Trans-Mississippi South." In *The Woodland Southeast*, edited by David G. Anderson and Robert C. Mainfort Jr., pp. 90–112. Tuscaloosa: University of Alabama Press, p. 112. Girard, Jeffrey S. 2020. "Interactions Between the Caddo and Cahokia Regions." In *Cahokia in Context:*

Hegemony and Diaspora, edited by Ryan M. Parish and Charles H. McNutt, pp. 205–215. Gainesville: University Press of Florida.

31. Romain, William F. 2015. "Moonwatchers of Cahokia." In *Medieval Mississippians: The Cahokian World*, edited by Timothy R. Pauketat and Susan M. Alt, pp. 33–41. Santa Fe, NM: School for Advanced Research Press.
32. Twain, Mark. 1883. *Life on the Mississippi*. New York: Bantam Dell, p. 114.
33. Norris, F. Terry, and Timothy R. Pauketat. 2008. "A Pre-Columbian Map of the Mississippi?" *Southeastern Archaeology* 27: 78–92.
34. Emerson, Thomas E., Dale L. McElrath, and Andrew C. Fortier, eds. 2000. *Late Woodland Societies: Transition and Transformation Across the Midcontinent*. Lincoln: University of Nebraska Press.
35. Walthall, John A., ed. 1991. *French Colonial Archaeology: The Illinois Country and the Western Great Lakes*. Urbana: University of Illinois Press.

CHAPTER 9

1. LaDuke, Winona. 2005. *Recovering the Sacred: The Power of Naming and Claiming*. Cambridge, MA: South End Press, pp. 34–35.
2. Kehoe, Alice B. 1998. *Land of Prehistory: A Critical History of American Archaeology*. London: Routledge. See also Pauketat, Timothy R., and Kenneth E. Sassaman. 2020. *The Archaeology of Ancient North America*. Cambridge: Cambridge University Press.
3. Alt, Susan M. 2019. "From Weeping Hills to Lost Caves: A Search for Vibrant Matter in Greater Cahokia." In *New Materialisms Ancient Urbanisms*, edited by Susan M. Alt and Timothy R. Pauketat, pp. 19–39. London: Routledge.
4. Alt, "From Weeping Hills," 33.
5. Weston, Jennifer. 2017. "Water Is Life: The Rise of the Mní Wičóni Movement." *Cultural Survival Quaterly Magazine*, March. https://www.culturalsurvival.org/publications/cultural-survival-quarterly/water-life-rise-mni-wiconi-movement. Willis, John, Shaunna Oteka-McCovey, and Terry Tempest Williams. 2019. *Mni Wiconi/Water Is Life: Honoring the Water Protectors at Standing Rock and Everywhere in the Ongoing Struggle for Indigenous Sovereignty*. Staunton, VA: George F. Thompson.
6. Dickens, Charles. 2004. *American Notes*. London: Penguin Books, p. 197.
7. Dickens, *American Notes*, p. 197
8. Oliver, William. 2002. *Eight Months in Illinois, with Information to Immigrants*. Carbondale: Southern Illinois University Press, p. 182.

9. Dickens, *American Notes*, p. 201.
10. Pauketat, Timothy R., Susan M. Alt, and Jeffery D. Kruchten. 2017. "The Emerald Acropolis: Elevating the Moon and Water in the Rise of Cahokia." *Antiquity* 91: 207–222.
11. Heidorn, Keith, and Ian Whitelaw. 2010. *The Field Guide to Natural Phenomena: The Secret World of Optical, Atmospheric and Celestial Wonders.* Richmond Hill, ON: Firefly Books.
12. Cummings, Marisa Miakonda. 2015. "An Umonhon Perspective." In *Medieval Mississippians: The Cahokian World*, edited by Timothy R. Pauketat and Susan M. Alt, pp. 43–46. Santa Fe, NM: School for Advanced Research Press.
13. Alt, Susan M. 2018. "The Emerald Site, Mississippian Women, and the Moon." In *Archaeology of the Night: Life After Dark in the Ancient World*, edited by Nancy Gonlin and April Nowell, pp. 223–246. Boulder: University of Colorado Press. Romain, William F. 2015. "Moonwatchers of Cahokia." In *Medieval Mississippians: The Cahokian World*, edited by Timothy R. Pauketat and Susan M. Alt, pp. 33–41. Santa Fe, New Mexico: School for Advanced Research Press.
14. Miller, Jay. 1996. "Changing Moons: A History of Caddo Religion." *Plains Anthropologist* 41, no. 157: 243–259.
15. Rother, Hubert, and Charlotte Rother. 1996. *Lost Caves of St. Louis.* St. Louis: Virginia.
16. Pauketat, Timothy R., Robert F. Boszhardt, and Danielle M. Benden. 2015. "Trempealeau Entanglements: An Ancient Colony's Causes and Effects." *American Antiquity* 80: 260–289. Pauketat, Timothy R., Robert Boszhardt, and Michael Kolb. 2017. "Trempealeau's Little Bluff: An Early Cahokian Terraformed Landmark in the Upper Mississippi Valley." *Midcontinental Journal of Archaeology* 42, no. 2: 168–199.
17. Friberg, Christina M., Gregory D. Wilson, Dana N. Bardolph, Jeremy J. Wilson, John S. Flood, Scott D. Hipskind, Matthew D. Pike, and Duane Esarey. 2021. "The Geophyics of Community, Place, and Identity in the Mississippian Illinois River Valley." *Journal of Archaeological Science: Reports* 36: 102888. https://doi.org/https://doi.org/10.1016/j.jasrep.2021.102888.
18. Theler, James L., and Robert F. Boszhardt. 2003. *Twelve Millennia: Archaeology of the Upper Mississippi River Valley.* Iowa City: University of Iowa Press.
19. Brennan, Tamira K., Alleen M. Betzenhauser, Michael Brent Lansdell, Luke A. Plocher, Victoria E. Potter, and Daniel F. Blodgett. 2018. "Community Organization of the East St. Louis Precinct." In *Revealing Greater Cahokia, North America's First Native City: Rediscovery and*

Large-Scale Excavations of the East St. Louis Precinct, edited by Thomas E. Emerson, Brad H. Koldehoff and Tamira K. Brennan, pp. 147–202. Studies in Archaeology 12. Urbana: Illinois State Archaeological Survey, University of Illinois. Pauketat, Timothy R., and Neal H. Lopinot. 1997. "Cahokian Population Dynamics." In *Cahokia: Domination and Ideology in the Mississippian World*, edited by Timothy R. Pauketat and Thomas E. Emerson, pp. 103–123. Lincoln: University of Nebraska Press.

20. Milner, George R. 1998. *The Cahokia Chiefdom: The Archaeology of a Mississippian Society.* Washington, DC: Smithsonian Institution Press.
21. Baires, Sarah E. 2016. "A Microhistory of Human and Gastropod Bodies and Souls During Cahokia's Emergence." *Cambridge Archaeological Journal* 27, no. 2: 245–260.
22. Ashley, Keith, and Robert L. Thunen. 2020. "St. Johns River Fisher-Hunter-Gatherers: Florida's Connection to Cahokia." *Journal of Archaeological Method and Theory* 27: 7–27. https://doi.org/https://doi.org/10.1007/s10816-019-09439-5.
23. Baires, Sarah E. 2017. *Land of Water, City of the Dead: Religion and Cahokia's Emergence.* Tuscaloosa: University of Alabama Press.
24. Pauketat, Timothy R., Thomas E. Emerson, Michael G. Farkas, and Sarah E. Baires. 2015. "An American Indian City." In *Medieval Mississippians: The Cahokian World*, edited by Timothy R. Pauketat and Susan M. Alt, pp. 20–31. Santa Fe, NM: School for Advanced Research Press.
25. Romain, William F. 2018. "Ancient Skywatchers of the Eastern Woodlands." In *Archaeology and Ancient Religion in the American Midcontinent*, edited by Brad H. Koldehoff and Timothy R. Pauketat, pp. 304–341. Tuscaloosa: University of Alabama Press.
26. Emerson, Thomas E. 1983. "The Bostrom Figure Pipe and the Cahokian Effigy Style in the American Bottom." *Midcontinental Journal of Archaeology* 8: 257–267.
27. Almere Read, Kay, and Jason J. Gonzolez. 2000. *Mesoamerican Mythology: A Guide to the Gods, Heroes, Rituals, and Beliefs of Mexico and Central America.* Oxford: Oxford University Press, p. 124 n. 18.
28. Hall, Robert L. 2000. "Sacrificed Foursomes and Green Corn Ceremonialism." In *Mounds, Modoc, and Mesoamerica: Papers in Honor of Melvin L. Fowler*, edited by Steven R. Ahler, pp. 245–253. Scientific Papers XXVIII. Springfield: Illinois State Museum.
29. Alt, Susan M. 2015. "Human Sacrifice at Cahokia." In *Medieval Mississippians: The Cahokian World*, edited by Timothy R. Pauketat and Susan M. Alt, p. 27. Santa Fe, NM: School for Advanced Research Press.

30. Fowler, Melvin L., Jerome C. Rose, Barbara Vander Leest, and Steven R. Ahler. 1999. *The Mound 72 Area: Dedicated and Sacred Space in Early Cahokia.* Reports of Investigations, no. 54. Springfield: Illinois State Museum.
31. Hargrave, Eve A. 2007. "Human Remains." In *The Archaeology of the East St. Louis Mound Center, Part Ii: The Northside Excavations*, edited by Andrew C. Fortier, pp. 77–83. Transportation Archaeological Research Reports no. 22, University of Illinois. Urbana: Illinois Transportation Archaeological Research Program.
32. Skousen, B. Jacob. 2012. "Posts, Places, Ancestors, and Worlds: Dividual Personhood in the American Bottom Region." *Southeastern Archaeology* 31: 57–69. Ridington, Robin, and Dennis Hastings. 1997. *Blessing for a Long Time: The Sacred Pole of the Omaha Tribe.* Lincoln: University of Nebraska Press.
33. Reed, Nelson A. 2009. "Excavations on the Third Terrace and Front Ramp of Monks Mound, Cahokia: A Personal Narrative." *Illinois Archaeology* 21, no. 1–89.
34. Gipson, Rosemary. 1971. "Los Voladores, the Flyers of Mexico." *Western Folklore* 30, no. 4: 269–278.
35. For a contrasting view, see Phillips, Philip, and James A. Brown. 1978. *Pre-Columbian Shell Engravings from the Craig Mound at Spiro, Oklahoma.* Cambridge, MA: Peabody Museum of Archaeology and Ethnology, Harvard University.
36. Reilly, F. Kent, III. 2007. "The Petaloid Motif: A Celestial Symbolic Locative in the Shell Art of Spiro." In *Ancient Objects and Sacred Realms*, edited by F. Kent Reilly, III and James F. Garber, pp. 39–55. Austin: University of Texas Press, figure 3.1.
37. Fowler, Melvin L. 1997. *The Cahokia Atlas: A Historical Atlas of Cahokia Archaeology.* Studies in Archaeology, no. 2. Urbana: Illinois Transportation Archaeological Research Program.

CHAPTER 10

1. Cabeza de Vaca, Álvar Núñez. 2002. *Chronicle of the Narváez Expedition.* Translated by F. Bandelier and H. Augenbraum. New York: Penguin, p. 61. See also Carson, David. 2018. *The Account of Cabeza de Vaca: A Literal Translation with Analysis and Commentary*. Friendswood, TX: Living Water Specialties, p. 131. Carson notes the possibility that this story referenced a visit by the bearded Spanish explorer Alonzo Álvarez de Pineda in 1519. Of course, the god Tezcatlipoca, who personified Flint

Knife, was also depicted with a beard in humanoid form, as was his sometime brother Ehecatl-Quetzalcoatl.

2. However, one recent study places the origins of the Osages and Omahas up the Ohio River: Cook, Robert A. 2017. *Continuity and Change in the Native American Village: Multicultural Origins and Descendants of the Fort Ancient Culture.* Cambridge: Cambridge University Press.
3. Hall, Robert L. 1997. *An Archaeology of the Soul: Native American Indian Belief and Ritual.* Urbana: University of Illinois Press.
4. Hamilton, Henry W., J. T. Hamilton, and Eleanor F. Chapman. 1974. *Spiro Mound Copper.* Memoir 11. Columbia: Missouri Historical Society, p. 92.
5. Emerson, Thomas E. 1989. "Water, Serpents, and the Underworld: An Exploration into Cahokia Symbolism." In *The Southeastern Ceremonial Complex: Artifacts and Analysis*, edited by Patricia Galloway, pp. 45–92. Lincoln: University of Nebraska Press.
6. Kehoe, Alice B. 2005. "Wind Jewels and Paddling Gods: The Mississippian Southeast in the Postclassic Mesoamerican World." In *Gulf Coast Archaeology: The Southeastern United States and Mexico*, edited by Nancy M. White, pp. 260–280. Gainesville: University Press of Florida.
7. Miller, Mary, and Karl Taube. 1993. *An Illustrated Dictionary of the Gods and Symbols of Ancient Mexico and the Maya.* London: Thames and Hudson, p. 88.
8. Kehoe, "Wind Jewels."
9. Hamilton, Hamilton, and Chapman, *Spiro Mound Copper.*
10. Phillips, Philip, and James A. Brown. 1978. *Pre-Columbian Shell Engravings from the Craig Mound at Spiro, Oklahoma.* Cambridge, MA: Peabody Museum of Archaeology and Ethnology, Harvard University.
11. Pauketat, Timothy R. 1983. "A Long-Stemmed Spud from the American Bottom." *Midcontinental Journal of Archaeology* 8: 1–12.
12. Romero, J. 1970. "Dental Mutilation, Trephination, and Cranial Deformation." In *Handbook of Middle American Indians, Vol. 9, Physical Anthropology*, edited by T. D. Stewart, pp. 50–67. Austin: University of Texas Press.
13. Hedman, Kristin M., Julie A. Bukowski, Dawn E. Cobb, and Andrew R. Thompson. 2017. "Modified Teeth, Cultural Diversity, and Community Building at Cahokia (AD 900–1400)." In *A World View of Bioculturally Modified Teeth*, edited by Scott E. Burnette and Joel D. Irish, pp. 229–249. Gainesville: University Press of Florida.
14. Girard, Jeffrey S., Timothy K. Perttula, and Mary Beth Trubitt. 2014. *Caddo Connections: Cultural Interactions Within and Beyond the Caddo World.* Lanham, MD: Rowman and Littlefield.

15. Moorehead, Warren K. 2000. *The Cahokia Mounds.* Tuscaloosa: University of Alabama Press.
16. Pauketat, Timothy R. 2009. *Cahokia: Ancient America's Great City on the Mississippi.* New York: Viking Penguin.
17. Pauketat, Timothy R., Andrew C. Fortier, Thomas E. Emerson, and Susan M. Alt. 2013. "A Mississippian Conflagration at East St. Louis and Its Historical Implications." *Journal of Field Archaeology* 38: 208–224.
18. Pauketat, Timothy R., ed. 2005. *The Archaeology of the East St. Louis Mound Center, Part I: The Southside Excavations.* Transportation Archaeological Research Reports no. 21. Urbana: Transportation Archaeological Research Program.
19. Kehoe, "Wind Jewels."
20. Antoniuk, Caitlyn. 2021. "Cahokia's Influence in the Yazoo Basin: A Ceramic Analysis of Early Mississippian Features at the Carson Site." *Southeastern Archaeology* 40, no. 2: 116–134. Johnson, Jay K., and John M. Connaway. 2020. "Carson and Cahokia." In *Cahokia in Context: Diaspora and Hegemony,* edited by C. H. McNutt and R. M. Parish, pp. 276–300. Gainesville: University Press of Florida.
21. Perino, Gregory. 1967. *The Cherry Valley Mounds and Banks Mound 3.* Memoir no. 1. St. Louis: Central States Archaeological Societies, p. 68.
22. Morse, Dan F., and Phyllis A. Morse. 1983. *Archaeology of the Central Mississippi Valley.* New York: Academic Press, pp. 245–246.
23. Morse and Morse, *Archaeology.*
24. Morse and Morse, *Archaeology.*
25. Dickens, Charles. 2004. *American Notes.* London: Penguin Books, p. 203.
26. Dickens, *American Notes,* p. 203.

CHAPTER 11

1. Three Legs, Bobbi Jean. 2017. "Water Is Life, Water Is Sacred: Standing Rock's Bobbi Jean Three Legs Speaks out Against Trump." *Democracy Now!, January 25.* https://www.democracynow.org/2017/1/25/water_is_life_water_is_sacred.
2. Deloria, Vine, Jr. 2006. *The World We Used to Live In: Remembering the Powers of the Medicine Men.* Golden, CO: Fulcrum.
3. LaDuke, Winona. 2005. *Recovering the Sacred: The Power of Naming and Claiming.* Cambridge, MA: South End Press.
4. Neihardt, John G. 2008. *Black Elk Speaks: Being the Life Story of a Holy Man of the Oglala Sioux.* Albany: State University of New York Press, p. 149.

5. Kerouac, Jack. 2007. *On the Road: The Original Script*. New York: Penguin, p. 393.
6. Ross Hassig long ago described Ehecatl-Quetzalcoatl to me as an actual storm god.
7. White, Mathew, Amanda Smith, Kelly Humphryes, Sabine Pahl, Snelling Deborah, and Michael Depledge. 2010. "Blue Space: The Importance of Water for Preference, Affect, and Restorativeness Ratings of Natural and Built Scenes." *Journal of Environmental Psychology* 30: 482–493.
8. Houston, Stephen D. 1996. "Symbolic Sweatbaths of the Maya: Architectural Meaning in the Cross Group at Palenque, Mexico." *Latin American Antiquity* 7, no. 2: 132–151.
9. Hall, Robert L. 1997. *An Archaeology of the Soul: Native American Indian Belief and Ritual*. Urbana: University of Illinois Press.
10. Tommila, Pekka. 1994. *Sauna: Suomalaisen Saunan Rakentaminen*. Helsinki: Rakennusalan Kustantajat.
11. Child, Mark B. 2006. "The Archaeology of Religious Movements: The Maya Sweatbath Cult of Piedras Negras." PhD dissertation, Yale University.
12. Pepper, George H. 1996. *Pueblo Bonito*. Albuquerque: University of New Mexico Press.
13. Hargrave, Michael L., R. Berle Clay, Rinita A. Dalan, and Diana M. Greenlee. 2021. "The Complex Construction History of Poverty Point's Timber Circles and Concentric Ridges." *Southeastern Archaeology* 40, no. 3: 192–211. https://doi.org/10.1080/0734578X.2021.1961350.
14. Cowan, Frank. 2005. "Stubbs Earthworks: An Ohio Hopewell 'Woodhenge.'" In *Ohio Archaeology: An Illustrated Chronicle of Ohio's Ancient American Indian Cultures*, edited by Bradley T. Lepper, pp. 18–151. Wilmington, OH: Orange Frazer Press.
15. Waselkov, Gregory A., and Kathyrn E. Holland Braund, eds. 1995. *William Bartram on the Southeastern Indians*. Lincoln: University of Nebraska Press.

CHAPTER 12

1. Glowacki, Donna M., and Scott Van Keuren, eds. 2011. *Religious Transformation in the Late Pre-Hispanic Pueblo World*. Tucson: University of Arizona Press.
2. Lankford, George E. 2004. "Some Southwestern Influences in the Southeastern Ceremonial Complex." *Arkansas Archeologist* 45: 1–25. See also Phillips, Philip, and James A. Brown. 1978. *Pre-Columbian Shell*

Engravings from the Craig Mound at Spiro, Oklahoma. Cambridge, MA: Peabody Museum of Archaeology and Ethnology, Harvard University.

3. Krieger, Alex D. 1945. "An Inquiry into Supposed Mexican Influence on a Prehistoric 'Cult' in the Southern United States." *American Anthropologist* 47, n.s., no. 4: 483–515. Waring, Antonio J., Jr., and Preston Holder. 1945. "A Prehistoric Ceremonial Complex in the Southeastern United States." *American Anthropologist* 47, no. 1: 1–34. Willey, Gordon R., and Philip Phillips. 1944. "Negative-Painted Pottery from Crystal River, Florida." *American Antiquity* 10, no. 2: 173–185.
4. Contrast statements published in 2005 by Alice Kehoe (in "Wind Jewels and Paddling Gods: The Mississippian Southeast in the Postclassic Mesoamerican World," in *Gulf Coast Archaeology: The Southeastern United States and Mexico*, edited by Nancy M. White, pp. 260–280 [Gainesville: University Press of Florida]) with those made by James Brown in 2005 ("6,000 Years of Mound Building," *Cambridge Archaeological Journal* 15: 113–115).
5. There were likely more Mesoamerican gods involved, including Xipe Totec, the Aztec flayed-skin lord that celebrated renewal and was connected to pole rituals, as discussed at length by Robert L. Hall in his 1997 book *An Archaeology of the Soul: Native American Indian Belief and Ritual.* Urbana: University of Illinois Press.
6. Castillo, Bernal Díaz del. 2008. *The History of the Conquest of New Spain.* Translated by David Carrasco. Albuquerque: University of New Mexico Press, pp. 19–20.
7. Witthoft, John. 1949. *Green Corn Ceremonialism in the Eastern Woodlands.* Occasional Contributions 13. Ann Arbor: University of Michigan, Museum of Anthropology, pp. 3–4.
8. Emerson, Thomas E., Kristin M. Hedman, Mary L. Simon, Matthew A. Fort, and Kelsey E. Witt. 2020. "Isotopic Confirmation of the Timing and Intensity of Maize Consumption in Greater Cahokia." *American Antiquity* 85, no. 2: 241–262. https://doi.org/10.1017/aaq.2020.7.
9. Helms, Mary W. 1988. *Ulysses' Sail: An Ethnographic Odyssey of Power, Knowledge, and Geographical Distance.* Princeton, NJ: Princeton University Press.
10. Markman, Robert H., and Peter T. Markman. 1992. *The Flayed God: The Mythology of Mesoamerica—Sacred Texts and Images from Pre-Columbian Mexico and Central America.* San Francisco: Harper.
11. Almere Read, Kay, and Jason J. Gonzolez. 2000. *Mesoamerican Mythology: A Guide to the Gods, Heroes, Rituals, and Beliefs of Mexico and Central America.* Oxford: Oxford University Press, p. 251.

12. Almere Read and Gonzolez, *Mesoamerican Mythology*, pp. 70–71.
13. Tedlock, Dennis, trans. 1996. *Popol Vuh: The Mayan Book of the Dawn of Life.* New York: Simon and Schuster.
14. Hall, Robert L. 1989. "The Cultural Background of Mississippian Symbolism." In *The Southeastern Ceremonial Complex*, edited by Patricia Galloway, pp. 239–278. Lincoln: University of Nebraska Press.
15. Parsons, Elsie Clews. 1939. *Pueblo Indian Religion.* Chicago: University of Chicago Press.
16. Parsons, *Pueblo Indian Religion*, p. 212.
17. Lankford, George E. 2008. *Looking for Lost Lore: Studies in Folklore, Ethnology, and Iconography.* Tuscaloosa: University of Alabama Press.
18. Mathiowetz, Michael D. 2011. "The Diurnal Path of the Sun: Ideology and Interregional Interaction in Ancient Northwest Mesoamerica and the American Southwest." PhD dissertation, Department of Anthropology, University of California, Riverside.
19. Emerson, Thomas E. 2015. "The Earth Goddess Cult at Cahokia." In *Medieval Mississippians: The Cahokian World*, edited by Timothy R. Pauketat and Susan M. Alt, pp. 55–60. Santa Fe, NM: School for Advanced Research Press. Emerson, Thomas E., Randall E. Hughes, Mary R. Hynes, and Sarah U. Wisseman. 2002. "Implications of Sourcing Cahokia-Style Flintclay Figures in the American Bottom and the Upper Mississippi River Valley." *Midcontinental Journal of Archaeology* 27: 309–338. Emerson, Thomas E., Randall E. Hughes, Mary R. Hynes, and Sarah U. Wisseman. 2003. "The Sourcing and Interpretation of Cahokia-Style Figurines in the Trans-Mississippi South and Southeast." *American Antiquity* 68: 287–313. Prentice, Guy. 1986. "An Analysis of the Symbolism Expressed by the Birger Figurine." *American Antiquity* 51, no. 2: 239–266.
20. Prentice, "Analysis," pp. 55–59.
21. Sharp, Robert V., Vernon J. Knight, Jr., and George E. Lankford. 2011. "Woman in the Patterned Shawl: Female Effigy Vessels and Figurines from the Middle Cumberland River Basin." In *Visualizing the Sacred: Cosmic Visions, Regionalism, and the Art of the Mississippian World*, edited by George E. Lankford, F. Kent Reilly III, and James F. Garber, pp. 177–198. Austin: University of Texas Press.
22. Radin, Paul. 1948. *Winnebago Hero Cycles: A Study in Aboriginal Literature.* Indiana University Publications in Anthropology and Linguistics, Memoir 1. Baltimore: Waverly Press, pp. 8–9.
23. Radin, *Winnebago Hero Cycles*, pp. 49, 115–132.
24. Witthoft, *Green Corn Ceremonialism*, pp. 79–80.

25. Hall, Robert L. 1997. *An Archaeology of the Soul: Native American Indian Belief and Ritual.* Urbana: University of Illinois Press. Hall, Robert L. 2000. "Sacrificed Foursomes and Green Corn Ceremonialism." In *Mounds, Modoc, and Mesoamerica: Papers in Honor of Melvin L. Fowler,* edited by Steven R. Ahler, pp. 245–253. Scientific Papers, volume XXVIII. Springfield: Illinois State Museum.
26. Hall, *Archaeology of the Soul*, pp. 80–81.
27. Neihardt, John G. 2008. *Black Elk Speaks: Being the Life Story of a Holy Man of the Oglala Sioux.* Albany: State University of New York Press, p. 149.
28. Hall, *Archaeology of the Soul.*
29. Gipson, Rosemary. 1971. "Los Voladores, the Flyers of Mexico." *Western Folklore* 30, no. 4: 269–278.
30. Wissler, Clark, and Herbert J. Spinden. 1916. "The Pawnee Human Sacrifice to the Morning Star." *American Museum Journal* 16, no. January: 49–55.

Further Reading

CHAPTER 1

Carballo, David M. 2020. *Collision of Worlds: A Deep History of the Fall of Aztec Mexico and the Forging of New Spain*. Oxford: Oxford University Press.

Matos Moctezuma, Eduardo. 1988. *The Great Temple of the Aztecs: Treasures of Tenochtitlan*. London: Thames and Hudson.

Minnis, Paul E., and Michael E. Whalen. 2016. *Discovering Paquimé*. Tucson: University of Arizona Press.

Murdy, Ann. 2019. *On the Path of Marigolds: Living Traditions of Mexico's Day of the Dead*. Staunton, VA: George F. Thompson.

CHAPTER 2

Cabeza de Vaca, Álvar Núñez. 2002. *Chronicle of the Narváez Expedition*. Translated by F. Bandelier and H. Augenbraum. New York: Penguin.

Diaz del Castillo, Bernal. 1963. *The Conquest of New Spain*. Translated by J. M. Cohen. New York: Penguin.

Hassig, Ross. 2006. *Mexico and the Spanish Conquest*. Norman: University of Oklahoma Press.

Pauketat, Timothy R., and Kenneth E. Sassaman. 2020. *The Archaeology of Ancient North America*. Cambridge: Cambridge University Press.

CHAPTER 3

Coe, Michael, and Stephen D. Houston. 2015. *The Maya*. London: Thames and Hudson.

Houston, Stephen D., and Takeshi Inomata. 2009. *The Classic Maya*. Cambridge: Cambridge University Press.

Martin, Simon, and Nikolai Grube. 2008. *Chronicle of the Maya Kings and Queens*. 2nd ed. London: Thames and Hudson.

Miller, Mary, and Karl Taube. 1997. *An Illustrated Dictionary of the Gods and Symbols of Ancient Mexico and the Maya*. London: Thames and Hudson.

CHAPTER 4

Faust, Katherine A., and Kim N. Richter, eds. 2009. *The Huasteca: Culture, History, and Interregional Exchange.* Norman: University of Oklahoma Press.

Hassig, Ross. 2001. *Time, History, and Belief in Aztec and Colonial Mexico.* Austin: University of Texas Press.

Nichols, Deborah L., and Christopher A. Pool, eds. 2012. *The Oxford Handbook of Mesoamerican Archaeology.* Oxford: Oxford University Press.

Pollock, Harry Evelyn Dorr. 1936. *Round Structures of Aboriginal Middle America.* Publication 471. Washington, DC: Carnegie Institution.

CHAPTER 5

Brown, Dee. 1970. *Bury My Heart at Wounded Knee: An Indian History of the American West.* New York: Henry Holt.

Englehardt, Joshua D., Verenice Y. Heredia Espinoza, and Christopher S. Beekman, eds. 2020. *Ancient West Mexicos: Time, Space, and Diversity.* Gainesville: University Press of Florida.

Faugère, Brigitte, and Christopher S. Beekman. 2020. *Anthropomorphic Imagery in Mesoamerican Highlands: Gods, Ancestors, and Human Beings.* Boulder: University Press of Colorado.

CHAPTER 6

Fish, Suzanne K., and Paul R. Fish, eds. 2007. *The Hohokam Millennium.* Santa Fe, NM: School for Advanced Research Press.

Fish, Suzanne K., and Paul R. Fish. 2012. "Hohokam Society and Water Management." In *The Oxford Handbook of North American Archaeology*, edited by Timothy R. Pauketat, pp. 571–584. Oxford: Oxford University Press.

Haury, Emil W. 1976. *The Hohokam, Desert Farmers and Craftsmen: Excavations at Snaketown, 1964–1965.* Tucson: University of Arizona Press.

Nelson, Margaret C., and Michelle Hegmon, eds. 2010. *Mimbres Lives and Landscapes.* Santa Fe, NM: School for Advanced Research Press.

CHAPTER 7

Lekson, Stephen H. 2015. *The Chaco Meridian: Centers of Political Power in the Ancient Southwest.* 2nd ed. Lanham, MD: Rowman and Littlefield.

Lekson, Stephen H. 2009. *A History of the Ancient Southwest.* Santa Fe, NM: School for Advanced Research Press.

Noble, David Grant, ed. 2004. *In Search of Chaco: New Approaches to an Archaeological Enigma*. Santa Fe, NM: School for Advanced Research Press.

Noble, David Grant, ed. 2006. *The Mesa Verde World: Explorations in Ancestral Pueblo Archaeology*. Santa Fe, NM: School for American Research Press.

Sofaer, Anna. 2008. *Chaco Astronomy: An Ancient American Cosmology*. Santa Fe, NM: Ocean Tree Books.

CHAPTER 8

Girard, Jeffrey S. 2018. *The Caddos and Their Ancestors: Archaeology and the Native People of Northwest Louisiana*. Baton Rouge: Louisiana State University Press.

Girard, Jeffrey S., Timothy K. Perttula, and Mary Beth Trubitt. 2014. *Caddo Connections: Cultural Interactions Within and Beyond the Caddo World*. Lanham, MD: Rowman and Littlefield.

La Vere, David. 2007. *Looting Spiro Mounds: An American King Tut's Tomb*. Norman: University of Oklahoma Press.

Schultes, Richard Evans, Albert Hofmann, and Christian Ratsch. 1992. *Plants of the Gods: Their Sacred, Healing, and Hallucinogenic Powers*. Rochester, VT: Healing Arts Press.

CHAPTERS 9 AND 10

Emerson, Thomas E., Brad H. Koldehoff, and Tamira K. Brennan, eds. 2018. *Revealing Greater Cahokia, North America's First Native City: Rediscovery and Large-Scale Excavations of the East St. Louis Precinct*. Studies in Archaeology 12. Urbana: Illinois State Archaeological Survey.

Pauketat, Timothy R. 2009. *Cahokia: Ancient America's Great City on the Mississippi*. New York: Viking-Penguin.

Pauketat, Timothy R., and Susan M. Alt, eds. 2015. *Medieval Mississippians: The Cahokian World*. Santa Fe, NM: School for Advanced Research Press.

CHAPTER 11

Lepper, Bradley T. 2004. *Ohio Archaeology: An Illustrated Chronicle of Ohio's Ancient American Indian Cultures*. Wilmington, OH: Orange Frazer Press.

Lynott, Mark J. 2014. *Hopewell Ceremonial Landscapes of Ohio: More than Mounds and Geometric Earthworks*. Oxford: Oxbow Books.

Waselkov, Gregory A., and Kathyrn E. Holland Braund, eds. 2002. *William Bartram on the Southeastern Indians*. Tuscaloosa: University of Alabama Press.

CHAPTER 12

Almere Read, Kay, and Jason J. Gonzolez. 2000. *Mesoamerican Mythology: A Guide to the Gods, Heroes, Rituals, and Beliefs of Mexico and Central America.* Oxford: Oxford University Press.

Hays-Gilpin, Kelley, and Polly Schaafsma. 2010. *Painting the Cosmos: Metaphor and Worldview in Images from the Southwest Pueblos and Mesoamerica.* Bulletin 67. Flagstaff: Museum of Northern Arizona.

Miller, Mary, and Karl Taube. 1993. *An Illustrated Dictionary of the Gods and Symbols of Ancient Mexico and the Maya.* London: Thames and Hudson.

Townsend, J. B., ed. 2004. *Hero, Hawk, and Open Hand: American Indian Art of the Ancient Midwest and South.* Chicago: Chicago Art Institute.

Index

For the benefit of digital users, indexed terms that span two pages (e.g., 52–53) may, on occasion, appear on only one of those pages.